The appendix of CLUES TO SUICIDE
consists of 33 genuine suicide notes matched
(by sex, age, and occupation) with 33
simulated notes from non-suicidal individuals.
You are asked to decide for yourself which
of each pair is genuine (a key appears elsewhere in the book), so that you can learn
yourself what it is that distinguishes genuine
suicidal intent. Earlier chapters deal with
psychologic and social work clues to suicide;
suicide in children, in old age, and in a
Catholic country; and suicide from the
legal standpoint.

Affiliations and degrees held by the editors
and participants in this investigation are
listed on pages v and vi.

Clues to Suicide

edited by
Edwin S. Shneidman
Norman L. Farberow

Foreword by
Karl A. Menninger, M.D.

McGraw-Hill Book Company, Inc.

New York   Toronto   London

From the Veterans Administration Neuropsychiatric Hospital and the Veterans Administration Mental Hygiene Clinic, Los Angeles

This investigation was supported in part by a research grant, M-1074, from the National Institute of Mental Health, of the National Institutes of Health, U.S. Public Health Service

Contributors

I. R. C. BATCHELOR, M.B., D.P.M., F.R.C.P.Ed.
Physician Superintendent, Dundee Royal Mental Hospital; Lecturer in Clinical Psychiatry, University of St. Andrews, Scotland

A. E. BENNETT, M.D.
Associate Professor of Psychiatry, University of California School of Medicine, San Francisco; Chief, Department of Psychiatry, Herrick Memorial Hospital, and Director, The A. E. Bennett Neuropsychiatric Research Foundation, Berkeley, California

O. SPURGEON ENGLISH, M.D.
Professor of Psychiatry, Temple University Medical Center, Philadelphia

NORMAN L. FARBEROW, Ph.D.
Clinical Psychologist, Veterans Administration Mental Hygiene Clinic, Los Angeles; Instructor, Extension Division, University of California at Los Angeles

HERMAN FEIFEL, Ph.D.
Research and Clinical Psychologist, Veterans Administration Mental Hygiene Clinic, Los Angeles; Research Associate in Psychology, Department of Medicine, City of Hope Medical Center, Duarte, California

FRANCO FERRACUTI, M.D.
Visiting Professor, Faculty of Social Sciences, University of Puerto Rico; Assistant, Istituto di Psicologia, University of Rome, Italy

DONALD M. HAMILTON, M.D.
Physician in Charge of Men, The New York Hospital, Westchester Division, White Plains, New York

ANDREW F. HENRY, Ph.D.
Associate Professor of Sociology, Vanderbilt University, Nashville, Tennessee

DON D. JACKSON, M.D.
Chief, Psychiatry Department, Palo Alto Medical Clinic; Consultant, Palo Alto Veterans Administration Hospital; Instructor in Psychiatry, School of Medicine, and Consultant, Department of Psychology, Stanford University, Stanford, California

DORTHEA M. LANE, B.A.

Assistant Chief, Social Work Service, Veterans Administration Center, Neuropsychiatric Hospital, Los Angeles

ROBERT E. LITMAN, M.D.

Psychiatrist, Beverly Hills, California; Consultant, Veterans Administration Neuropsychiatric Hospital, Los Angeles; Attending Psychiatrist, Mount Sinai Hospital, Los Angeles

LEONARD M. MOSS, M.D.

Assistant in Psychiatry, Cornell University Medical College; Assistant Psychiatrist to Outpatients, Payne Whitney Psychiatric Clinic, New York Hospital

SEYMOUR POLLACK, M.D.

Assistant Professor of Psychiatry, University of Southern California School of Medicine, Los Angeles

MARSHALL D. SCHECHTER, M.D.

Psychiatrist, Beverly Hills, California; Assistant Clinical Professor of Psychiatry, University of California School of Medicine, Los Angeles; Psychiatric Consultant for the Shriners' Hospital for Crippled Children, Los Angeles Unit

EDWIN S. SHNEIDMAN, Ph.D.

Chief for Research, Psychology Service, Veterans Administration Neuropsychiatric Hospital, Los Angeles; Research Associate and Clinical Associate, University of Southern California

JAMES F. SHORT, JR., Ph.D.

Assistant Professor of Sociology, State College of Washington, Pullman, Washington

HELEN SILVING, LL.B. (Columbia University), J.D., Dr.sc.pol. (University of Vienna)

Professor of Law, University of Puerto Rico; Member of the New York Bar

NORMAN TABACHNICK, M.D.

Psychiatrist, Beverly Hills, California

CHARLES WILLIAM WAHL, M.D.

Assistant Professor, Department of Psychiatry, University of California School of Medicine, Los Angeles; Attending Psychiatrist, Sepulveda Veterans Administration Hospital, Sepulveda, California; Consultant in Psychiatry, Camarillo State Hospital, Camarillo, California

Foreword

Once every minute, or even more often, someone in the United States either kills himself or tries to kill himself with conscious intent. Sixty or seventy times every day these attempts succeed. In many instances they could have been prevented by some of the rest of us.

Few people realize that suicide is more frequent than murder and more easily predicted. Early in my clinical experience I learned with astonishment how incredulous relatives and friends could be regarding the threats of patients and the warnings of doctors. To the normal person suicide seems too dreadful and senseless to be conceivable. There almost seems to be a taboo on the serious discussion of it. There has never been a wide campaign against it, as there has been against other less easily preventable forms of death. There is no organized public interest in it. There is very little scientific research concerning it.

That is why this is an important book. It is a research study in a neglected and important area. It is the joint production of a group of scientists who have observed and collated and checked. To anyone who reviews any considerable number of suicides, it is unmistakably clear that the assigning of *the* cause or even of *the causes* for the final act is naïvely absurd and grossly misleading. But the nature and degree of the internal stress and the external evidence of it—these are a different matter. These can be found if searched for, and it is such a search that the authors have conducted through a large collection of poignant material. What are the discernible manifestations, they asked themselves, of an internal personality disorder so great and so formulated as to lead to self-directed violence? What are the subtle hints of this possibility? And may such hints ever safely be ignored?

The titles of the many interesting chapters speak for themselves. No one can read them and the farewell notes without some new reflections—reflections about the meaning of life and the meaning of death and about the unimaginable extent of unseen human misery.

For those devoted to the diminution of that misery as a professional responsibility, this book is an assurance and a help.

Karl A. Menninger

Preface

The best available, although admittedly incomplete, statistics on the suicide rate in the United States indicate that at least 16,000 persons take their own lives each year. These statistics do not include deaths from complications induced by suicide attempts; nor do they include covert or concealed suicides—those who kill themselves gradually or subtly. Yet even this conservative figure ranks suicide among the first ten in the list of killers.

There is yet another fact about this important psychiatric, psychologic, sociologic, cultural, and medical phenomenon; it is that surprisingly little work has been done on it, considering its ubiquitous nature. Indeed, the major books on this topic, such as those by Durkheim, Cavan, Menninger, and Dublin and Bunzel, are veritable landmarks not only because of the high quality of their contents but also because of their rarity. Although this present book may contain many statements and conclusions which will be disputed, nevertheless every reader will almost certainly agree that suicide is an important clinical and scientific problem, and that the lowering of the suicide rate is a major mental health challenge.

Something of the history of this volume may be given. The editors have been engaged for a number of years in an investigation of the psychology of suicide in Los Angeles County. In 1955, considerable help was obtained for the project in the form of a three-year U.S. Public Health Research Grant. To accommodate the growing interest in the problem, a symposium on the psychology of suicide was organized by the editors and presented at the Western Regional Meeting of the American Psychological Association, Berkeley, California, in March, 1956. The papers presented at that symposium, reproduced here essentially in their original form, were by Drs. Bennett, Farberow, Jackson, Shneidman, Tabachnick, and Wahl. Subsequent to the symposium, requests for reprints and suggestions for publication were made. It was in response to these that this volume was initiated. Once publication was decided upon, the scope of the book was extended and the other participants were invited to make their contributions. The papers by the two editors constitute, at this point, only a sketchy first report of their own investigations to date. A full report of their study is planned as a separate volume.

Essentially this book is a series of essays on various theoretical and practical aspects of suicide. It is hoped that the book will have both practical and heuristic values. It is addressed primarily to the practitioner: the psychiatrist, the clinical psychologist, the physician in general practice, the psychiatric social worker, the lawyer, and the police officer. The student of personality, the sociologist, and all those interested in theories of maladaptation should find interest in its contents.

Part I, Theoretical and Experimental Considerations, includes chapters by the editors describing their theoretical and experimental approach to the problem; several chapters by others on the current theories and thinking about the nature of suicide, its cultural background, and its place within the broader problem of death itself; and chapters on the sociologic aspects of suicide. The chapter on suicide and law may be of especial interest inasmuch as it brings together for the first time the attitudes of law toward the suicidal act, traced from the beginnings of legal formulations to the present. Part II, Clinical Considerations, describes the challenging problems which occur in the psychotherapy, medical treatment, and administrative management of the suicidal person of various ages, in mental hospitals, general hospitals, clinics, and private practice. This part of the book ends with a number of feasible suggestions aimed toward the reduction of the suicide rate. The Appendix, which contains 33 pairs of matched genuine and simulated suicide notes collected by the editors, gives the reader the opportunity to compare genuine suicidal thoughts and feelings with simulated thoughts and feelings.

It should be stated that care has been taken, according to usual scientific practice, to change names, dates, and places, so that complete anonymity for all suicidal persons referred to in this book is carefully preserved.

The editors wish to express their sincere appreciation to three agencies without whose cooperation this volume and the research project which it reflects could not have been: the Veterans Administration, where both editors are staff members, for allowing time and providing an intellectual climate which fostered the study; the Los Angeles County Coroner's office, for sharing invaluable data with us and making us feel welcome in the process; and the U.S. Public Health Service, for giving tangible support to the study through their research grant.

Great appreciation is also extended to Dr. Karl A. Menninger, who wrote the foreword, and to each of the contributors, who worked so graciously and so willingly throughout the many phases of preparation that go into a volume of this kind. Specific credit is given to *Public Health Reports* for permission to reprint the chapter "Clues to Suicide," which was originally published there; to Henry Holt and Company and the Society of Authors, London, as the representative of the estate of the late A. E. Housman, and to Messrs. Jonathan Cape, Ltd., for permission to reprint from *The Collected Poems of A. E. Housman* two stanzas of "More Poems—XXVI" (beginning "Good creatures do you love your lives . . .") in Dr. Wahl's chapter "Suicide as a Magical Act"; and to the *American Journal of Psychiatry* for permission to reprint "Psychotherapy of the Suicidal Patient" by Drs. Moss and Hamilton, as well as to Dr. O. Spurgeon English for permission to include his discussion of that paper. Special appreciation is expressed to Susan Alexander, who prepared the manuscript and who helped in many ways too numerous to mention.

Edwin S. Shneidman
Norman L. Farberow

Contents

    Patient *by Edwin S. Shneidman and Dorthea M. Lane*   170
18. Suggestions for Suicide Prevention *by A. E. Bennett*   187

    Postscript   194
    Appendix: Genuine and Simulated Suicide Notes   197
    Name Index   217
    Subject Index   221

PART I

Theoretical and Experimental Considerations

Clues to Suicide*

EDWIN S. SHNEIDMAN AND NORMAN L. FARBEROW

The importance of the phenomenon of suicide is gauged by the large number of people who take their lives each year (1) and by the human suffering involved. Professional psychiatric, psychologic, and social services might save many potentially suicidal persons if the danger were anticipated. In our continuing study of suicide in Los Angeles County (5, 6, 9), we are attempting to discover a few of the danger signals.

A basic point of view implicit in our study is that we believe suicide to be motivated by sociologic, cultural, ecologic, psychologic, and many other factors (2–4, 7). Another basic point of view is our belief that meaningful studies of suicide can effectively use the scientific method of experimental control.

Our purpose at this time is to describe an experimental approach in the investigation of psychologic factors in suicide and to report a few tentative results. Although our study is limited to the psychologic aspects of suicide, it does not preclude other important aspects of the phenomenon studied by Cavan, Dublin and Bunzel, Durkheim (2–4), and others.

THREE TYPES OF RAW MATERIALS

Our raw materials are psychiatric case histories, psychologic test results, and suicide notes. We have attempted to obtain adequate control data for each category so that statistical comparisons might be made.

Case Histories

The names of adult male suicides were obtained from the weekly lists of all suicides in the Los Angeles County Coroner's Office for the period

* Reprinted (with minor editorial changes) with permission from *Public Health Reports*, 71: 100–114, 1956.

1944 through 1953. By checking the names of completed suicides with rosters of former patients of Veterans Administration neuropsychiatric hospitals in the county, we collected the psychiatric case histories of 32 adult male patients who, sometime after discharge from the hospital, had killed themselves.

The case histories of the 32 suicides were then checked with the case histories of an equal number of control cases in each of three comparable categories of neuropsychiatric hospitalized males: a group of 32 males who had attempted suicide, a group of 32 who had threatened suicide, and a group of 32 who had no suicidal tendencies. In the four groups selected, all 128 subjects were male and white, and most of them were from twenty to forty years old, although the ages ranged from twenty to sixty-nine.

We have analyzed the 128 case histories in terms of more than 100 different social, economic, cultural, and psychologic categories and have computed the statistical significance of the differences among the four groups. Samples of the categories used for analysis are family history details, economic level, parents' age at the time of various events in the subject's life, educational and vocational achievements, marital status, psychiatric diagnosis, and so forth.

Psychologic Tests

For our second type of raw data, we collected test results on the Rorschach ink-blot technique, the Thematic Apperception Test, the Make a Picture Story Test, and the Minnesota Multiphasic Personality Inventory, among others.

In collecting these data we followed much the same procedure used for obtaining the case histories. The lists of suicides in Los Angeles County were checked against the hospital rosters. Then the previously administered psychologic tests on individuals who had subsequently committed suicide were found. Psychologic tests on comparable groups of individuals who had attempted suicide, threatened suicide, or who were nonsuicidal were obtained next, and the test results among the four groups were compared.

However, only the test results for 96 of the 128 subjects—the nonsuicidal subjects and those who attempted or threatened suicide—have been analyzed so far. Data for those persons who had been tested and who subsequently committed suicide have not yet been collected in numbers sufficiently large to be subjected to statistical analysis.

Suicide Notes

For our third set of raw materials, we collected 721 genuine suicide notes with the cooperation of the Los Angeles County Coroner's Office. The notes were written during the period 1944 through 1953. Some were written by men, some by women, others by children. The writers were as young as thirteen and as old as ninety-six.

There are practical, as well as theoretical, difficulties in obtaining control data to match with genuine suicide notes. A practical difficulty is that notes written by people who have threatened or attempted suicide are hard to obtain, inasmuch as the notes are usually destroyed. To obtain control data, we asked certain individuals, carefully matched with the genuine suicide-note writers, to write the suicide note they would leave if they were going to take their own lives. The names of the people we asked to participate were obtained from such community sources as labor unions and fraternal groups. In recognition of the moral and ethical overtones associated with suicide, we employed preliminary screening tests, interviews, and other safeguards in order to screen out anyone who might be upset by writing a fictitious suicide note.

Our last step was to analyze the genuine and simulated suicide notes and to relate the statistically significant results to the major psychiatric, psychoanalytic, and psychologic hypotheses about suicide.

RESULTS OF RESEARCH

The following findings come from the research in process and are tentative in nature.

Case History Comparisons

From our studies of the four sets of psychiatric case histories (6), we concluded:

(1) It is practically impossible to distinguish a potentially suicidal person from the details of his case history alone, however stressful or traumatic it has been.

(2) Seventy-five per cent of the subjects who committed suicide had a history of having previously threatened or attempted suicide.

(3) Almost half of the individuals who committed suicide after leaving the hospital did so within ninety days after having been discharged.

As to the first finding, there were few statistically significant differences in the case history details among the four groups. For example, as many people in one group as in another were only children, came from broken homes, had a history of suicide in the family, and so forth.

From all the comparisons made of the four groups we found that only a diagnosis of reactive depression or paranoid schizophrenia differentiated the three suicidal groups (completed, threatened, and attempted suicide) from the nonsuicidal group. Only a history of mental hospitalization among members of the family distinguished the completed suicide group from the other three groups. All other comparisons yielded negative results.

Although it is true that not all people who have attempted or threatened suicide go on to commit suicide, the contrary fact—our second finding— is even more striking. That is, there is a large percentage of suicides, specifically, 75 per cent in our study, who have a history of having threatened or attempted suicide. This fact would seem to indicate that suicidal gestures (attempts or threats) may be considered as danger signals and must be taken seriously. The results of this study do not permit us to state whether the same percentage would apply in a general population. Nevertheless, the finding does suggest that suicidal threats and attempts are a danger signal in the type of suicidal population found in a neuro-psychiatric hospital or sanitarium.

Clinical observations in the psychiatric literature corroborate the finding that almost half of the individuals who did commit suicide after leaving the hospital did so within ninety days after discharge. Thus, it appears that even though persons of observed suicidal tendencies are judged to have improved sufficiently to be ready to function in the community again, they are in a dangerous period. It is not possible to state what might be the result of keeping such patients in the hospital another ninety days, without further detailed, controlled investigations. This third finding has implications for timing discharge from treatment and for continuing vigilance in behalf of these emotionally disturbed individuals. It would seem that if a person has been making suicidal attempts or threats, his physician and relatives must be especially cautious for at least three months after he appears to be improving and seems to be on his way to recovery.

Psychologic Test Comparisons

Our study (5) of the psychologic tests for those who attempted suicide, threatened suicide, or who were nonsuicidal resulted in the interesting finding that there are differences among individuals heretofore loosely classified as "suicidal."

There were some differences between people who attempted suicide and threatened suicide. Specifically, individuals who have threatened suicide show more guilt, aggression, irritability, and agitation—in a word, more emotional disturbance—than do individuals who have attempted suicide. Those who have attempted suicide are more like the nonsuicidal mental hospital patients, except perhaps more withdrawn. It is almost as though the attempt itself had operated in an abreactive and therapeutic manner and had lessened the immediate seriousness of the personality disturbance.

This temporary relief, however, does not mean the emotional state preceding suicide will not return.

Genuine and Simulated Notes

From our comparisons of genuine and simulated suicide notes (9), we are presenting only the results of our application of the Discomfort-Relief Quotient (DRQ), a technique developed by Mowrer (8).

Mowrer's technique is used to measure the relative amounts of discomfort thought units, relief thought units, and neutral thought units contained in case history materials or in statements made during psychotherapy sessions. The thought unit is a discrete idea, regardless of number of words. The DRQ was deemed to be applicable to the analysis of genuine and simulated suicide notes for indications of the current emotional and ideational state. Thirty-three male, white, Protestant, married, native-born, genuine-suicide-note writers were matched man-for-man, by age and occupation, with 33 nonsuicidal, simulated-suicide-note writers.

The total number of thought units was significantly higher in the 33 real notes than in the fictitious notes, indicating that the genuine-note writers apparently feel the need to say more in this last communication.

With respect to "discomfort" statements, or the statements of guilt, blame, tension, aggression, and the like, we found some difference between the prorated number of discomfort units expressed by the genuine-suicide-note writers and those expressed by the simulated-note writers. We noted that the discomfort statements in the simulated suicide notes were only mildly negative but that similar statements in the genuine notes were characterized by deeper and more intense feelings of hatred, vengeance, demand, and self-blame. As used at this time, however, the discomfort measure does not reflect these qualitative differences.

As for the number of "relief" statements, or statements which were pleasant, warm, loving, and which denoted relief from tension, we found no quantitative difference between the genuine notes and the simulated notes.

It was in regard to the "neutral" statements, the statements free of expressions either of tension or of release from tension, that the notes revealed the greatest significant difference. The genuine suicide notes contained much the higher percentage of neutral thought units. On inspection, we found them to be mostly statements giving instructions and admonitions and sometimes listing things to do.

What might our findings indicate about suicide-note writers?

We interpreted the higher percentage of neutral thoughts expressed by the genuine-note writers to indicate two important, although quite contradictory, feelings on their part and, in addition, to reflect a basic difference in the attitudes of the two groups of writers.

The genuine-note writer has, as one part of his thinking, apparently accepted and incorporated the idea that within a short time he will not be alive. In this connection, he instructs and admonishes in relation to the many details of continued living which he will not be able to pursue himself.

The fictitious-note writer, although he can apparently approximate in fantasy the "affect" of suicide (inasmuch as the number of relief statements is proportionately the same), does not take the additional step of converting his fantasy into the "reality" of imminent absence. In other words, only the genuine-suicide-note writer deals with the idea of his really being gone. At the same time, there is a distinct contradiction in the concept of the self reflected in his decision to die and his listing of things to do and his plans for the future. It is as though he were exercising power and command in these directions, as if somehow he were making sure his plans would be carried out. It is a kind of unrealistic feeling of omnipotence and omnipresence on the part of the suicidal individual which may reflect in part some of the confused, illogical, and paradoxical motivations in the entire act.[1]

SOME WORDS OF CAUTION

In addition to the fact that our project deals only with some of the psychologic aspects of suicide, as revealed in case histories, psychologic tests, and suicide notes, some other limitations of the study should also be made explicit.

The data we have analyzed so far are restricted to a specific period (1944 to 1953) and to a specific area (Southern California) and, therefore, cannot be representative of other times and other locations.

We wish to point out also that, although the 721 suicide notes in the study represent almost 100 per cent of the suicide notes written in Los Angeles County during the ten-year period 1944 to 1953, only about 15 per cent of the suicides in the county have left notes. Thus, the conclusions about the psychology of suicides from this source may possibly contain some as yet undisclosed sampling biases.

Our clues about suicide are to be taken only as an interim report of tentative findings from a continuing study. We hope, within the next few

[1] Chapter 4, The Logic of Suicide, elaborates on this and gives the statistics.

years, to report more definite information about the psychologic nature of suicide from which a clearer theoretical understanding of its motivations can be obtained and, perhaps, even some clues as to how its prevention and control can be evolved.

SUMMARY AND CONCLUSIONS

The following five points are offered as a summary of the findings and implications of this interim report:

(1) Three-fourths of our subjects who committed suicide had previously threatened or attempted to take their own lives. This means that suicidal behavior, whether attempted or threatened, must be taken seriously, inasmuch as the next suicidal gesture may be the final one.

(2) Almost half of the individuals who committed suicide did so within three months of having passed an emotional crisis and after they seemed to be on the way to recovery. This means that physicians and relatives must be especially cautious and watchful for at least ninety days after a person who has been suicidal appears to be improving.

(3) On the basis of comparisons among psychologic tests, it appears that the person who threatens suicide seems to be more emotionally disturbed than the person who attempts suicide, but both must be taken seriously and watched carefully for at least three months.

(4) The comparison of genuine suicide notes with simulated suicide notes indicates that the person about to take his own life includes orders and admonitions, as though he had reached a final decision in solving his problems but is confused and contradictory about whether he will continue to be around.

(5) Calling upon professional psychiatric, psychologic, and social work specialists for the treatment of a potentially suicidal person may mean the difference between life and death.

References

1. Why do people kill themselves? *Statistical Bulletin of the Metropolitan Life Insurance Company,* 26: 9–10, 1945.
2. Cavan, R. S., *Suicide.* Chicago: University of Chicago Press, 1926.
3. Dublin, L. I., and B. Bunzel, *To Be or Not to Be.* New York: Random House, Inc., 1933.
4. Durkheim, É., *Suicide.* (Originally published in France in 1897.) Glencoe, Ill.: Free Press, 1951.
5. Farberow, N. L., Personality patterns of suicidal mental hospital patients. *Genetic Psychology Monographs,* 42: 3–79, 1950.
6. ———— and E. S. Shneidman, A study of attempted, threatened, and completed suicide. *Journal of Abnormal and Social Psychology,* 50: 230, 1955.

7. Menninger, K. A., *Man Against Himself*. New York: Harcourt, Brace and Company, Inc., 1938.
8. Mowrer, O. H., *Psychotherapy: Theory and Research*. New York: The Ronald Press Company, 1953.
9. Shneidman, E. S., and N. L. Farberow, Comparison between genuine and simulated suicide notes by means of Mowrer's DRQ. *Journal of Genetic Psychology* (in press).

2

Theories of Suicide

DON D. JACKSON

In 1936, Zilboorg (31) said: "It is clear that the problem of suicide from the scientific point of view remains unsolved. Neither common sense nor clinical psychopathology has found a causal or even a strictly empirical solution." Freud had made a similar statement in 1918 in summarizing a psychoanalytic symposium on suicide in Vienna. Theories of suicide have not undergone sufficient amplification since the statement by these two authorities to deny the essential validity of their remarks. Perhaps the most that has been accomplished in the last twenty years has been a more happy blending of the sociologic and psychoanalytic data, and increased recognition that suicide is more a number of syndromes than a discrete psychologic entity.

The earliest theories of suicide were largely demonologic and theologic. A good deal of speculation and argument centered over the right of the individual to take his own life. That suicide was considered a conscious volitional act is evidenced by laws that existed against suicide, and by its being banned by some religions. However, both Hobbes and Berkeley, among others, discussed the intriguing quality of death because of its unknown aspects and the invitation for a new beginning which it offered in fantasy.

The breakthrough in the understanding of suicide occurred from two separate fields: Freud's psychodynamic elucidation and Durkheim's sociologic approach. Freud's paper "Mourning and Melancholia" (10), which depicted the dynamics of depression, also provided the framework for the psychoanalytic theory of suicide. This theory, in brief, is essentially one which posits the turning of sadism against the individual himself. As Freud said: "The ego sees itself deserted by the superego and lets itself die." Fenichel (8) extends Freud's ideas, stating, in essence, that suicide is

11

the outcome of a strong ambivalent dependence on a sadistic superego and the necessity to get rid of an unbearable guilt tension at any cost. He mentions that the desire to live means to feel a certain self-esteem, and to feel supported by the protective forces of the superego. When this feeling vanishes, the original feeling of annihilation which the individual experienced as the deserted hungry baby reappears. Since the superego is made up of introjects which represent incorporated love objects, suicide involves the murder of the original object whose incorporation helped to create the superego. Along with the self-murder goes the hopeful illusion that forgiveness and reconciliation will be attained by the killing of the punishing superego and the regaining of union with the protective superego. Anna Freud (9) has stressed that turning against the superego may be strengthened by identification with an aggressor.

On the other hand, Durkheim (6) approached the problem of suicide from a sociologic point of view. His interest was not in the individual but in the forces of society which affect the individual—much as the tides are at the mercy of the moon. The three types of suicide that Durkheim described are: *egoistic* suicide, in which the individual is not sufficiently integrated into his society; *altruistic* suicide, in which there is an overintegration of the individual with society and he sacrifices himself as in the case of a soldier on the battlefield; and *anomic* suicide, in which the individual's adjustment to society is suddenly disrupted, as through great economic depressions or by sudden wealth. In essence, Durkheim arrived at some conclusions which still hold good. He dismissed climate and certain other "extrasocial" influences as causes of suicide and suggested that a major factor was a lack of sympathetic acceptance of an individual by his social group.

From Freud and Durkheim until the present, many authors have written about suicide. Farberow (7) reviewed the literature and summarized many of the theories advanced on suicide under two broad categories: psychoanalytic theories and nonpsychoanalytic theories. For the purpose of completeness an abstract of his review is included here, despite the fact that some overlap will occur with the discussion which follows.

PSYCHOANALYTIC THEORIES

Most of the psychoanalytic theories stem from Freud's theory of depression and postulation of a death instinct, "Thanatos," to accompany his life instinct, "Eros." His theory of depression, as summarized by Zilboorg (31), states that when the patient has identified with a person whom he both loves and hates, these strong ambivalent feelings are turned in on himself and unconscious sadism is directed against himself. The suicides were thus the victims of strong aggressive impulses which they failed to express outwardly, and which, as a result, were turned inward. Menninger (21) is probably the best-known protagonist of Freud's proposal of a death instinct, visualizing suicide as the winning out of the destructive tendencies over the constructive tendencies. He analyzes three sources of suicide: (a) impulses derived from the primary aggressiveness crystallized as a wish to kill; (b) impulses derived from a modification of the primitive aggressiveness crystallized as the wish to be killed; and (c) impulses from primary aggressiveness and additional sophisticated motives crystallized as the wish to die. Pollack (26), Read (27), and Hendrick (13) are others who accept the Freudian theory. Pollack adds that instability of mood and difficulty in sex adjustment, with Oedipal and homosexual situations, occur frequently. Zilboorg (31, 32) adds his conception that suicide is a way of thwarting outside forces that are making living impossible. In his studies he has found that every potential case shows strong unconscious hostility combined with an unusual incapacity to love others. Another aspect which he emphasizes is the paradoxical effect of living by killing oneself. This is one method of gaining immortality and fame, thus maintaining the ego rather than destroying it. O'Connor (23) also stresses the immortality aspect, stating that the suicide of the depressed patient is a kind of return to early power-narcissism, wherein the person achieves omnipotence. He warns that when a depressive shows sudden improvement, suicide may be even more of a possibility because of the change in attitudes. Jamieson (18) stresses the early influences, interpreting the motives for suicide on the basis of infantile organizations, particularly aggressiveness and narcissism. Bender and Schilder (1) studied suicide in 18 children under thirteen years of age and found that there was hardly any case in which spite was not important. They concluded that suicide for children was an attempt to escape an unbearable situation, usually consisting of the deprivation of love. Aggressive tendencies were provoked which aroused guilt feelings, and these aggressive feelings were then directed against the self. These feelings may be increased by constitutional factors and/or identification with an aggressive parent. The attempt also constitutes a punishment against the surroundings and a method of getting a greater amount of love. Palmer (24), too, stresses early influences. His main contention is that arrest in psychosexual development is the basic mechanism in the majority of attempts. The arrest in development is most often due to loss of, or unavailability of, parents at crucial stages in the child's life. These are, particularly, the years during which the child is making identifications which allow him to progress through the various stages. Though he found spite to be present frequently, he felt that it was a rationalization of a deeper-lying defect in development, rather than a direct incitement. Garma (11) states that two of the major factors which lead a person toward suicide are the loss of a vitally important libidinous object and aggression secondarily turned against the ego. The act then becomes for the suicide a way of recovering the lost object and, at the same time, a way of freeing himself from the aggression of the environment and of influencing it. He also adds the hereditary constitution as an important factor. Bergler (2) feels that differentiation must be made between the types of suicide. He calls one type the *introjection* type, or that in which the patient has guilt feelings against which is mobilized pseudo aggression. A second type is called the *hysteric* type, which is an unconscious dramatization of how one does not want to be treated, accompanied by a childish misconception of death lacking finality. The third type is the *miscellaneous,* made up of other suicides, like paranoid schizophrenics, who project their superegos outwardly and hear voices commanding them to kill themselves. He doubts whether aggression leading to inner guilt is the basic principle and believes that inner passivity, masochistically tinged, is the decisive element.

NONPSYCHOANALYTIC THEORIES

Davidson (5) is one of the people who have offered nonpsychoanalytic theories concerning suicide. He feels that the person, at the time of his suicidal attempt, has reached the limit of his resources, and has lost his goal. The immediate situation acts as a "dominant," which restricts the field of consciousness to such an extent that there is an inattention to life itself. An "organic depression" results, and the higher centers are unable to comply with and control the incoming impulses to choose an action. He ceases to will, giving way to imagination, with the result that normal automatic rejection of what is unhealthy will cease. Crichton-Miller (4) attributes suicide to a failure of adaptation and feels that it constitutes a final regression from reality. Usually present in suicides, he says, are signs of social suffering and fears, doubts and dreads, and, to a smaller extent, physical pain. Anticipated pain is much more powerful than the pain itself. Clark (3) states that at the bottom of all suicides one almost invariably finds an onanistic, an incest, or an inversion motive. The result is a disturbance in the normal balance of the will to live, an increase of intrapsychic tension, and a suicidal act, because of the dynamic fixation of infantile attachment. Teicher (29) feels that attempted suicides have developed aggressive patterns of reaction to insecurity-provoking situations, and then turn these aggressions inward because of their insecurities. The act then becomes an infantile exhibitionistic protest and an act of hostility against a harsh restraining figure. He considered their insecurity so great that they were unable even to complete the aggressive act against themselves. Williams (30) felt that the dominant reasons for suicide are disappointment and frustration. But since these happen to everybody, there must be a personality factor in addition, which he called a strong narcissism in a rigid personality, and which prohibited easy adaptation. For Goitein (12), suicidal impulses occurred as compensations for homicidal impulses against members of the immediate family. Pessin (25) reported one case of a girl of fifteen with self-destructive tendencies. He noticed almost the same factors mentioned by Bender and Schilder (1), with the addition of strong erotic trends. Lewis (19, 20) approaches the problem of suicide more from the viewpoint of psychobiology and attributes the event to the final breakdown of the adaptive process. For him, the suicide is ". . . not able to adapt in the midst of so-called higher-level contradictions because of some lack of compensatory adjustment, which is in no way a conscious or deliberate proceeding, but . . . belongs in the realm of general patterns forming an integral part of the personality." Mills (22) recognizes weather as only one of many contributing factors, but feels that it is a major one. Suicides represent for him that section of the population which admits its inability to cope with the mental stress of life, and mental stress, he says, is always heightened with bad weather. Thus, he found that in a five year period sudden peaks of suicides coincided sharply with low-pressure weather crises. Hurlburt (15) felt that the suicide rate tended to fluctuate roughly in an inverse manner with the rate of business activity. Henry and Short (14) correlated both suicide and homicide data with fluctuations in economic cycles and found several interesting relationships.

Another way of classifying and discussing theories of suicide is in terms of the various emphases which are given to the underlying motives of the suicidal act. We propose the following outline:

(1) *Self-directed aggression.* This category may or may not include the concept of a death instinct. It does include partial suicide, such as multiple operations, accident proneness, and so forth.

(2) *Rebirth and restitution.* Authorities who discuss suicide in children and in schizophrenics are especially apt to mention the concept of doing away with the "bad me" in order to make a new beginning. Events ranging from running away from home to departing from life represent a continuum which includes the sorrow of those left behind and the joy of finding someone who really cares.

(3) *Despair, loss of self-esteem, and the real or imagined loss of the love object.* Many experts, especially those sociologically oriented, point to the loss of something that precedes a suicide. There may be the loss of health or facilities as in malignant cancer or old age; or the kind of loss that occurs in financial disaster, drop in social status or prestige, or the losing of a mate by death, separation, or divorce. There are some authorities who hold socioeconomic forces to be influential in the act of suicide and correlate suicide with business cycle fluctuations (14).

These various emphases point up the idea that suicide is a symptomatic act, not a discrete entity. Thus, it may be artificial, even misleading, to describe suicide from the point of view of a single motivation, inasmuch as all the above categories may be present in an individual who kills himself. From another point of view, the suicidal phenomena may be viewed as a continuum; at one extreme would be the "irrational" suicide who kills himself entirely because of inner emotional make-up (an example would be a psychotic who feels that the world is coming to an end), while at the other extreme would be a "rational" suicide who destroys himself because of external conditions (an example would be a cancer victim in extreme pain); in between would be the "neurotic suicide" under some daily emotional strain and the lonely aged person. Thus suicide can be viewed as a combination of the individual's inner emotional make-up and external stress or extreme social pressures—a concatenation of "psychic forces" and "environmental factors." The psychic forces (of dependence, hostility, identification, and so forth) stem from childhood conditioning based on biologic and cultural factors; the environmental factors (such as pain, wartime heroic sacrifice, cultural suttee or hara-kiri) stem from unfortunate current stressful situations which recapitulate childhood trauma or emphasize cultural mores.

In the following section, various aspects of the suicidal phenomenon, following the outline, are commented upon and summarized.

Self-directed Aggression

Perhaps the best-known theory of suicide since Freud's original work is that elucidated by Karl Menninger (21) and subscribed to by numerous psychoanalytic writers. As described above, Menninger feels that there are three elements in any suicide—the wish to kill, the wish to be killed, and the wish to die. Thus, a person who expresses a wish to live after being saved from suicide would be lacking in the third element, the wish to die. The first two points are an expression of the talion law: "An eye for an eye and a tooth for a tooth." The third element, however, involves the controversial death instinct. Despite intriguing speculation and argument, Thanatos still seems to remain a highly nebulous concept. Zilboorg and certain other authorities have stressed unchanneled aggression rather than the death instinct as being of prime importance in motivating suicide. Hence, Zilboorg (32) stresses the high suicide rate in children and primitive people. Other authorities feel that the suicide rate in children is low, and the evidence for a high rate among primitive people is questionable, especially in view of insufficient data. Psychiatric authorities who quote anthropologic evidence in support of their theories run the danger of biased selection.

Rebirth and Restitution

This concept is exemplified by a schizophrenic patient who made a serious suicide attempt which, by accident, did not succeed. After he had recovered from the major psychotic manifestations of his illness, he recalled the following thoughts about the suicide attempt.

I wouldn't have done it if everyone (the family) weren't there to see it. I was obsessed with thoughts of Heaven and Hell—getting free from them was Heaven and being trapped by them was Hell. Father had said there are lots of people who go into these places (mental hospitals) and get out of them. I thought he was really saying "our mad son—he'll never get out of here." My brother seemed to me to be saying that he wanted to get this mess off his hands and lock me up for good. I had to be a carbon copy of him in order that he wouldn't be disappointed in me. When he told me that I could do anything I wanted to in life, that I wouldn't have to spend the day working in the family business if I didn't want to, it was his way of saying: "You'll never get out of this hospital." I remember it seemed like a repetition of an incident that had happened a couple of days before. I had gone swimming with my brother and his girl friend and figured that I would try to make the shore from the boat. I felt I was too weak to do it and might be drowned but if I made it I would be saved. They paid no attention to me and it seemed like an invitation to drown. I still get angry at them because they walked away. Making the shoreline meant that I might be free to live again; not making it was death which was all right since being tied to them was death.

In this account, as well as in other material from this patient, the idea of the new beginning and of being told to die played a large part. Numerous authorities have noted, particularly in regard to the suicides of children and schizophrenics, that the idea of making a new start by destroying the old (bad) self seems to play a part. There is also the belief that through death one is joined with the love object—as portrayed in *Romeo and Juliet*. Obviously in children such ideas can be strengthened if there is identification with an actual dead love object. Some studies indicate that sometimes there is a dead or absent parent in families of those committing suicide (24).[1] This fact might also be a partial explanation for the infrequency of suicide at an early age, when the parents are alive, and the increased rate with older age groups, after the parents or spouse

[1] Reference is made to Chap. 10, by Moss and Hamilton, The Psychotherapy of the Suicidal Patient, in which they remark on the "death trend" noted in suicidal patients and in which they state that they found a very high percentage of individuals closely related to the patient who had died under dramatic and often tragic circumstances.

are dead. It might also play a part in the clinical observation that suicidal attempts or feelings may result from fear of the mother's becoming pregnant again and being lost to a younger sibling. It has been felt that suicide is related to the feelings about birth of a new cycle—a new season, a new year, and so forth. It is as if the individual might feel: "I cannot face another birth, a time when other people are happy. I cannot face the creative feel of a new day or a new week when I am so alone and unwanted." The idea of being alone and left to die connects suicide with sleep. For example, the child goes to sleep for the "good mother" and eagerly awaits the reunion next morning. The child who is sent to sleep by the "bad" mother feels himself to be bad and unloved, and may fear sleep much as the adult fears death, since the good mother may be permanently gone. Once asleep, however, wish-fulfilling processes may ease the pain, and in the morning there may be a joyous reunion and the reappearance of the good mother. Hence, ideas about sleep can be intimately connected with later unconscious preoccupation with death. The idea of a new beginning with the original love object is supported also by observations on suicide occurrences or attempts on the anniversary of the death or departure of a loved one.

A woman committed suicide by cutting her throat and wrists a year from the day her husband had left her. During her childhood her mother had died of suffocation due to a throat tumor.

Attempts at suicide, although they form a continuum with completed suicide, also show different motivational emphasis. Here the intent seems to be to manipulate and force and to get revenge. Suicide attempts are more common, in our culture, in women and rather uncommonly occur in the aged.

A young woman who had made several suicide attempts came into a psychotherapeutic session with her face apparently horribly bruised. She was attempting to act out in the transference with the aid of facial make-up similar feelings to those that had led to her suicide attempts.

Socioeconomic Theories of Suicide

These theories range from those which propose a one-to-one relationship between economic factors and suicide to those which correlate socioeconomic forces with the knowledge of human psychology. Unfortunately, an adequate operational socioeconomic theory of suicide does not exist. In the first place, present sociologic data are selective and incomplete and lack valid controls. Second, cause-and-effect relationships are virtually impossible to sort out. For example, a sociologic study of suicide in London (28) reveals that a suicide map and a map of the poorest single-unit dwellings are nearly identical. Are lonely poor people more prone to suicide? Or, do potential suicides become lonely poor people as a way station in their downward path? Probably it is not an "either-or" matter but a concatenation of events that is capped by an x factor which includes time, chance, and some "last straw" type of precipitating cause.

Finally, it should be mentioned that there is a tendency (not limited to sociologic researchers) to accept external causes as one of the more frequent explanations for suicide. This tendency, at its unfortunate extreme, is typified by the usual newspaper account: "So-and-so killed himself because of illness [or financial disaster, or the like]." However, despite its extensive use as a naïve explanation of suicide, it is possible that the victim of a painful, crippling illness, for example, is mentally healthy rather than masochistic in arranging his own demise. We need to know more about so-called "rational" suicide.

The discussion of the theories of suicide can be concluded by indicating some important implications of theoretical points of view in respect to patients in psychotherapy. It is doubtful if suicide, apart from its rational form, can ever occur where adequate communication exists between the therapist and his patient. There is probably a real event, whether of omission or commission, which, however fantastically interpreted, actually triggers the act of suicide. Such an event involves a real or fantasied death wish and in psychotherapy may be represented by a communication difficulty or block between patient and therapist. Such a block in the relationship produces just enough feeling of abandonment in the patient to recapitulate old feelings of hate and fear over loss of the love object, and perhaps most importantly, allows him to interpret this as a deliberate but subtle attempt to withdraw love or support. This point may not be sufficiently understood by therapists dealing with demanding, hysterical patients who attempt suicide. The patient may be trying to force involvement by suicide threats and at the same time be fearful that his manipulativeness and hatefulness will lead the therapist to abandon him. The trigger point may be the indication of helplessness on the therapist's part, either by rigid firmness of behavior or by reluctant permissiveness. Helplessness or fear on the therapist's part, just as in the parent, indicates to the patient abandonment and an inability to tolerate his hatefulness.

References

1. Bender, L., and P. Schilder, Suicidal preoccupation and attempts in children. *American Journal of Orthopsychiatry*, 7: 225–234, 1937.
2. Bergler, E., Problems of suicide. *Psychiatric Quarterly* (supplement), 20: 261–275, 1946.
3. Clark, L. P., A study of the unconscious motivations in suicides. *New York Medical Journal*, 116: 254–263, 1922.
4. Crichton-Miller, H., The psychology of suicide. *British Medical Journal*, 2: 239–241, 1931.
5. Davidson, G. M., The problem of suicide. *Medical Record*, 139: 24–28, 1934.
6. Durkheim, E., *Le Suicide*. (Translated by Spalding.) Glencoe, Ill.: Free Press, 1950.
7. Farberow, Norman L., Personality patterns of suicidal mental hospital patients. *Genetic Psychology Monographs*, 42: 3–79, 1950.
8. Fenichel, Otto, *The Psychoanalytic Theory of Neurosis*. New York: W. W. Norton & Company, Inc., 1945.
9. Freud, Anna, *The Ego and the Mechanisms of Defense*. London: Hogarth Press, Ltd., 1937.
10. Freud, S., Mourning and Melancholia. (In *Collected Papers*, volume IV.) London: Hogarth Press, Ltd., 1925. (Originally published in *Zeitschrift für Psychoanalyse*, Band IV, 1917.)
11. Garma, A., Sadism and masochism in human conduct (part II). *Journal of Clinical Psychopathology and Psychotherapy*, 6: 355–390, 1944.
12. Goitein, P. L., Mind of murder. *Journal of Criminal Psychopathology*, 3: 625–647, 1942.
13. Hendrick, I., Suicide as wish-fulfillment. *Psychiatric Quarterly*, 14: 30–42, 1940.
14. Henry, Andrew F., and James F. Short, Jr., *Suicide and Homicide*. Glencoe, Ill.: Free Press, 1954.
15. Hurlburt, W. C., Prosperity, depression, and the suicide rate. *American Journal of Sociology*, 37: 714–719, 1932.
16. Jackson, Don D., Suicide and the physician. *The Prescriber*, March, 1955.
17. ———, Suicide. *Scientific American*, 191: 88–96, 1954.
18. Jamieson, G. R., Suicide and mental disease: A clinical analysis of one hundred cases. *Archives of Neurology and Psychiatry*, 36: 1–12, 1936.
19. Lewis, N. D. C., Studies on suicides, I. Preliminary survey of some significant aspects of suicide. *Psychoanalytic Review*, 20: 241–273, 1933.
20. ———, Studies on suicide, II. Some comments on the biological aspects of suicide. *Psychoanalytic Review*, 21: 146–153, 1934.
21. Menninger, K. A., *Man Against Himself*. New York: Harcourt, Brace and Company, Inc., 1938.
22. Mills, C. A., Suicide and homicides in their relation to weather changes. *American Journal of Psychiatry*, 91: 669–677, 1934.
23. O'Connor, W. A., Some notes on suicide. *British Journal of Medical Psychology*, 21: 222–228, 1948.
24. Palmer, D. M., Factors in suicidal attempts: A review of 25 consecutive cases. *Journal of Nervous and Mental Disease*, 93: 421–442, 1941.

25. Pessin, J., Self-destruction tendencies in adolescence. *Bulletin of the Menninger Clinic*, 5: 13–19, 1941.
26. Pollack, B., A study of the problem of suicide. *Psychiatric Quarterly*, 12: 306–330, 1938.
27. Read, C. S., The problem of suicide. *British Medical Journal*, 1: 631–634, 1936.
28. Romilly, S., *Suicide*. London: Hogarth Press, Ltd., 1939.
29. Teicher, J. D., A study in attempted suicide. *Journal of Nervous and Mental Disease*, 105: 283–298, 1947.
30. Williams, E. Y., Some observations on the psychiatric aspects of suicide. *Journal of Abnormal and Social Psychology*, 31: 260-265, 1936.
31. Zilboorg, G., Differential diagnostic types of suicide. *Archives of Neurology and Psychiatry*, 35: 270–291, 1936.
32. ———, Suicide among civilized and primitive races. *American Journal of Psychiatry*, 92: 1347–1369, 1936.
33. ———, Considerations in suicide with particular reference to that of the young. *American Journal of Orthopsychiatry*, 17: 15, 1937.

3

Suicide as a Magical Act

CHARLES WILLIAM WAHL

It is a most interesting and instructive task to survey the literature on suicide of fifty years ago and to contrast it with that of recent times. Even the most cursory examination shows that there are two striking features of the writings of those days. First, there seems to have been an almost universal conviction that the causes of suicide were patently evident and certainly presented no real mystery, and, second, there was almost ubiquitous concurrence that suicide is effected for essentially one of two reasons, namely, "worry over ill health" or because one had "lost one's mind." These two reasons seem to have been the only ones accepted at that time as valid and cogent, and it is noteworthy that there was a marked lack of interest and curiosity in pursuing the matter further. The paradox between these two views did not then appear to be perceived. For the first infers that "naturally" anyone might take his life because of worry over ill health: "What value is life if your health is not good," the common folk cliché of the time succinctly summarized it. And yet, the second view antithetically infers that to take one's life under any circumstance, to fly in the face not only of one's self-preservative "instincts" but also of the generally accepted tenets of society and religion, was to perform an uncanny, unnatural, and wholly irrational act. It was craziness—an act only considered or effected by the dement.

With even a cursory examination of the literature on suicides of the present day, we see an immense change in attitude and perspective. Not only is there a fascinated interest about suicide—which is certainly antipodal to the apathy of yesterday—but there is also a widespread concurrence that suicide, far from being simple or easily understood, is an extremely complex act, and is effected for a variety of reasons and purposes. We now know that we are only beginning to understand some of the

22

complexities of its motivation, and indeed, we are learning that we know very little about why suicide is adopted as a solution for the impelling conflict rather than an employment of some other remedial act or symptom. Is the purpose of suicide to "bind anxiety"? Many neurotic symptoms and defense mechanisms do this superlatively well. Is it to alleviate guilt? A wide variety of neurotic symptoms, as well as many philosophic and religious systems, may do the same. Why indeed does not the suicide become instead a zealot or a "true believer"? Is its purpose to discharge an otherwise invincible hostility? Why then cannot antisocial behavior or revolutionary activity be adopted? Does it represent a need to escape from an intolerable life situation? Why then is there not recourse to the withdrawal and dereism of a schizophrenic, the nomadism of the derelict, or the needle of the drug addict?

It is unfortunately the painful truth that as yet we have no satisfying answers to any of these questions.

The act of suicide becomes all the more puzzling if we believe, as does Silverberg (4), that the ego's main purpose and motive is to ensure survival and that this drive for survival is omnipresent, irrational, and not easily foiled or flouted. All of us could cite instances of beings who are seemingly reduced to utter degradation, squalor, ignominy, and misery but who, even so, wish to live and are loath to end their lives. For, as Bettelheim (1) discovered, even in the horrors of a German concentration camp, the majority of persons, under the most desperate and benighted conditions, will cling tenaciously to life. What then accounts for the ease with which the suicide gives up a life which the rest of us cling to so doggedly? What are the ends and goals which the suicide pursues and which are to him stronger than life itself? Most of us are probably in essential agreement with Silverberg and would hold that the wish to live is a powerful and constant force, not to be gainsaid by any series of rational remonstrances; our task is to address ourselves to the problem of just what are the irrational concepts which make the termination of life possible or even desirable.

The view to be presented in this paper is that suicide is not preeminently a rational act pursued to achieve rational ends, even when it is effected by persons who appear to be eminently rational. Rather, it is a magical act, actuated to achieve irrational, delusional, and illusory ends. Magic is used here as it is defined by Schopenhauer, namely, an objectification of desire outside the causal nexus; an act of attempted control, or delusion of such control, of physical forces normally peripheral to human mastery. Suicide, like the other neurotic symptoms which it resembles, is a symbolic, reified solution of a conflict, and the purposes of this symbolic solution are largely unconscious and only minimally within the limits of conscious awareness.

The major conflict, which is the primary one that the act of suicide is an attempt to solve, is an identification conflict. By identification is meant that process by which the child during the prelogical stage of his development comes to take within himself, by a process essentially magical and unwitting in character, the habits, patterns, and methods of problem solution characteristic of the primary socializers, usually the parents. He obtains by this process, moreover, his basic conceptions of himself as a person; or, since he is unable, owing to his limited past experience and proto-irrational concept formation, to evaluate his own merit, any conceptions of his adequacy and worth and, indeed, of his very nature are obtained by an uncritical acceptance of the prevailing attitudes held toward him by his parents. Hence, if they derogate and reject him, or if they themselves are weak and vacillating, or if they are lost to him for some reason such as death or abandonment, he is almost certain to develop a conception of himself as a debased and inadequate person. Because this is an unendurably painful state of affairs, he reacts with strong hatred and hostility, which usually takes the form of death wishes toward the depriving parent, and in time these themselves evoke strong and often unremitting guilt. Repression is the usual and most pathologic mechanism for handling the anxiety, self-hatred, hostility, and guilt which result from this identification dilemma.

It is, of course, obvious that this is an oversimplified schema and that these painful effects may be produced in other ways or take other forms, and, moreover, we know that the parental situation described above need not eventuate in this manner. Also, the identification dilemma outlined above is known to be a common antecedent of most disturbed populations, and many different kinds of neurotic and psychotic disorders will serve to "bind" and repress the unacceptable affects which such a prior environment might induce. As yet, we have only suggestive data on the familial and personal antecedents of a sufficiently large number of persons who attempt to perform suicide to determine what relevance, if any, these factors may have in the genesis of this phenomenon (2, 5, 6).

Suicide, or ruminations about it, compare with neurotic symptoms in that they are magical and symbolic attempts to solve an exigent conflict and to achieve comfort thereby. Suicide also resembles other neurotic symptoms in that it is complexly and severally motivated. These motivations seem to vary in nature and in strength and significance from one person to another, and they are in varying degrees conscious or unconscious in each subject. Some of the motives in which the magical aspect of suicide is most strongly suggested are as follows:

First, a wish to punish a depriving figure by the induction of guilt. Such figures usually prove to be the parents or the siblings but are sometimes the extrapolation of them, that is, society or mankind. In this connection, one is reminded of the story in Mark Twain's *Tom Sawyer*. Tom, being painfully frustrated by his aunt, was strongly comforted by the fantasy of committing suicide by drowning himself in the Mississippi. He thought to himself of how sad and piteous a spectacle he would make when his body would be brought into his aunt's presence, with his curls all wet, and how consequently sorry and remorseful she would be. She would then say to herself, "Oh, if I had only loved him more. How differently I would have treated him if I had only known." We read that this picture brought tears of self-pity to his eyes. There are reasons to believe that fantasies of this character are ubiquitous among children. This appears to be true not only because children have intense expectations and needs from the parents, some of which are bound to be unfulfilled, but also because children are almost totally impotent physically and mentally. They can therefore best repay the hostility which this frustration induces by acts of their own which induce guilt, since, because of their weakness, they are largely deprived of a more direct means of aggression. The entertainment of such a maneuver involves also a denial of death as a finite and terminal act. It is as though they could remain behind to see and relish the discomfiture and remorse their act would induce. Presumably, therefore, when impotence of a physical, mental, or social nature persists far into adult life, then the individual, like the child, is more prone to utilize this method of being hostile to others, since a more direct means of aggression is generally impossible. For example, in Japan, if one has been unsufferably injured, or if the person who has done this injury is of an unapproachable social class, one still has recourse to the highly aggressive device of committing suicide on the enemy's doorstep. And Malinowski (3) relates that among the Trobriand islanders there is a similar reaction to an inadmissible affront. There, the aggrieved person climbs a high palm tree, and after haranguing the audience on the evils of the affronting person, he dives, head foremost, to his death. Also, suicide for such a motive is by no means isolated from our own culture. Presumably, in these instances, the wish for revenge by inducing guilt and remorse exceeds the desire to live and is seemingly related to a denial of the infinitude and irreversibility of death.

A second motive for suicide is the wish to reduce personal guilt, which is by general concurrence the most painful of all affect states. These suicide attempts seem to be usually an act of self-punishment, an attempt to expiate the fantasied act of murder (death wishes) by operation of the talion law. It must be remembered that in the unconscious the thought is equally comparable with the deed and is equated with it. It says in effect, "You wish the death of a person and therefore you must die." Often, subsequent stresses in a patient's life trigger-off and actuate latent, repressed conflicts of this nature, which then sum with the current stress and produce a resultant act of physical self-destruction. Zilboorg (7) has commented on the interesting phenomenon of persons who commit suicide on the anniversary of their parents' or siblings' death, as though to expiate through their own demise the parental or fraternal death which they unconsciously perceived as resultant from their death wishes. The wish had then become hypostatized and equated unconsciously with the deed. It appears that expiation of personal guilt and achievement of a hostile wish by guilt induction are almost invariably present in every suicidal attempt or act.

A third motive, and one more recondite, is the employment of suicide as an aid in coping with an overpowering thanatophobia, or fear of death. Suicide in this sense serves as a reaction formation to the morbidly feared eventuality of death by embracing it rather than running from it. An example is an adolescent boy who had a prolonged history of an intense fear of death and who attempted to hang himself. He accounted for his actions by saying he tried to find out if death was as bad as he had been told. He had resolved to be a man and face the thing he feared. A more complete explanation of his act revealed, of course, that it was much more complexly motivated; it developed that in part he unconsciously felt toward death as do children who play "cops and robbers," that death is a reversible and temporary rather than a permanent and irreversible process and, therefore, not "really dangerous." These magical aspirations may constitute largely overlooked motives for suicide.

One cannot truly understand the deeper dynamics of suicide until he comprehends its relationship to death, and the unconscious significance and meaning which death has to us. There are cogent reasons to believe that, unconsciously, we do not consider (as most of us do consciously) death to be the end of our existence or a permanent state from which there is no returning. But rather because of the innate, unconscious narcissism of the ego, our own demise is not considered even to be a possible eventuality. In our deepest selves we believe as did the psalmist, who said confidently, "A thousand shall fall at thy right hand, ten thousand at thy left, but it shall not come nigh thee." Hence, most of us do not fear death because on the deepest level we cannot even conceive of it. We have created a vast number of philosophic and religious systems which convince us, no less than they did the ancient Egyptians, that we cannot ever cease to exist, but that instead we are merely translated from one form of existence to another. This denial of death and conviction of immortality the religious person entertains consciously, but the remainder of persons appear to entertain it unconsciously, however strongly they may protest and believe that they are reconciled to an eventual termination of their existence.

This may be an answer to the question phrased previously, namely, how can the suicide value life so cheaply when there are such manifold examples of lengths to which the average man will go to preserve his life? Can it be that death may be perceived in a different fashion by the suicide—that he is able to encompass his self-destruction because unconsciously he does not perceive death as the to-be-avoided thing which most of us so regard it? There is evidence from some of my own cases that the manifestly deprived and frustrated person, who is more prone than others to employ grandiose fantasies of a compensatory character, exalts thereby his sense of narcissistic immortality and omnipotence. Death then, by one's own hand, not only serves the motives of expiating self-guilt and inflicting it on others but is not even conceived in the usual terms of fear and dread. The possibility of his own not-being is unconsciously so distant and remote that he can entertain and effect an act of self-destruction without the sense of self-preservative horror which it so commonly induces in others.

There are also reasons to believe that death is conceived not only as a surcease from pain in this world and a translation to a happier one, but also as an act whereby one acquires powers, qualities, and advantages not possessed in the living state. The dead man is conceived by the act of dying to become a spirit, ghost, or poltergeist, possessing a whole new hierarchy of powers, even capable of transcending time and space and so wreaking vengeance upon his enemies. If one credits and identifies with these beliefs, which exist as almost universal superstitions, one can thereby achieve a vengeance by dying which one's impotence has denied him while living. The ubiquity of this belief among primitive races and small children and its widespread presence as a present-day superstition attests to its unconscious omnipresence, attested to also by the cliché "When I die, I'll come back and haunt you." Just as the ghosts of the small and weak children whom Hercules inadvertently destroyed pursued and tormented him, securing a vengeance on him which they could never have achieved in life, so in modern man the unconscious acceptance of this possibility may serve to motivate an act of self-destruction for the purpose of securing a revenge and harassment on his erstwhile tormentors and on all those who have ever deprived and injured him. A variant of this view is the expectant wish that death gives one immediate access to the Godhead, where one can make a personal appeal for divine redress against those who have wronged him.

Finally, there is the phenomenon of infantile cosmic identification, and its possible relevance to suicide. It is an amply demonstrated fact that when we are faced with situations and obstacles which appear insurmountable to us, when we are required to deal with situations and circumstances in which we feel ourselves to be manifestly impotent, we are perforce constrained into a retrospective scrutiny of our own past for aiding memories of those times and places in which we *were* able to so cope with such situations. This is, of course, the phenomenon of regression, and in states of exigent and compelling need, we are powerfully impelled to regress to that portion of our childhood in which we did indeed have a power and capacity which in adulthood is largely denied to the conscious mind. This is, of course, the period of infantile omnipotence.

This response of an automatic retrospection in extreme situations to those times in which we may have encountered similar difficulties is demonstrated by the often described circumstance of one's life flashing before view in that moment when one is faced with the circumstance of an impending, sudden, or violent death. This may be envisioned as the organism's desperate attempt to "rack its brain" for memory of a solution to similar extraordinary and life-threatening situations.

Situations, therefore, which we must face with a conviction of intense and extreme impotence incite us to the employment of the heavy artillery of defense, namely, a regression to infantile omnipotence. This use of magical defenses is obvious to us when it adopts the form of the solipsistic dereism of the hebephrenic or catatonic schizophrenic, but is not so obvious when the conscious rational superstructure is left largely intact, as is the case in the average suicide candidate. When rationality fails, or when we think it has failed, to solve exigent and insuperable problems, we then have recourse to magic; when this is a conscious act, it takes the form of spell, incantation, ritual, and dogmatic belief; if unconscious, however, it takes the form of the employment of magical symptoms which are reifications or hypostatizations which serve to bind, alleviate, or attenuate the anxiety, hostility, and guilt.

In the early stage of the ego development of the child, there is a period when he cannot differentiate himself from persons or objects in this world of which he is a part. He, his thoughts, and his body constitute all of reality. These feelings appear to be unconsciously persistent in all of us as latent concepts of cosmic identification and the belief that retaliation toward others can be effected by self-punishment, as though all persons were a part of our own substance. As an example, a young schizophrenic boy frequently tried to slash himself with a knife, and he would smile gleefully as he watched his blood flow. Asked why he did this, he replied, "All the world bleeds when I'm cut, but I have more blood than they do and I'll live when they are all bled out." "But," he added, "my parents and sister bleed most of all when I cut myself."

The potential suicide, too, faces grave, and to him, insurmountable problems. As his resources to alter himself in the world are exhausted, he is forced to employ magic and dereism, to use hypostatic reality as does the child, and by so doing is thereby enabled to fulfill many of his wishes which could not be gratified in real life. The suicide achieves, as does the infant, a kind of cosmic identification. By equating the world with self, he affirms the same fallacy as the medieval mystics who said, as did St. Eustace, "Nothing outside my own mind is real; the world and all persons in it are, in reality, me." Therefore, to kill oneself is to kill everything that there is, the world and all other persons. Not only then is the suicide committing an aggressive act against the specific person who is himself and against the introjected parents whom he wishes to murder, but also against that extension of the parents—society, which the aggrieved individual has found to be nonnurturant and nonsuccoring. As is so often the case, it is the poet who shows us the royal road to the unconscious, and this delusion of annihilation, which has its origin in the depths of the infantile omnipotence, is admirably demonstrated in a poem by A. E. Housman [1]:

> Good creatures, do you love your lives
> And have you ears for sense?
> Here is a knife like other knives,
> That cost me eighteen pence.
>
> I need but stick it in my heart
> And down will come the sky
> And earth's foundations will depart
> And all you folk will die.

[1] A. E. Housman, *The Collected Poems of A. E. Housman.* New York: Henry Holt and Company, Inc., 1946.

Like Sampson in the temple, the suicide may unconsciously believe that by an act of self-destruction he is encompassing the destruction of myriads of others who, by ignoring the irrational demands which he has placed on them to be his substitute parents, have earned his hatred and his anger. The suicide, when he dies, kills not one person but many. He commits not only suicide but vicarious matricide, patricide, sororicide, fratricide, and even genocide. Did medieval man not subliminally realize this when he made an attempt at self-destruction a legal crime? Indeed, it was entitled *felo-de-se* and it still remains such in the British law books. By the fifteenth-century man, the suicide was treated legally as a murderer—as unconsciously he may have been—and his body would be carried nude through the streets, to be buried at a crossroads with a stake driven through his heart. Apparently the citizens of five centuries ago were expressing the baffled rage which they must have felt at this person whom they regarded as a murderer, and so deserving death, but who had escaped.

But perhaps the saddest thought of all is to see the suicide as he really is, a forlorn, beaten, and deprived person who has peopled his emptiness with malefactors and villains of his own making. His small ingrown self becomes an empty cosmos peopled with his tormentors and detractors. In an immense moment of fantastic grandiosity he lays them, and all the world, to ruin. But instead of leaving the world as he fantasies it, desolated and sere, stricken and laid waste by the magnitude of his act, he gains only a personal surcease from pain and a small footnote on the inside pages of a newspaper. He goes out "not with a bang but a whimper," a dupe to the irrationality within himself.

References

1. Bettelheim, Bruno, *Love Is Not Enough.* Glencoe, Ill.: Free Press, 1951.
2. Farberow, Norman L., Personality patterns of suicidal mental hospital patients. *Genetic Psychology Monographs,* 42: 3–79, 1950.
3. Malinowski, Bronislaw, *The Sexual Life of Savages.* New York: Halcyon House Publications, 1929.
4. Silverberg, William V., *Childhood Experience and Personal Destiny.* New York: Springer Publishing Company, Inc., 1952.
5. Wahl, Charles W., Some antecedent factors in the family histories of 568 male schizophrenics of the U.S. Navy. *American Journal of Psychiatry,* 113: 201–210, 1956.
6. ———, Some antecedent factors in the family histories of 109 alcoholics. *Quarterly Journal of Studies on Alcohol,* 17: 643–654, 1956.
7. Zilboorg, Gregory, Considerations on suicide, with particular reference to that of the young. *American Journal of Orthopsychiatry,* 7: 15–31, 1937.

4

The Logic of Suicide *

EDWIN S. SHNEIDMAN AND NORMAN L. FARBEROW

On superficial thought, one of the outstanding characteristics of the suicidal act is that it is illogical. Yet one can take the position that there is an implicit syllogism or argument in the suicidal act. Although we cannot be sure that our logical reconstructions of suicidal logic are correct, it remains that the suicidal person behaves *as if* he had reasoned and had come to certain—albeit, generally unacceptable—conclusions.

Parenthetically, it is recognized that suicidal reasoning has unconscious motivations and psychodynamic determinants, but those areas are not the subject of this paper. This logical analysis of suicide is not an alternative to a psychodynamic accounting but rather is meant to provide a formal framework within which the specific nature of the psychodynamics must be specified. Thus, the purpose of this paper is to elucidate some details of suicidal logic. The implication is that if one knew the lethal modes of reasoning and the suppressed premises (or beliefs) which lead to a deadly conclusion, then one might have effective clues to use in the prediction and prevention of suicide.

The materials for the development of this paper come from the over 700 suicide notes we have collected as part of our larger study on the psychology of suicide.

In formal, or symbolic, logic, there are a number of errors, called logical fallacies, which can be made. One of many types of fallacy is illustrated in the deductive logic implicit in schizophrenic thinking—first described by Storch (5) and then by von Domarus (6) and recently called "paleologic" by Arieti (1). In normal logic, before identity can be made, certain conditions have to be satisfied. "Paleologic" sweeps aside these conditions and

* Appreciation is expressed to Professor Abraham Kaplan, Department of Philosophy, University of California at Los Angeles, for his logical and philosophical comments.

arrives at fallacious identities. Two examples of this type of reasoning, from von Domarus, can be given. "Switzerland loves freedom; I love freedom; therefore I am Switzerland" and "The Virgin Mary was a virgin; I am a virgin; therefore I am the Virgin Mary." [1]

Another type of logical fallacy, other than the deductive fallacy, wherein the error is dependent on the form of the argument, is the semantic fallacy, wherein the error is dependent on the meaning of the terms occurring in the premises or conclusion. Our examination of the suicide notes indicated that the fallacies of reasoning committed were primarily of this latter type. An example of a semantic fallacy is as follows: "Nothing is better than hard work; a small effort is better than nothing; therefore a small effort is better than hard work." Here the fallacy is not dependent upon the form of the argument but rather on the ambiguous meaning of a specific term, namely, "nothing." Another example of a semantic fallacy, this time with suicidal content, is as follows: "If anybody kills himself then he will get attention; I will kill myself; therefore I will get attention." Deductively, this argument is sound, but the fallacy is concealed in the concepts contained in the word "I." Here the logical role of this pronoun is related to the psychology of the conception of the self.

We see then that in addition to the logic of the normal person and the "paleologic" of the schizophrenic person, we have the reasoning of the suicidal person. We call this type of thinking "destructive logic" or "catalogic." It is destructive not only in the sense that it disregards the classical rules for semantic clarity and formal reasoning but also in that it destroys the logician.

As a result of our analysis of the semantic qualities exhibited in the suicidal notes, it appeared that the logic could be understood best in terms of two implied components of the "I," or the self. The first we call I_s. This is the self as experienced by the individual himself. I_s refers to the person's own experiences, his pains and aches, and sensations and feelings. He says in the note "I can see you crying" and adds (by implication from the tenor of the rest of the note) "I'll be glad this is going to trouble you." The

[1] These two syllogisms illustrate the process of identification in terms of the attributes of the predicate, but it can be pointed out that they can be seen in quite another way: that is, they also demonstrate straightforward Aristotelian reasoning if one only supplies the missing or suppressed premises. What these two syllogisms have in common is that the focus of attention is narrowed to only one attribute of the class. Consider: If Switzerland were the *only* class that loved freedom, and if I loved freedom, then I would indeed have to be Switzerland. Psychologically, this narrowing of focus may reflect the difficulty that the emotionally disturbed person has in grasping other than what is immediately before his mind.

second aspect of the semantic self is called I_o. This is the individual as he feels himself thought of or experienced by others. This would be what he considers his reputation, based on other people's attitudes, other people's actions, ideas, remarks; that is, what others think of him. This comes out in the notes in the extreme concern with practical and trivial details, such as the repair of the automobile, the distribution of goods, the canceling of appointments, and so forth. The suicide says in effect, "I_o will get attention, that is, certain other people will cry, go to a funeral, sing hymns, relive memories, and the like." But he also implies or states that even after death, I_s will go through these experiences, that is, "I will be cried over; I will be attended to"—as though the individual would be able to experience these occurrences. This is the heart of the semantic fallacy or ambiguity.[2]

More accurately, it is not a fallacy in the words of the reasoning, but rather it is a fallacious identification. Hence, we call it a *psychosemantic fallacy*. Parenthetically, we believe that this confusion or ambiguity might indeed occur whenever an individual thinks about his death, whether by suicide or otherwise. It may arise because an individual cannot imagine his own death, his own cessation of experience, a state where there is no more I_s after death. A rare example wherein an individual experienced both the I_o satisfactions of the response from others, as well as the I_s satisfactions of experiencing the reactions of others to his death, is in *Tom Sawyer*, where the boys hide out in the balcony of the church and listen to their own funeral service; but it must be pointed out that they could do this only because they were in point of fact not dead.

This semantic confusion in suicidal logic is similar to the "atmosphere effect" described by Woodworth (7) and Sells (3). They describe the tendency of individuals to accept negative conclusions because of the negative

[2] It will be possible for the philosophically inclined reader to attribute existentialist implications to this point of view. As far as the authors are concerned, these are not necessarily implied. Nevertheless, it may be of interest to quote from Sartre, who states the following: "The lie is also a normal phenomenon of what Heidegger calls the '*Mitsein*' (a 'being-with' others in the world). It presupposes my existence, the existence of the *other*, my existence *for* the other, and the existence of the other *for* me. Thus there is no difficulty in holding that the liar must make the project of the lie in entire clarity and that he must possess a complete comprehension of the lie and of the truth which he is altering. It is sufficient that an opaqueness of principle hides his intentions from *the other*. It is sufficient that the other can take the lie for truth. By the lie, consciousness affirms that it exists by nature as hidden from the other; it utilizes for its own profit *the ontological duality of myself and myself in the eyes of others*." (Last italics ours.) (Sartre, J. P., Self-Deception. In Kaufman, Walter [Ed.], *Existentialism from Dostoevsky to Sartre*. New York: Meridian Books, 1956.)

impression created by the premises. An example would be: "None of my relatives is wealthy; no wealthy person loves me; therefore none of my relatives loves me." In the present context, we label this the "noose effect," that is, it is Thorndike's well-known "halo effect" which has slipped.

The question of the role of anticipation and anticipatory goal responses arises. There is a form of satisfaction to I_s in the following sense: although it is true that I_s ceases to exist after death and thus could not be the subject of the remorse felt toward I_o at that time, I_s can experience a satisfaction through the anticipation of the remorse felt toward I_o. This anticipation, of course, takes place before death, when I_s still exists. It is a fallacy because in order to achieve the anticipation (of the pleasurable experience), he cannot achieve the result (experience it), except that the anticipation of pleasure can itself be a pleasure. It is this psychologic reward which may be one of the prime motivating aspects of suicide. Also, it has been said that all motivations of suicide (both psychodynamic and sociologic) involve anticipation of rejection. An individual's taking of his own life can thus be a way of protecting himself from anticipated punishment and trauma. There may be implications in the above for an exploration of suicide from the point of view of learning-theory concepts.

Some important exceptions to our general hypothesis about suicidal logic can be given. They are three in number:

(1) Some individuals desire nothingness—surcease from pain—and do not confuse I_s with I_o. They apparently understand that, with the commission of suicide, I_s will cease. They realistically face the termination of I_s. Such an individual says, "I cannot stand this excruciating pain." We call these individuals "surcease suicides." Our work with suicide notes of the more aged persons illustrates this phenomenon.

(2) Another exception is those individuals who believe in the continuation of I_s, that is, a belief in a life after death or a hereafter. In this case, owing to the belief in the continued I_s, the psychosemantic ambiguity with I_o need not arise. They say in their notes that they will come back and haunt the individual, or that they will be looking down from above, or they will see loved ones in heaven. This means that beliefs in the hereafter are often very relevant to the suicidal logic, inasmuch as an individual who believes in a life after death may not commit the semantic fallacy discussed in this chapter.

Also related to this category are persons who put a tremendous emphasis on the I_o. Examples would be the kamikaze pilots of the last war, Seneca's suicide at his emperor's suggestion, and so forth. We call these "cultural suicides."

(3) A third exception to the above generalizations would be in relation to individuals who are schizophrenic. One obvious implication of this statement is that not all suicide is psychotic. Certainly some psychotics do commit suicide (and, although in the minority, they are the most unpredictable of all suicides). Here, the hypothesis concerning suicidal logic would be subservient to the notions of schizophrenic "paleologic"; one would expect the reasoning of a schizophrenic suicide to reflect more the semantics and logic of the schizophrenic than of the suicide.

How may these instances of suicidal semantic confusion be identified? The following criteria can be stated, although they are not definite and provide only the initial clues that may indicate that the suicidal semantic fallacy is being committed.

(1) Concern with minor details, trivia, and neutral statements in the suicide note would be one indication that the semantic fallacy is being committed.

(2) Another indication would be concern with the direct or indirect reaction of others, specifically what explicit thoughts are being entertained toward the individual. For example, "Don't think badly of me."

The following two criteria are negative criteria:

(3) Concern with one's own suffering and physical discomfiture or pain, where the focus is on ending it all, would seem to indicate that this error or confusion is not taking place.

(4) An indication of the belief in a hereafter also would tend to preclude the presence of this semantic error.

Thus it is possible to diagram four types of suicide, each with its own implications for treatment, as indicated in Table 4-1.

What evidence do we have for this general hypothesis about suicidal logic? We believe that we have some empirical, experimental data which are relevant to it. In another publication (4), we have compared 33 genuine suicide notes left by Caucasian, Protestant, native-born males between the ages of twenty-five and fifty-nine, with an equal number of suicide notes elicited from comparable nonsuicidal subjects matched man-for-man in terms of similar occupations and in terms of almost identical chronologic age.

It is reasonable to assume that the ideational content (including syntax and semantics) of any individual contemplating suicide would be present immediately antecedent to the actual suicidal event. This ideation ought

TABLE 4-1

OUTLINE OF TYPES OF SUICIDE AND SUGGESTED TREATMENTS

Logical Type	Personal Characteristics	Psychologic Label	Suggested Mode of Treatment
Catalogic: the logic is destructive; it confuses the self as experienced by the self with the self as experienced by others	Individuals who are lonely, feel helpless and fearful, and feel pessimistic about making meaningful personal relationships	*Referred suicides:* the confusion in logic and in the identification is "referred" (like referred pain) from other root problems	Dynamic psychotherapy wherein the goal would be to supply the patient with a meaningful, rewarding relationship, so that his search for identification would be stabilized
Normal logic: the reasoning is acceptable according to Aristotelian standards	Individuals who are older, or widowed, or who are in physical pain	*Surcease suicides:* persons desire surcease from pain and reason that death will give them this	Treatment is in terms of giving freedom from pain through analgesics and sedatives, and providing companionship by means of active milieu therapy
Contaminated logic: the logical or semantic error is in the emphasis on the self as experienced by others	Individuals whose beliefs permit them to view suicide as a transition to another life or as a means of saving reputation	*Cultural suicides:* their concept of death plays a primary role in the suicide	Treatment has to do with deeply entrenched religious and cultural beliefs and would have to deal with and clarify the semantic implications of the concept of death
Paleologic: makes logical identifications in terms of attributes of the predicates rather than of the subjects	Individuals who are delusional and/or hallucinatory	*Psychotic suicides:* not all suicides are psychotic, but psychotics can be unpredictably suicidal	Treatment has to do primarily with the psychosis and only subsequently with suicidal tendencies; treatment would include protecting the individual from his own impulses

to be found, concretely, in his suicide note. It is also possible to employ one of Mill's canons of inductive logic, specifically the method of difference, and make comparisons between genuine suicide notes and pseudo suicide notes. This was done by asking nonsuicidal individuals to compose the notes that they would write if they were going to take their own lives. It should be stated that, recognizing the moral and ethical overtones associated with suicide, we employed several safeguards so as to screen out carefully any person who might have been upset by this task. These elicited notes we call simulated suicide notes or pseudo-suicidal notes. It is our belief that the comparison of genuine suicide notes with simulated suicide notes seems to offer the most potentialities for a pointed and relevant analysis.

These 66 notes were analyzed in terms of "discomfort," "relief," and "neutral" statements as defined by O. Hobart Mowrer (2). We assumed that the Discomfort-Relief Quotient (DRQ) would reflect the ways in which an individual expressed feelings about himself. Specifically, we believed that discomfort and relief statements could be held to be comparable to our I_s concept and that neutral statements could be thought similar to our I_o concept.

All the notes were typed and coded by a secretary and then scored by the two authors in terms of discomfort thought units, relief thought units, and neutral thought units, according to Mowrer's method, without knowledge by us of the true category of the note. Our inter-rater reliability was substantially high in the 66 notes. One rater found a total of exactly 600 thought units, the other rater found 619. Of these, 528 thought units, or approximately 86 per cent were rated in common. Of these 528 thought units, 375, or 71 per cent, were scored identically by the two raters as discomfort, relief, or neutral. By Tschuprow's formula (8), the significance of the agreement between the two raters was determined from the chi-square (χ^2) of the formula. The χ^2 was 154.73, far in excess of the .01 level of significance, and indicated that the inter-rater scoring was similar beyond chance. At this point, the two raters pooled their judgments and arrived at a single label for each thought unit in each of the 66 notes, being guided by the scoring of a few of the notes which Dr. Mowrer had sent in a personal communication.

A sample scoring by Dr. Mowrer of the discomfort (D), relief (R), and neutral thought units (N) in one suicide note is reproduced below: [3]

[3] This note is number 18-B of the total set of 66 notes. All 33 pairs of genuine and simulated notes are reproduced in the Appendix.

Dearest Mary: / Well, dear—it's the end of the trail for me.^{D}/ It has been a fairly long and reasonably pleasant life, all in all—especially fine that part in which you played a part.^{R}/ You have been wonderful.^{R}/ No man could have asked for a better wife than you have been.^{R}/

Please understand that if I didn't feel that this course would be the best for you and the girls I certainly would have waited for nature to take her course.^{D}/ It would not have been long anyhow,^{D}/ for the clot I coughed up was from the lungs and I know there's activity there—of an ominous nature.^{D}/

Be good to your mother, girls.^{D}/ You have the finest mother in the world;^{R}/ even as I have had the most wonderful wife and two wonderful daughters.^{R}/ Bye–by Mary, Betty, and Helen.^{N}/ How I do love you all.^{R}/ And may God help and guide you from here on in.^{R}/ Daddy.

The results of our analyses were as follows: the total number of mutually agreed upon thought units as a result of this joint procedure was 553. Of this total there were 369 in the 33 genuine notes and 184 in the 33 elicited notes; the χ^2 was 8.7, significant beyond the .01 level, indicating that the genuine-note writers were significantly more verbose.

For the *discomfort* (tension, pain, hostility) statements, the genuine notes had 226 and the simulated notes had 137; the χ^2 was 9.5, significant beyond the .01 level and indicating that the genuine-note writers expressed significantly more discomfiture.

For the *relief* (pleasant, warm, loving) statements, the genuine notes had 65 and the pseudo notes had 34; the χ^2 was .06, which was not significant, indicating that neither the genuine- nor the pseudo-note writers expressed more relief.

For *neutral* statements, the genuine notes had 78 and the pseudo notes had 13; the χ^2 was 17.7, significant beyond the .01 level and indicating that the genuine-note writers expressed a significantly greater number of neutral statements. The content of these neutral statements typically had to do with giving instructions and admonitions and sometimes included lists of things to do.

The focus of our attention was on the difference in the neutral statements between the genuine suicide notes and the simulated suicide notes. This was so for two reasons: there was no significant statistical difference in the relief statements between the two sets of notes, and although there was a difference with regard to the greater amount of discomfort shown by the two kinds of suicide notes, it was also true that, when we analyzed the differences in quality of affect relating to the discomfort statements between the two groups, we noted that the discomfort statements in the genuine notes were characterized more by deeper feelings of hatred, vengeance, and self-blame, as compared with the more mildly negative statements of the simulated notes. We were forced to conclude that the quality of the discomfort statements is not accurately represented in the Mowrer scoring system.

We interpret the larger number of neutral statements on the part of the genuine-note writers as indicative of unrealistic feelings of omnipotence and omnipresence on the part of the suicidal individual. He cannot successfully imagine his own death and his own complete cessation. It also epitomizes the illogicality of the entire suicidal deed—thinking simultaneously and contradictorily of being absent and of giving orders as though one were going to be present to enforce them. Although the suicide is able to imagine his absence from the scene more successfully than the nonsuicide, he shows, paradoxically, the greater inability to comprehend his complete cessation of influence and effect. The larger number of neutral statements in the genuine notes—wherein reputation, or the self as experienced by others, is the primary characteristic—would seem definitely to imply this paradox.

To the extent that these neutral statements do indeed contain implied semantic confusions, we have support from our data for the hypothesis that the logical processes of the genuinely suicidal person are characterized (at least to a statistically significant extent greater than in the case of nonsuicidal individuals given a suicidal *Aufgabe*) by proneness to commit the particular kind of psychosemantic fallacy discussed in this chapter. Specifically, we mean the suicide's confusion relating to the concept of the self revolving around the multiple logical components and meanings contained in the pronoun I, *das Ich,* the ego.

One may speculate about the psychologic significance of the confused suicidal logic. It may well be that the confusion relating to the subject of the premise manifested by the suicide reflects his problems having to do primarily with identification. It is this fallacious identification between the self as experienced by the self (I_s) and the self as it feels itself experienced by others (I_o) which enables the suicide to accept erroneous premises and invalid conclusions and which accounts for his making his tragic deductive leap into oblivion.

References

1. Arieti, Silvano, *Interpretation of Schizophrenia.* New York: Robert Bruner, 1955.
2. Mowrer, O. Hobart, *Psychotherapy: Theory and Research.* New York: The Ronald Press Company, 1953.
3. Sells, S. B., The atmosphere effect. *Archives of Psychology,* 1936, no. 200.
4. Shneidman, E. S., and N. L. Farberow, Comparison between genuine and simulated suicide notes by means of Mowrer's DRQ. *Journal of General Psychology,* 56: 251–256, 1957.
5. Storch, A., *The Primitive Archaic Forms of Inner Experiences and Thought in Schizophrenia.* Washington, D.C.: Nervous and Mental Disease Publishing Company, 1924.
6. Von Domarus, E., The Specific Laws of Logic in Schizophrenia. (In Kasanin, J. S. [Ed.], *Language and Thought in Schizophrenic.*) Berkeley, Calif.: University of California Press, 1944.
7. Woodworth, R. S., and S. B. Sells, An atmosphere effect in formal syllogistic reasoning. *Journal of Experimental Psychology,* 18: 451–460, 1935.
8. Yule, G. U., and N. Kendall, *An Introduction to the Theory of Statistics.* New York: Hafner Publishing Company, 1950.

5

Suicide and Age

NORMAN L. FARBEROW AND EDWIN S. SHNEIDMAN

Suicide is a phenomenon which does not limit itself to any particular age. Statistics show it as an ever-increasing proportionate problem with the advance in age, the phenomenon occurring in all ages from the young child to the very old adult. There are many speculations about the psychodynamics of suicide. It has been noted, in our examination of these formulations, that there have been no differentiations in these theories for the age of the suicidal person, the assumption generally being made that such psychodynamic formulations as are proposed apply to all suicides regardless of age. The authors' investigations to date have caused them to question this assumption, and this study is an attempt to determine whether the question raised, that is, whether the dynamics, or the pattern of dynamics, varies with the age of the suicidal subject, is a legitimate and necessary one.

The material used in this particular study to investigate this question consisted of suicide notes obtained through the kind cooperation of the Los Angeles County Coroner's Office. These are the genuine suicide notes which, along with other data, have been the raw data in the authors' investigation of the phenomenon of suicide in the Southern California area. By viewing such notes as similar or equivalent to projective material, it is possible through various methods of analysis to infer much information about the note writer. Of the over 700 notes collected covering the years from 1944 to 1953, 619 notes, consisting of all the notes written by the male and female, Caucasian, native-born suicide-note writers, were examined in this study.[1] The males (489 notes) ranged in age from twenty

---

[1] The remainder of the notes were from non-Caucasian or foreign-born persons. Some notes by persons below age twenty were excluded because there were so few. Another group consisted of a number of notes randomly selected and held out for a cross-validation study.

through ninety-six, while the females (130 notes) ranged in age from twenty through seventy-eight.

In order to examine the possible variation in motives with the age of the suicidal subject, a number of the various theories most frequently found in the psychiatric and psychologic literature were examined. On the basis of this survey, Karl Menninger's theory of suicide, as described in his book *Man Against Himself* (1), was selected. This theory lent itself to the purpose of the present study; that is, it broadly categorized the assumed psychodynamic motivations underlying the act of killing oneself, and the motivations were readily inferred from the raw data of the study—the suicide notes. Menninger's theory states that there are three components to the suicidal act and that all are present in varying degrees in any given case. These three components are (a) the wish to kill, (b) the wish to be killed, and (c) the wish to die. In translating these three components operationally, considerable help was obtained from a written communication from Dr. Menninger in which he stated, "... I think you might use as a very rough criterion, conscious hate, conscious guilt feelings, and conscious hopelessness, or discouragement as roughly determining the three components that I suggested." In further describing his three factors in his book, Menninger uses additional descriptive terms, such as, for "wish to kill"—aggression, accusation, blame, eliminating, driving away, disposing of, annihilating, and revenge; for "wish to be killed"—submission, maso-chism, self-blame, and self-accusation; and for "wish to die"—hopelessness, fear, fatigue, and despair. References to illness and pain as motives for doing away with the self were included in the last component.

All 619 notes were grouped according to the age of the writer into three age groups, twenty to thirty-nine, forty to fifty-nine, and sixty and over, or what might be broadly conceived as young, middle-aged, and older groups (Table 5-1). The notes were then classified under one of the above

TABLE 5-1

DISTRIBUTION OF MALE AND FEMALE SUICIDE-NOTE WRITERS
ACCORDING TO AGE

Ages	Male	Female	Number
20–39	99	38	137
40–59	215	52	267
60+	175	40	215
Total	489	130	619

three categories, or in an unclassifiable category if the note did not give enough information to allow any classification. Though Menninger hypothesizes that all three of these factors, in varying strengths, are present in each suicidal act, the procedure was followed of classifying each note in terms of one component, that is, the major, predominant motive that was judged to be expressed. This was done to focus more clearly on any changes in motivations which might appear in the notes for the various ages.

The following notes are examples of the four rubrics into which all of the notes were categorized. They are not chosen as characteristic of any particular age group, but are selected to illustrate each of the categories.

Wish to Kill

Male, married, age 53.

1.

I hereby Will all the property to my son, anything that you can get as Jane did not have anything in the place. She just took me for a ride. If she gives you any trouble find Joe as she has checked up on Jim and a lot of other. See Jack 1000 Main Street. She will tell you or her little girl that Oscar and her have been living together out at her place as man and wife. Also go to the Beach and see how long her and Jim lived here as man and wife. You know where I said to look. I have 2 small policys (that Insurance I mean) they made out to you.

John Smith

2.

Jane:

You 25¢ chippy I hope this makes you happy. All the time that you could spent here you had to be shacked up with someone else. Now you tell me to get the hell out from the bar. You have brought this on your self. When ever you think that you can be married to me 9 mo. and only live with me 1½ mo. the rest of the time you have been sleeping with some one else. I could go from here to and through the state of Washington and find out with who and what day & nite you spent with some other man, and now you are telling me to get the hell out.

John

Wish to Be Killed

Female, married, age 24.

I've proved to be a miserable wife, mother and homemaker—not even a decent companion. Johnny and Jane deserve much more than I can ever offer. I can't take it any longer. This is a terrible thing for me to do, but perhaps in the end it will be all for the best. I hope so.

Mary

Wish to Die

Male, divorced, age 50.

To The Police—

This is a very simple case of suicide. I owe nothing to anyone, including the World; and I ask nothing from anyone. I'm fifty years old, have lived violently but never committed a crime.

I've just had enough. Since no one depends upon me, I don't see why I shouldn't do as I please. I've done my duty to my Country in both World Wars, and also I've served well in industry. My papers are in the brown leather wallet in my gray bag.

If you would be so good as to send these papers to my brother, his address is: John Smith, 100 Main Street.

I enclose five dollars to cover cost of mailing. Perhaps some of you who belong to the American Legion will honor my request.

I haven't a thing against anybody. But, I've been in three major wars and another little insurrection, and I'm pretty tired.

This note is in the same large envelope with several other letters—all stamped. Will you please mail them for me? There are no secrets in them. However, if you open them, please seal them up again and send them on. They are to the people I love and who love me. Thanks.

George Smith

Unclassifiable

Female, widowed, age 70.

In case of my death notify Charles Smith, Smith Funeral Home, 100 Main Street.

This letter to be opened by him.

Mary Jones

It is my wish that my funeral be strictly private. Just a minister to say a prayer for me.

The notes were classified independently by the two authors and the reliability of their ratings was checked by means of a χ^2 analysis. A four-by-four contingency table was formed, in terms of the four categories used. That the two judges agreed quite well in their classification of the notes is shown by the fact that the obtained χ^2 was 751.47, which, for 9 degrees of freedom, is significant beyond the .001 level. When the obtained χ^2 is expressed in terms of Tschuprow's coefficient (2), a value of .64 is obtained, which constitutes a substantial correlation. After reliability in scoring was ascertained, those notes where discrepancies in scoring had appeared were reread, and the differences resolved so that a single classification was obtained. The percentage of notes scored as wish to kill, be killed, to die, or unclassifiable were then computed for each age group of note writer. These results may be seen for males and females in Tables 5-2 and 5-3 respectively. The following trends for males may be noted:

TABLE 5-2

NUMBER AND PERCENTAGES OF 489 MALE SUICIDE NOTES CLASSIFIED ACCORDING TO MENNINGER'S HYPOTHESIS

Ages	To Kill		To Be Killed		To Die		Unclassifiable	
	Number	%	Number	%	Number	%	Number	%
20–39	31	31	27	27	23	23	18	18
40–59	50	23	35	16	75	35	55	26
60+	20	11	18	10	99	57	38	22
Total	101	21	80	16	197	40	111	23

The general trend for each of the components indicated that the two factors, the wish to kill and the wish to be killed, decreased with age, and the factor, wish to die, increased with age. The category of "unclassifiable" was scored for about one-quarter of the notes for each age group.

The specific trend for each of the individual motives for the male suicide-

TABLE 5-3

NUMBER AND PERCENTAGES OF 130 FEMALE SUICIDE NOTES CLASSIFIED ACCORDING TO MENNINGER'S HYPOTHESIS

Ages	To Kill		To Be Killed		To Die		Unclassifiable	
	Number	%	Number	%	Number	%	Number	%
20–39	12	32	8	21	8	21	10	26
40–59	15	29	9	17	15	29	13	25
60+	6	15	2	5	30	75	2	5
Total	33	25	19	15	53	41	25	19

note writers showed that the wish to kill appeared in 31 per cent of the notes of the young group, declined to 23 per cent for the middle age group, and then fell to 11 per cent in the notes of the older group. The differences between the proportions in the various age groups indicated no significant difference between the young and the middle age group, but the differences between the middle age and the older groups, and between the young and older age group, were statistically significant (Table 5-4).

TABLE 5-4

CRITICAL RATIOS BETWEEN PROPORTIONS OF AGE GROUPS OF MALE
AND FEMALE SUICIDE-NOTE WRITERS

Age Groups	To Kill		To Be Killed		To Die	
	M	F	M	F	M	F
Young—middle age	1.47	0.30	2.15 *	0.48	2.25 *	0.88
Middle age—older	3.23 †	1.66	1.78	1.92	4.43 †	4.95 †
Young—older	3.83 †	1.80	3.40 †	2.15 *	6.02 †	5.68 †

* A *t* value of 1.968 is necessary for significance at the 5% level.
† A *t* value of 2.592 is necessary for significance at the 1% level.

The wish to be killed appeared in 27 per cent of the notes of the young group, fell to 16 per cent for the middle age group, and then to 10 per cent for the older group. The differences between the proportions for the young and the middle age and between the young and the older groups were found to be statistically significant, but the difference between the middle age and the older groups was not.

The wish to die appeared in 23 per cent of the notes of the young group, increased to 35 per cent for the middle age group, and rose to 57 per cent in the older age group. Here, all the differences between the various age groups were found to be statistically significant.

At first glance, the general trend for the women's notes seems to follow somewhat the same pattern, with the wish to kill and to be killed decreasing with advancing age and the wish to die increasing with advancing age. The difference between these proportions, however, is statistically significant only between the young and the older group for the factor "wish to be killed," and between the middle age and the older, and the young and the older, age groups for the factor, "wish to die" (Table 5-4).

It is apparent that the results of this study emphasize the meaningfulness of the question raised at the beginning of this chapter; that is, that the pattern or the constellation of the various dynamics motivating the suicidal person tends to show marked shifts depending on his age. The pattern for the male suicide-note writers, particularly, changes with age. As may be seen from Table 5-2, the younger males are expressing all the factors fairly equally—31, 27, and 23 per cent for wish to kill, to be killed, or die, respectively. The older males, however, are expressing the wish to kill and to be killed only 11 and 10 per cent of the time, respectively, while the wish to die appears in 57 per cent of their notes. Another way of stating this is by combining the data for the wish to kill and to be killed (the intense affects) and contrasting these with the percentage for the wish to die (the more chronic and less intense affect). The younger males then show the wish to kill and be killed in 58 per cent of their notes and the wish to die in 23 per cent. The pattern reverses itself in the older age group with 21 per cent and 57 per cent, respectively. One must conclude that the younger males, between twenty and thirty-nine, apparently are much more concerned than the older males, sixty and above, with the highly charged, more affect-laden, and, at the same time, more transient motives, "kill" or "be killed". They are inclined to be much more intensely angry and hostile, full of hate and bitterness toward another person; or more depressed, self-disparaging, self-abasing, and guilt-ridden than the older males. In the suicide of older men these more interpersonal motives seem to decrease in intensity and the affect shifts to the less acute but more chronic feelings of discouragement—pain, illness, mild despair, and so on. The older suicide is tired, either of life or of pain and suffering, and he writes that he is physically and/or mentally exhausted. The scores of the middle age group point up the trends in the shifts of these motives, showing that the anger and hostility tend to persist longer and to appear in the notes fairly often through the age of fifty-nine, before the frequency begins to lessen noticeably. On the other hand, the guilt and self-blame lessens markedly by age thirty-nine and then does not decrease much more after that.

While for the female suicide-note writers the pattern does not show the same distinct shifts in all factors as for the male note writers, there are the same relative shifts in the patterns for the various age groups (Table 5-3). Thus, the younger females also show somewhat the same percentages of motives—32, 21, and 21 for wish to kill, to be killed, and to die, respectively, and then a very marked shift in the older age group to percentages of 15, 5, and 75, respectively. Or again, it might be stated that the wishes to kill and to be killed appear in 53 per cent of the notes as contrasted to 21 per cent for wish to die for the younger females, with the pattern reversing itself even more markedly, with 20 and 75 per cent, respectively, for the older females.

However, viewed from age group to age group, the feelings of anger and hostility do not change remarkably (statistically) with advancing age, but tend to persist in somewhat the same proportions regardless of whether the woman is young, middle-aged, or old. The older women do tend, however, to show much less guilt and self-blame, and considerably more discouragement, despair, feelings of being a burden, and depressed feelings about pain and illness than the younger women. Again the middle age group gives some clues as to the time when these shifts occur. Their scores indicate that it is at age sixty and above that guilt decreases to a point significantly less than the younger group expresses, and that the decline up to that age is a gradual and apparently steady one. The despair and discouragement increase tremendously once age sixty is passed, whereas from ages twenty to fifty-nine there is not too much difference in its presence as a motive for the destruction of the self.

Some words of caution should be expressed at this point. One cannot help but wonder whether the results would have been changed much if it were possible to know the motives in the "unclassifiable" notes. Twenty-three per cent and nineteen per cent male and female notes, respectively, could not be classified, and if these notes had fallen primarily into any one of the other categories, they would have caused a marked change in the pattern. Certainly, this must be kept in mind in drawing any conclusions. However, the trends themselves seem remarkably consistent and the probability must also be considered that the already noted trends might have been further emphasized. One other caution to be kept in mind is that these results are based upon a "selected" sample, namely, suicide-note writers. In Los Angeles County, note writers make up around 15 per cent of the total number of people who commit suicide and may not actually be representative of the total group. However, comparisons of sociologic, economic, and other available statistics indicated that the suicide-note writers seemed to be similar to the entire group of suicidal individuals in Los Angeles County for the period studied.

It should be stated here that the results of this study do not in any way indicate that Menninger's hypotheses are invalid for different ages. This study is not designed to test the validity of this theory, but simply takes advantage of its operational usefulness in serving as a vehicle for examining the motives expressed in the notes. As stated earlier, Menninger emphasizes that these are elements which are all present in all suicides, but in varying degrees, a fact which actually is verified by the data. These results do stress the important fact, however, that apparently the pattern of the motives shifts and that there is a relationship between these changes with differences in age. They also point to a need to reexamine and to modify the current theories about suicide in order to take into account the variations in the constellations of dynamics of the suicidal patient, depending upon his age.

Though the theoretical examination and modification of the phenomenon remain a task for the future, it seems possible to draw some immediate practical implications for treatment and management of the suicidal person.

In general, when persons between twenty and thirty-nine years of age come to the attention of the therapist because of suicidal urges or attempts, the therapist might expect to find the more intense interpersonal motives operating in over half of his patients, while the chronic depressive feelings will be dominant in only about one-quarter of the cases. The method of choice for treatment, once the necessary medical measures have been taken, seems to be a type of dynamic psychotherapy. The aim would be to provide patients with the opportunity for working out and gaining insight into the tensions and the intense feelings which had been operating in their interpersonal relationships. In the case of older patients, both male and female, the therapist must be prepared to institute more of the environmental and milieu therapy and to treat with the purpose of offering a great deal of physical relief for pain and suffering. In addition to providing analgesics and sedatives, he must be prepared to offer much support aimed at relieving feelings of discouragement, of uselessness, and of being a burden. This means he may have to take a much more active part than generally he might by actually entering into the patient's environment in dealing with relatives and friends in helping to reestablish fading environmental bonds and lost feelings of usefulness and belonging.

References

1. Menninger, K. A., *Man Against Himself*. New York: Harcourt, Brace and Company, Inc., 1938.
2. Yule, G. U., and N. Kendall, *An Introduction to the Theory of Statistics*. New York: Hafner Publishing Company, 1950.

6

Some Aspects of the Meaning of Death

HERMAN FEIFEL

The person who commits suicide meets death more precipitously than most of us. Information about attitudes toward death can throw a helpful spotlight on understanding the psychology of suicide. The problem of death is something which each one of us must come to grips with sooner or later. Life insurance, reactions to the death of a parent or close friend, Memorial Day, thoughts about life after death—all attest to our concern. A discerning fifteenth-century author remarked that "as soon as a man comes to life, he is immediately old enough to die." The ideas and attitudes that persons hold concerning death are potential guiding forces of their present behavior.

Historical and ethnologic information (5) reveals that reflection concerning death extends back to earliest civilization and exists among practically all peoples. Some investigators (4, 6, 24) hold that fear of death is a universal reaction and that no one is quite free from it. Freud (12), for instance, postulates the presence of an unconscious death wish in people which he connects with certain tendencies to self-destruction. Teicher (22) feels that "war neuroses" are essentially neurotic forms of the fear of death. Heidegger (14) states that time has meaning for us only because we know we have to die. Stekel (21) goes so far as to express the hypothesis that every fear we have is ultimately a fear of death. Death themes and fantasies are also prominent in psychopathology (1, 3, 22). Ideas of death are recurrent in some neurotic patients and in the delusions and hallucinations of many psychotic patients. The stupor of the catatonic patient, for example, has sometimes been likened to a death state. Caprio (4) thinks that all nervous and mental disorders can be regarded as forms of "psychic death." In addition, a number of psychoanalysts (11, 13, 17, 19) are of the opinion that one of the main reasons that shock treatments produce positive effects in many patients is that these treatments provide them with a kind of death-and-rebirth fantasy experience.

Both theology and philosophy have grappled with the problem of death and its meaning. Nevertheless, a review of the literature indicates few studies of an empirical nature dealing with attitudes toward death. The author, for example, could find none which focused on hospitalized mentally ill patients or persons sixty-five years of age and over. The studies that have been reported emphasize the attitudes toward death of children (16, 18), college students (15, 20), and a small number of psychoanalyzed neurotic patients (3) in whom ideas of death were noticeable.

The major purpose of this chapter is to augment the limited available data regarding the attitudes toward death of mentally ill persons and to present some findings on the attitudes of older individuals toward death. Many of these data have been previously reported (9, 10). The findings constitute part of a continuing series of research endeavors in this area now being carried on by the author. They will have to be considered as tentative and in the nature of an interim report because of present sampling limitations, group control inadequacies, and so forth. It should also be kept in mind that they pertain to conscious and "public" attitudes more than they do to the deeper layers of the personality.

The study (9) relating to mentally ill persons investigated the attitudes toward death of 38 acutely disturbed closed-ward patients in partial remission and 47 open-ward cases diagnosed as psychoneurotic and character disorders. The essential findings were as follows: (a) Most patients in both groups viewed death in a philosophic vein as the natural end process of life. The next predominating outlook was of a religious nature, perceiving death as physical and, in reality, a preparatory stage for another life. (b) Many patients depicted death as occurring through violent means. The conjecture was that violent conception of death mirrors self-held feelings of aggressiveness toward others as well as toward oneself. (c) When faced with hypothetical situations suggesting the imminence of death, the characteristic choice tendencies of both groups of patients gave priority to activities of a social and religious type. This was in contrast to reported findings on "normals" (2), whose responses, in similar situations, emphasized personal pleasures and gratifications. (d) The *degree* of mental disturbance per se in the patients had little seeming effect on their over-all attitudes toward death.

The remainder of this chapter deals with the attitudes toward death of some older persons. The major portion of what follows was previously printed as "Older Persons Look at Death" (10).

The subjects consisted of 40 white male veterans of World War I, living at a Veterans Administration Domiciliary Home. All were American-born except four, and these had been in the United States for over forty years. None had ever been mentally disturbed or had any apparent incapacitating brain involvement. They were living in the Domiciliary because of physical illness and inability to support themselves. Major diagnostic categories were as follows: cardiovascular, 25 per cent; arteriosclerosis, 23 per cent; respiratory, 20 per cent; hypertension, 10 per cent; arthritis, 8 per cent; and miscellaneous, 14 per cent.

The mean age of the group was sixty-seven; mean educational level, seven and one-half years; and mean IQ, based on the Shipley-Hartford test, 99.1. Skilled and semiskilled job backgrounds—73 and 15 per cent, respectively—prevailed in the group with a smattering of professionals, businessmen, and farmers. Of the group, 44 per cent were married, 28 per cent were divorced, and 28 per cent were single. Seventy per cent had been in the Domiciliary less than a year; the other 30 per cent, an average of three years.

The subjects were individually seen and interviewed by means of a questionnaire technique and rating scales. Reliability of the response categories, where appropriate, was determined by having an independent judge score the answers. Agreement ranged from 86 to 94 per cent, indicating a good degree of consistency in response classification.

The findings were as follows:

(1) When asked "What does death mean to you?" 40 per cent of the group answered "the end of everything"; "you're through." Another 40 per cent saw death in a religious aspect as "the beginning of a new existence"; "a new life in the hereafter." Ten per cent visualized death as "relief from pain"; "a peaceful sleep." The remaining 10 per cent responded "I'm not clear what happens"; "don't know." The choice of categories and the percentage favoring each is rather similar to the results obtained on the previously mentioned mentally ill patients who were in their middle thirties. The only difference is that the older group showed a somewhat more religious outlook. This might be related to the age difference between the groups.

(2) In the replies to the question "What do you think happens to us after we die?" there was a definite turn toward perceiving death in religious terms. Twenty-five per cent of the group still felt that "when you're

dead, you're dead," but 60 per cent now expressed a religious orientation, such as "you are judged for your life on earth"; "your spirit exists in some way in some kind of hereafter." The 10 per cent who originally stated "don't know" remained steadfast; the remaining 5 per cent saw life after death as "a long, sound sleep." The increase in religious emphasis was mainly due to a shift in the answers of those who stated that death was "the end" to the "meaning of death" question. When faced with the concrete inquiry of what happens to us after death, 15 per cent of this group now asserted a belief in "some kind of hereafter."

(3) An overwhelming majority of the group, 96 per cent, wanted to die quickly with little suffering—"peacefully in your sleep," as most put it. The remainder wanted to have plenty of time in order to make farewells to family and friends. "Bed" was specifically mentioned by 55 per cent of the group as the preferred place of death. Eighteen per cent stated that it did not make any difference to them where they died, and 13 per cent expressed the desire to die at home in the midst of their families. With reference to the time of death, 65 per cent answered that this didn't matter to them at all. Twenty-five per cent stated "at night" because "it would mean less trouble for everyone concerned." One waggish comment was "after dinner, since I'll feel better then."

(4) About half the group, 48 per cent, said they "occasionally" thought about death, 32 per cent answered "rarely," and 20 per cent stated "frequently." A religious outlook was significantly evident, at the .05 level, in those persons responding "occasionally" and "frequently." Older persons who are religiously inclined seem to give more thought to concepts about death than do those to whom death represents the inexorable end. It should be remembered that no necessary relationship exists between frequency of thought about death and fear of death. Nevertheless, the speculative implication that some older persons attempt to master their anxiety about death by thinking of it as the precursor of a new life should be studied further. The "judgment" aspect might also be an important variable in explaining why religiously inclined persons are more concerned with death than nonreligious individuals.[1]

One should be cautious in considering the religious person as invariant. A variety of people are undoubtedly subsumed under the concept of "religious person." Some people may profess religious tenets but not practice

[1] Data now being gathered on this point by the author suggest that a positive relationship does exist between being personally afraid of death and expecting "divine judgment" after death.

them. Others may adopt religion as a kind of defense against "the slings and arrows of outrageous fortune." Then, there are those individuals who incorporate their religious beliefs into everyday living activities. Sharper and more definitive categorization is needed in this area. Attitudes toward death may well vary among the different categories, as well as among differing denominational groups.

(5) When asked "How many years do you think you have yet to live?" 50 per cent stated they thought they had another seven to ten years; 30 per cent thought three to six years. The rest felt they would live eleven years or more, except for one person who expected to die within two years. These estimates seem to be fairly realistic in terms of actuarial studies and the known life spans of the group's parents. There was no significant relationship between the meaning of death and the choice of the number of years yet to live.

(6) In response to the query "What specific disease do you most often think of in connection with your own death?" 50 per cent answered "none in particular"; 35 per cent replied "heart failure" because "I'm having trouble with it"; and 9 per cent stated "cancer" because "my parents died from it—it's in the family." Interestingly, no one thought he would die as the result of an accident. This is in contrast to the findings for the mentally ill patients, a good proportion of whom saw themselves as dying by violent means.

(7) The group was asked when people most and least fear death, and the following age periods were listed: childhood, up to twelve; adolescence, thirteen to nineteen; twenties; thirties; forties; fifties; sixties; and seventy and over. Almost half the group, or 45 per cent, ranked the period of seventy and over as the time when people are most afraid of death, followed by 15 per cent who ranked the forties, and 15 per cent who ranked the twenties. One of the findings of Bromberg and Schilder (2) is pertinent in this regard. They discovered little difference between subjectively held attitudes toward death and those generally attributed to other persons.[2] The seventy-and-over period was chosen because "you're close to it then" and "you're at the end of the rope"; the forties, because "you have a family to take care of" and "you really start to think about it then"; and the twenties, because "you have your whole life ahead of you yet." Thirty-five per cent selected both childhood and the seventy-and-over category as the periods when people *least* fear death. Childhood was chosen

[2] This has been recently substantiated by the author for a group of 51 normal adults. The correlation between age periods assigned to others and those self-chosen was .89.

because "you don't think about it"; "you don't know what it is"; and "life seems all ahead of you." The frequent singling out of old age in this connection is somewhat less expected. The main reasons for selecting the seventy-and-over period were "by then you don't give a rap"; "you've lived your life and accept it"; and "you have least to live for." The notion was entertained that some relationship might exist between these rankings and a specific outlook on death, but no significant differences were discovered. No reliable differences in outlook on death were in evidence between those ranking the seventy-and-over period as the time when people *most* fear death and those ranking it as the time when people *least* fear death. Nevertheless, a religious trend was apparent in those who felt that people most feared death in old age. The implication again suggests itself that certain older persons may resort to a religious outlook in order to cope with their fears concerning death.

(8) The generally negative orientation to old age (8, 23) was also conspicuous in our group. When asked "What does old age mean to you?" the great majority, 77 per cent, saw it as "the end of the line" and as "a time when you have to depend on others." Only 15 per cent thought of it as a period of "leisure," "peace," and "contentment." One seventy-two-year-old stated, "I'll cross that bridge when I come to it." No significant relationship was found between a specific outlook on death and attitude toward old age, but once again, a religious trend was prevalent in those viewing old age with a gloomy eye.

(9) In describing themselves, over half of the group, or 52 per cent, perceived themselves as "kind and considerate to others"; "loyal and honest"; "easy to get along with"; and "people like me." Another 20 per cent felt they were "average" and "ordinary guys no different than most." A hard core of 28 per cent regarded themselves as "crabby," "old bucks," and "hard-headed Yankees." The need of these older persons to be liked, accepted, and considered the same as anyone else is striking. Personal experiences, apparently, have convinced them of their "minority" status in society.

The frenetic accent on and continual search for the fountain of youth in many segments of our society reflect, to a certain degree, anxieties concerning death. We tend to reject the aged because they remind us of death. Professional people who come in contact with chronic and terminally ill patients have noted parallel avoidant tendencies in themselves. They often reject this kind of patient because he reactivates or arouses their own fears about dying. The onslaught of the patient's hostility makes them feel guilty and defensive for outliving him. One's narcissism also becomes wounded when "our medicine, our prayers" cannot help or save him. Conscious denial of death permeates a good deal of our thinking. Geoffrey Gorer, the English anthropologist, has commented that death has become as unmentionable to us as sex was to the Victorians. Forest Lawn, a cemetery in Los Angeles, proudly claims to minister "not to the dead, but to the living."

Research in progress indicates that people respond differently to oncoming death. For most religious persons, death represents "the dissolution of bodily life" and "the doorway to a new life." For some, death is a "rest" and "peaceful sleep" (it is interesting to note that in Homer's *Iliad*, Sleep [Hypnos] and Death [Thanatos] are alluded to as twin brothers); also, the emphasis in our experimental populations on dying "at night while asleep" should be noted. To others, death is perceived as an adventure—so well expressed in Lord Balfour's dying words, "This is going to be a great experience." Then there are those who put up a desperate fight against death—so beautifully described by Dylan Thomas, the Welsh poet, "Do not go gentle into that good night . . . rage, rage, against the dying of the light." Just as there is no universal rule for living, there is probably none for dying.

Birth is an uncontrolled event but the manner of one's departure from life may bear a definite relation to one's philosophy of life and death. Man's behavior may be influenced more than we assume by his outlook and hopes and fears regarding the nature and meaning of death. We would indeed err grievously to consider death as a purely biologic event. Its meaning for the individual can serve as an important organizing principle in determining how he conducts himself in life, including his attitudes toward taking his own life. Death may never assume for us the role it did for medieval man to whom it represented the beginning of a moment infinitely more important than the moment of birth (7)—but it is an area of meaning which requires and demands broader and deeper investigation.

References

1. Boisen, A., R. L. Jenkins, and M. Lorr, Schizophrenic ideation as a striving toward the solution of conflict. *Journal of Clinical Psychology,* 10: 389–391, 1954.
2. Bromberg, W., and P. Schilder, Death and dying: A comparative study of the attitudes and mental reactions toward death and dying. *Psychoanalytic Review,* 20: 133–185, 1933.
3. ―――― and ――――, The attitudes of psychoneurotics toward death. *Psychoanalytic Review,* 23: 1–28, 1936.
4. Caprio, F. S., A psycho-social study of primitive conceptions of death. *Journal of Criminal Psychopathology,* 5: 303–317, 1943.

5. ———, Ethnological attitudes toward death: A psychoanalytic evaluation. *Journal of Criminal Psychopathology,* 7: 737–752, 1946.

6. ———, A study of some psychological reactions during prepubescence to the idea of death. *Psychiatric Quarterly,* 24: 495–505, 1950.

7. Eissler, K. R., *The Psychiatrist and the Dying Patient.* New York: International Universities Press, Inc., 1955.

8. Feifel, H., Psychiatric patients look at old age: Level of adjustment and attitudes toward aging. *American Journal of Psychiatry,* 111: 459–465, 1954.

9. ———, Attitudes of mentally ill patients towards death. *Journal of Nervous and Mental Disease,* 122: 375–380, 1955.

10. ———, Older persons look at death. *Geriatrics,* 11: 127–130, 1956.

11. Fenichel, O., *The Psychoanalytic Theory of Neuroses.* New York: W. W. Norton & Company, Inc., 1945.

12. Freud, S., *Beyond the Pleasure Principle.* London: International Psycho-Analytic Press, 1922.

13. Grotjahn, M., Psychiatric observations of schizophrenic patients during metrazol treatment. *Bulletin of the Menninger Clinic,* 2: 142–150, 1938.

14. Heidegger, M., *Sein und Zeit.* Halle: Max Niemeyer Verlag, 1927.

15. Middleton, W. C., Some reactions toward death among college students. *Journal of Abnormal and Social Psychology,* 31: 165–173, 1936.

16. Nagy, M., The child's theories concerning death. *Journal of Genetic Psychology,* 73: 3–27, 1948.

17. Schilder, P., Notes on the psychology of metrazol treatment of schizophrenia. *Journal of Nervous and Mental Disease,* 89: 133–144, 1939.

18. ——— and D. Wechsler, The attitudes of children towards death. *Journal of Genetic Psychology,* 45: 406–451, 1934.

19. Silbermann, I., The psychical experiences during the shocks in shock therapy. *International Journal of Psychoanalysis,* 21: 179–200, 1940.

20. Stacey, C. L., and K. Markin, The attitudes of college students and penitentiary inmates toward death and a future life. *Psychiatric Quarterly* (supplement), 26: 27–32, 1952.

21. Stekel, W., *Conditions of Nervous Anxiety and Their Treatment.* New York: Liveright Publishing Corporation, 1949.

22. Teicher, J. D., "Combat fatigue" or death anxiety neurosis. *Journal of Nervous and Mental Disease,* 117: 234–243, 1953.

23. Tuckman, J., and I. Lorge, The best years of life: A study in ranking. *Journal of Psychology,* 34: 137–149, 1952.

24. Zilboorg, G., Fear of Death. *Psychoanalytic Quarterly,* 12: 465–475, 1943.

7

The Sociology of Suicide *

ANDREW F. HENRY AND JAMES F. SHORT, JR.

INTRODUCTION

Sociologic study of suicide began in systematic fashion with the publication of Émile Durkheim's *Le Suicide* in 1897 (3). Durkheim's was the first theoretical and empiric exploration of the persistent variations of suicide in relation to sociologic variables. His theoretical types of suicide and his frame of reference for their interpretation remain basic to all research by sociologists in this area. Following Durkheim, his student Halbwachs (6) undertook a larger statistical investigation of suicide which substantiated in large part Durkheim's theoretical formulations and added considerably to our empiric knowledge. Later students of the phenomenon, particularly in the United States, have concentrated on empiric studies of the ecologic distribution of suicide and of the relation between suicide and economic cycles (1, 7, 11, 14, 15, 16).

A recent sociologic monograph (8) has attempted a synthesis of disparate theories about suicide by sociologists, psychologists, and psychiatrists suggesting that both suicide and homicide might profitably be handled within a single conceptual framework. This formulation suggests that both suicide and homicide are acts of aggression consequent to frustration. Suicide is viewed as the end product of aggression directed inwardly against the self.

In the treatment which follows, the theoretical constructs of Durkheim will be presented, together with later empiric findings and the theoretical reformulations which they suggest.

* The material in this chapter is taken largely from a previous work by the authors (8). The reader is referred to this work for a more detailed presentation and analysis of the data treated in this chapter. For a synthesis of sociologic and psychologic theories of suicide, see especially chapter 7 of the reference cited.

DURKHEIM'S THEORY

Durkheim isolated three "etiological types" of suicide—"anomic," "egoistic," and "altruistic." The most fruitful of these types for the understanding of suicide in modern society are the first two. Anomic suicide, said Durkheim, results when the equilibrium of society is severely disturbed, as for example, when the business cycle drops suddenly and rapidly.

In the case of economic disasters, indeed, something like a declassification occurs which suddenly casts certain individuals into a lower state than their previous one. Then they must reduce their requirements, restrain their needs, learn greater self-control. All the advantages of social influence are lost so far as they are concerned; their moral education has to be recommenced. But society cannot adjust them instantaneously to this new life and teach them to practice the increased self-repression to which they are unaccustomed. So they are not adjusted to the condition forced on them, and its very prospect is intolerable; hence the suffering which detaches them from a reduced existence before they have made a trial of it.... This explanation is confirmed by the remarkable immunity of poor countries. Poverty protects against suicide because it is a restraint in itself.... The enormous rate of those with independent means (720 per million) sufficiently shows that the possessors of most comfort suffer most. Everything that enforces subordination attenuates the effects of this state. At least the horizon of the lower classes is limited by those above them, and for this same reason their desires are most modest. Those who have only empty space above them are almost inevitably lost in it, if no force restrains them. [Ref. 3, pages 252–257.]

Egoistic suicide, according to Durkheim, results from a lack of integration of the individual with other members of his society. The absence of group solidarity and consensus frees the individual from the control of the group. Durkheim clarified the distinction between egoistic and anomic suicide, as follows:

Certainly, this [anomic] and egoistic suicide have kindred ties. Both spring from society's insufficient presence in individuals. But the sphere of its absence is not the same in both cases. In egoistic suicide it is deficient in truly collective activity, thus depriving the latter of object and meaning. In anomic suicide, society's influence is lacking in the basically individual passions, thus leaving them without a check-rein. In spite of their relationship, therefore, the two types are independent of each other. We may offer society everything social in us, and still be unable to control our desires; one may live in an anomic state without being egoistic, and vice versa. [Ref. 3, page 258.]

Durkheim's "altruistic" type of suicide results from "insufficient individuation"—a condition directly opposite to the one producing egoistic suicide. While later investigation has questioned some of Durkheim's theoretical formulation and challenged the accuracy of part of his supporting data, his study remains as the first important sociologic contribution to the understanding of suicide.

SUICIDE AND STATUS

More than 17,000 persons decided life was no longer worth living and committed suicide in the United States in 1950, producing a suicide rate of 11.4 per 100,000 population (17, 18).

White persons are about three times more likely to kill themselves than are Negroes [1] and males have a rate about three times the rate for females; women are less prone to suicide than men and Negroes are less susceptible than whites.

Suicide is more common among the privileged groups in American society than among the downtrodden. Commissioned officers in the United States Army kill themselves with greater frequency than enlisted men of the same race (2). While suicides occur in substantial numbers at both extremes of the socioeconomic scale, data from the life insurance companies show that they are concentrated among the well-to-do (2).

A common theme runs through the differences in susceptibility to suicide of these groups. In every case, the category with highest status position is the category with the highest suicide rate. Males, because of their greater involvement in the occupational system, enjoy a status position somewhat higher than females. The superior status position of whites as compared with Negroes is obvious. Those at the top of the economic scale enjoy high status as compared with those less fortunate, and the commissioned officers "outrank" the enlisted men. These data show that susceptibility to suicide rises with status position.[2]

---

[1] In a recent study of completed and attempted suicides in Seattle, Washington, during the five-year period 1948 to 1952, Schmid and Van Arsdol (15) confirm the finding that Negroes have lower suicide rates than whites. They find, however, that the *attempted* suicide rate among Negroes is *higher* than that of whites. Data on attempted suicides are, of course, more difficult to evaluate than are data on completed suicides. The racial findings, as well as other structural correlates of attempted suicides presented in the Schmid–Van Arsdol study, suggest that the attempted suicide may be an act conceptually and motivationally quite different from the completed suicide, a point made by both Farberow (4) and Rosen (12). For this reason, our treatment is restricted to completed suicides.

[2] The status structure of our society is not static. Recent changes suggest that the

SUICIDE AND STRENGTH OF THE RELATIONAL SYSTEM

Durkheim and others (8) have suggested that suicide varies with the strength of the relational system in which the person is enmeshed. Persons deeply and intimately involved with others should be low suicide risks, while those isolated from meaningful relationships with their fellow men should be high risks. There are four possible tests of this hypothesis using data available for the United States population.

The central transitional sectors of cities are characterized by high residential mobility and extremes of personal and social disorganization. Anonymity, loneliness, and isolation from meaningful interpersonal relationships reach their extremes. On the streets in these areas are found the "homeless men" and cheap apartment-hotel dwellings with a very high rate of turnover. Inhabitants of these "disorganized" areas are not deeply enmeshed in meaningful interaction with other persons. The relational system typically is very weak. Suicide rates in these areas are higher than in outlying residential areas of the city. Studies of the distribution of suicide in Chicago (1), Seattle and Minneapolis (14), and London (13) all reveal extreme concentrations of suicide in the central, disorganized sectors of the city.

There is a direct relation between degree of urbanization and suicide rates. The suicide rate in the United States falls steadily from its high point in cities of over 100,000 population to its low point in rural areas. One of the critical differences between rural and urban living is in the stability and continuity of family and neighborhood life. The strong control exercised by the neighbors on the farm or in the small town contrasts sharply with the anonymity and impersonality of life in the city. These characteristics of the city are magnified in the central, disorganized sectors. The steady rise in suicide from the tightly knit rural community to the anonymity of the city may reflect the strong relational systems of the rural small-town dweller and the relative isolation from meaningful relationships of many of the inhabitants of large cities (8).

A third measure of the relation between suicide and strength of the relational system can be derived from statistics on suicide by marital status. The degree of involvement in meaningful relationships with other persons

distinctions between the pairs in our four status categories are decreasing. With such changes in relative status, we expect suicide rates to change correspondingly. The difference in suicide between the two racial groups is greater in the Southern states, where the status differential is also greater. Conversely, the suicide differential is smaller in the Northern states, where the status of the two groups is more nearly equal.

is greater, on the average, for the married than for the single, widowed, or divorced. The married are by definition involved in at least one more meaningful relationship than the nonmarried. When the effects of age and sex are held constant, the suicide rate of the married is lower than the suicide rate of the single, the widowed, or the divorced (8). Suicide is highest for the divorced. When the factor of age is held constant, suicide is higher for the widowed than it is for the single, up to the age of thirty-five. From age thirty-five on, however, the suicide rate of the single is higher than that of the widowed. Strength of the relational system is related to the widowed and single categories in an extremely complex manner. It is probably weaker for the widowed than for the single at the younger ages, when widowhood comes as a greater shock and young family responsibilities are most likely to be disrupted. On the other hand, it is probably stronger for the widowed during the older age periods, when they are more likely to have the benefit of relations with their children grown to adulthood and when the single find their relationships curtailed by increasing mortality of their age group. These are all complex relationships, and our marital status classifications are only relative measures, or indexes, of strength of the relational system (5, 10). The findings, however, are congruent with the hypothesis that susceptibility to suicide will be lowest for those immersed in a meaningful network of interaction with other persons.

The relation between suicide and age provides a final test of the effect on suicide of involvement in meaningful relationships with other persons. Gerontologists point out that one of the chief problems of the aged is that of finding meaningful groups with which to associate. Our culture, with its emphasis on conjugal relationships, makes it more difficult for family bonds to remain intact and strong with the aging process. Further, the degree of involvement in relationships within the "family of orientation" varies with age simply as a function of parental mortality. By age fifty-five to sixty-four, the probability that at least one of the two parents will be dead is virtually 1.0 (8). Death of the parents certainly weakens the strength of the relational system of those persons who maintain contact with their parents through the years. The suicide rate rises sharply with age from a low of 4.5 per 100,000 for those aged fifteen to twenty-four, to 27.0 per 100,000 aged fifty-five to sixty-four, and maintains its high level up to age eighty-five and over (17). Part of the increase may be due to departure of children from the home; yet this fact does not explain the rise adequately, since the increase occurs for the single as well as for the married. The direct relation between suicide and age is also to some extent a function of sex. Schmid and Van Arsdol find that the suicide of males in Seattle increases with age, but suicide of females rises to middle age and decreases thereafter (15). It seems probable that our cultural pattern of female dependency is reflected in the lowered suicide rates of aged females. That is, while aged males may be allowed to drift, thus weakening the strength of their relational bonds, the aged mother is more likely to be taken care of by one of her children. Much further research on this question is needed before this interpretation can be given more than very tentative standing.

In summary, the suicide rate is higher in the central, disorganized sectors of cities than in the outlying residential areas; it is higher in cities than in rural areas; it is higher for the single, widowed, and divorced than for the married; and, finally, it is higher for the old than the young. These relationships may reflect differences in the degree of isolation from meaningful relationships of those in the categories we have examined.

SUICIDE AND EXTERNAL RESTRAINT

Since the suicide rate is related both to status position and to strength of the relational system, it becomes reasonable to ask whether these two variables include some common element which might explain their association with suicide. What is common to high status position and isolation from social relationships which might account for the very high suicide rates accompanying these conditions? And conversely, what is common to low status position and intense involvement in relationships with others which might account for the relative immunity these two conditions provide against suicide? Henry and Short suggest a common element in their concept of "external restraint."

Weber has defined the term "social relationship" to denote "the behavior of a plurality of actors insofar as, in its meaningful content, the action of each takes account of that of the others and is oriented in these terms." If the action of each "takes account of that of the others," the behavior of one party to a "social" relationship must, by definition, suffer some degree of restraint to make it conform to the wishes and expectations of the other party to the relationship.

Let us assume: (a) that present in every "social" or "cathectic" relationship is an element of restraint which acts to curb action or behavior of parties to the relationship; (b) that this element arises directly out of the relationship and is external to the personalities of the individuals who are a party to the relationship; (c) that acceptance of the element of restraint by each party to the relationship is a condition of the continuation of the relationship. [Ref. 8, page 74.]

With these assumptions, it follows that behavior of a person involved in a "social" relationship as defined will be subject to a greater degree of "horizontal external restraint" than behavior of a person not involved in a social relationship. Further, as the number of social relationships in which the person is involved increases, the amount of horizontal external restraint over his behavior will increase. The degree to which the person's behavior is required to conform with the demands and expectations of others increases with the number of social relationships in which the person is involved. We have shown that the risk of suicide decreases as the number of social relationships increases. Since the degree of horizontal external restraint over behavior increases with the number of relationships, let us suggest tentatively that the risk of suicide decreases as the degree to which behavior is required to conform to the demands and expectations of others increases. Behavior of the isolated person is freed from the requirement that it conform to the expectations of others. And the risk of suicide for the isolated is very high.

We have argued that behavior of a person who is more involved in social relationships is subject to greater horizontal external restraint than is behavior of a person not so involved in social relationships. Let us suggest further that behavior of a person playing the subordinate role in a social relationship is subject to greater "vertical" external restraint than behavior of the person playing the superordinate role. Negroes, women, enlisted men, and low income persons, in their relationships with whites, men, officers and high income persons on the average play the subordinate roles in the relationships. Members of the high status categories tend to play the superordinate role in their relationships with others.

The risk of suicide increases as position in the status hierarchy rises. Since the degree of "vertical" external restraint over behavior is greater, on the average, for the low status than for the high status category, we may suggest that the risk of suicide decreases as the degree of "vertical" external restraint over behavior increases. Behavior of the high status person playing many superordinate roles—like behavior of the isolated person—is freed from the requirement that it conform to the demands and expectations of others. External restraints over behavior are minimal and the suicide risk is high. Behavior of the low status person playing many subordinate roles—like behavior of the person immersed in social relationships with others—is subject to heavy requirements that it conform to the demands and expectations of others. External restraints over behavior are maximal and the risk of suicide is low. This formulation has been summarized elsewhere as follows:

We have grouped the correlates of suicide in two variables, position in a status hierarchy and degree of relational involvement with other persons. We have further deduced a common element of these two variables which we have labelled external restraint.

Behavior of subordinate status groups is restrained by the weight of the demands and expectations imposed by other groups higher in the status hierarchy. Behavior of the Negro is subject to the demands of white persons to a greater extent than behavior of the white person is subject to the demands of Negroes. The behavior of an employee is subject to greater restraint than behavior of his superior. Power is associated with status position and this is recognized by both parties to the relationship, subordinate and superordinate. But it is the behavior of the subordinate which must conform to the expectations of his superior. The superior is not similarly limited. The vertical restraint demanded by subordinate status is of a different order from the restraint demanded as a condition of collective living. Whether a person is of the highest or the lowest status, as long as he is operating in a network of interpersonal relationships, his behavior must also conform to the demands and expectations of other parties to the relationship. And this conformity requires that he restrain his behavior. He must control and modify his impulsive behavior to meet the definitions operating in the relationship.

But whether the restraint derives from subordinate status or from interpersonal relations with other persons, it seems to provide relative immunity from suicide. [Ref. 8, page 80. Italics added.]

Why does external restraint over behavior provide this immunity? As the degree to which behavior is determined and controlled by the demands and expectations of others increases, the share of others in responsibility for the consequences of the behavior also increases. If a person commits an act primarily because others want him to commit it, others must share in the responsibility for the consequences of the act. The restraining persons can easily be blamed if the consequences of the act are unfortunate. But when an act is determined exclusively by the self and is independent of the wishes and expectations of others, the self must bear sole responsibility if it results in frustration. Others cannot be blamed since others were not involved in the determination of the act.

We have noted elsewhere that homicide, in contrast with suicide, tends to occur among those groups where behavior typically is subject to high levels of external restraint. If suicide is the result of aggression flowing inwardly against the self and if homicide results from the outward discharge of aggression against others when aggression is aroused by frustration, it will tend to flow inwardly against the self when the source of the frustration is the self and outwardly against others when the source of frustration is viewed as lying outside the self. The likelihood that the source of frustration will be perceived as lying outside the self is high when a wide sphere of the person's total behavior is determined by the demands and expectations of others. The likelihood that the self will be blamed is high when a person's behavior is determined by his own demands and expectations. Aggression will flow against the perceived source of frustration. When external restraints are strong, others will be perceived as the source of frustration, and aggression consequent to frustration will flow outwardly. When external restraints are weak, the self will be perceived as the source of frustration, and the aggression consequent to it will flow inwardly against the self. In extreme cases, it will produce suicide.

SUICIDE AND THE BUSINESS CYCLE

If suicide is a form of aggression and if aggression is one consequence of frustration, the suicide rate should increase with increase in frustration and decrease with decrease in frustration. A major source of frustration in the United States is the decline in income experienced during economic depressions. Therefore, we would expect the suicide rate to rise during business depression and to fall during business prosperity. This relationship is so strong, in fact, that about two-thirds of the variation in the suicide rate through time in the United States can be accounted for by economic fluctuations.

Ogburn (11), Thomas (16), Dublin and Bunzel (2), and Henry (7) all have demonstrated the existence of this high negative relationship between suicide and the business cycle in the United States, in England, and Wales. The fact that this relationship has been demonstrated with the use of a variety of business and suicide indices during different time periods and in different countries firmly establishes the finding in empirical fact.

Economic data suggest that high income groups suffer the greatest relative loss of income when the business cycle turns downward (9). If we assume that frustrations accompanying business cycles are generated by failure to maintain a constant or rising position in the status hierarchy relative to the status position of others in the same status reference system —and if the upper status groups experience these frustrations more than lower status groups—we would expect suicide of upper status groups to be more sensitive to changes in economic conditions than suicide of lower status groups. Henry has shown this to be the case (7). Suicide of males is more sensitive to the business cycle than suicide of females; suicide of whites is more sensitive than suicide of nonwhites; suicide of persons living in high-median-rental census tracts in Chicago is more sensitive than suicide of persons living in low rental tracts. Finally, suicide of persons in the young and middle age groups is more sensitive to business fluctuation than suicide of those subject to the relatively low status position of the older age groups in American society.

In each of these four cases, the suicide rate of the higher status category fluctuates with economic conditions more closely than the suicide rate of the lower status category with which it is compared.

It is necessary to point out that the homicide rate also fluctuates with economic conditions. Since homicide also is a form of aggression, the frustration-aggression theory would require that murder rates should respond to frustrations accompanying business cycles in the same way as suicide rates. Persons who commit homicide are, on the average, from low status groups. And since the sharpness of relative loss of income during depression is lower for low status than for high status groups, we are not surprised that the homicide rate is less sensitive to depression than the suicide rate. Among white persons, homicide does increase along with suicide during business depression (8). But among Negroes, the homicide rate *decreases* during business depression and increases during business prosperity. Negroes who commit homicide represent probably the lowest point in the status hierarchy in the United States. We have noted that suicide of Negroes rises less during depression than suicide of whites, and have argued that this results from the fact that Negroes suffer less frustration (as defined) [3] during business contraction. Low status Negroes suffer frustration not during business contraction but during business expansion. Lying at the very bottom of the status hierarchy, they experience a gain of status *relative* to whites when whites, through economic misfortune, lose their relative position of superiority during business contraction. Distinctions between the races become blurred when there are representatives of each in the bread lines. Frustration comes to the low status Negro when business starts to improve and the whites are able to regain their position of relative superiority. Whites relative to Negroes experience more frustration during business contraction and less frustration during business expansion, and this fact is reflected in both the suicide and homicide rates of these groups as they are affected by business cycles. Both suicide and homicide are acts of aggression and both increase with frustration.

---

[3] The frustration to which we refer is that resulting from interference with the assumed "goal response" of maintaining a constant or rising position in the status hierarchy relative to the status position of others in the same status reference system.

CONCLUSION

The sociologic evidence suggests that suicide is a form of aggression against the self aroused by some frustration, the cause of which is perceived by the person as lying within the self. Failure to maintain a constant or rising position in the status hierarchy relative to others in the same status reference system is one—but by no means the only—important frustration arousing aggression. When this frustration is perceived as being the fault of the self, the aroused aggression may flow against the self. This is most likely when the person is relatively freed from the requirement that his behavior conform to the demands and expectations of others. Persons of high status and those isolated from meaningful relationships are most likely to blame themselves and commit suicide when frustration occurs, since their behavior is relatively independent of the demands and expectations of others.

References

1. Cavan, Ruth S., *Suicide*. Chicago: University of Chicago Press, 1928.
2. Dublin, Louis I., and B. Bunzel, *To Be or Not to Be*. New York: Random House, Inc., 1933.
3. Durkheim, Émile, *Le Suicide*. Paris: Librairie Felix Alcan, 1897. (Translated by John A. Spaulding and George Simpson, and published as *Suicide*. Glencoe, Ill.: Free Press, 1951.)
4. Farberow, Norman L., Personality patterns of suicidal mental hospital patients. *Genetic Psychology Monographs*, 42: 3–79, 1950.
5. Goode, William J., *After Divorce*. Glencoe, Ill.: Free Press, 1956.
6. Halbwachs, Maurice, *Les Causes de suicide*. Paris: Librairie Felix Alcan, 1930.
7. Henry, Andrew F., The Nature of the Relation between Suicide and the Business Cycle. (Unpublished Ph.D. dissertation, Department of Sociology, University of Chicago, 1950.)
8. ———— and James F. Short, Jr., *Suicide and Homicide: Some Economic, Sociological and Psychological Aspects of Aggression*. Glencoe, Ill.: Free Press, 1951.
9. Mendershausen, Horst, *Changes in Income during the Great Depression*. New York: National Bureau of Economic Research, Inc., 1946.
10. Nye, F. Ivan, Child adjustment in various types of broken homes and in unhappy unbroken homes. (Paper prepared for the Annual Meeting of the American Sociological Society, 1956.)
11. Ogburn, William F., and Dorothy S. Thomas, The influence of the business cycle on certain social conditions. *Journal of the American Statistical Association*, 18: 305–350, 1942.
12. Rosen, Albert, William M. Hales, and Werner Simon. Classification of "suicidal" patients. *Journal of Consulting Psychology*, 18: 359–362, 1954.
13. Sainsbury, Peter, *Suicide in London: An Ecological Study*. London: Chapman & Hall, Ltd., 1955.

14. Schmid, Calvin F., *Suicide in Seattle, 1914–1925: An Ecological and Behavioristic Study*. (University of Washington Publications in the Social Sciences.) Seattle: University of Washington Press, 1928.
15. ——— and M. D. Van Arsdol, Jr., Completed and attempted suicides. *American Sociological Review*, 20: 273–283, 1955.
16. Thomas, Dorothy S., *Social Aspects of the Business Cycle*. New York: Alfred A. Knopf, Inc., 1927.
17. National Office of Vital Statistics, *Vital Statistics of the United States*, vol. I, table 8.43, pp. 209–216. U.S. Public Health Service, 1950.
18. National Office of Vital Statistics, *Vital Statistics of the United States*, vol. III, table 56. U.S. Public Health Service, 1950.

8

Suicide in a Catholic Country

FRANCO FERRACUTI

The relationship between Catholicism and suicide has often been treated in the literature on suicide, particularly in sociologic studies. The importance of religion as a social factor makes it necessary to assess its value and influence in the baffling social phenomenon of suicide.

Émile Durkheim (7), using data from Morselli (14), reached the conclusion many years ago that suicide "is very little developed in purely Catholic countries (Spain, Portugal, Italy), while it is at its maximum in Protestant countries." A careful analysis of the data from countries with a mixed religious situation, especially Germany and Switzerland, confirmed that, even when all other cultural and economic facts are similar, Catholics do commit suicide less often than non-Catholics. There is general agreement on this point, although some data remain to be explained, such as the very low suicide rate in Norway, a Protestant country, and in England.

Durkheim's study represents one of the first significant analyses of the manner in which society influences a highly individualistic aspect of human activity (12). Durkheim tries, after a detailed discussion, to explain the difference in suicide rates between Protestants and Catholics on the basis of the prophylactic effect of religion as a social phenomenon, in the sense of the "existence of a certain number of beliefs and practices common to all, faithful, traditional and thus obligatory." Catholicism is more a society than Protestantism; Judaism is even more traditional. (And Jews, under normal conditions, kill themselves less frequently than people belonging to any other religion, even though Judaism does not formally forbid suicide.) Durkheim's faith in the degree of integration of religious societies, instead of the religious dogmas, as a deterrent to suicide was taken up by Halbwachs (11) and enlarged to include the kind of life and the types of civilization, emphasizing the conservative, traditional aspect of religion.

Durkheim, Halbwachs, and Dublin and Bunzel (6) are the most important representatives of the sociologic approach in the study of suicide. The psychopathologic or psychiatric approach, even in its neo-Freudian form, generally studies single cases or limited groups and, as a rule, has attempted generalizations of only limited interest for the problem of the relationship between Catholicism and suicide. Besides, the statements of Esquirol, Darwin, Strahan, Delmas, and others, attempting to consider suicide only a case of mental imbalance and delirium, appear oversimplified and peremptory. Without discarding psychopathology and taking into account the relevant difficulties of a study of the problem at an individual level, we may say that the sociologic approach, up to now, appeared to be the one most likely to help us to explain those cases of suicide in which no mental disease was apparent.

This opinion is shared by a recent author, Deshaies (5), who is particularly important because he comes from the psychiatric profession. Also, less recent writers, like Altavilla (1), have taken this point of view. Deshaies, on the problem of the relationship between suicide and religion, expresses some doubts as to the reliability of the data on religious affiliation, trying to reconsider the problem on a more personal and individualistic basis. It is not so much, in his opinion, a matter of religious affiliation as it is a matter of religious faith and knowledge of religious dogmas— a very different thing indeed.

It might be of some interest, and it might provide a more firm basis for discussion, to investigate exactly what the Catholic doctrine does say about suicide, and how its official point of view derives from former philosophies. The pre-Catholic Mediterranean societies had a varied pattern in this regard; the Egyptians, Greeks, and Romans did not take a firm stand on the issue. Plato condemned suicide, but the Cynic and Stoic philosophic schools asserted its lawfulness and even its advisability. The ancient Roman code punishes suicide only in two cases: military personnel (the penalty was serious, the so-called *missio ignominiosa;* attempted suicide was also punished) [1] and slaves (no fixed penalty). In the case of free Roman citizens committing suicide, the state could confiscate the property, in payment for taxes, and the like. It appears that the only

---

[1] *De re militari* 1.6, 7D. *De poenis* D.1.38, 12: ... miles, qui sibi manus intulerit, nec factum peregit, nisi impatientia doloris, aut morbi, luctusve alicuius, vel alia causa fuerit, capite puniendus est; alias ignominia mittendus est.

concern of the Roman law for suicide was economic or military. No other consideration was given to the phenomenon (15).

With the coming of the Catholic Church, a slow change took effect in the attitude of society toward suicide. In the first centuries the problem was ignored, but later, with St. Augustine, the old thesis of Plato, condemning suicide as proof of not accepting the divine will of being bound to one's own body, was taken up again and strictly enforced. The Council of Toledo (693 A.D.) provided excommunication for attempted suicide, and suicide in the form of a sort of search for martyrdom was also criticized and discouraged. St. Augustine and St. Thomas Aquinas are very definite on this issue.[2]

The Catholic Church denies to man the right of committing suicide on the basis of the Commandment, "Thou shalt not kill," stating that only God has the right of separating body from soul, and also as an interpretation of the natural law. This opinion of the Church is so firmly stated that no room for doubt is left. Suicide in any form and for any reason is forbidden and penalties are stated for it.

The Canonic Code,[3] the basic law of the Church, has a number of articles on suicide and self-mutilation. The practical consequences of this code are as follows: (a) a person who has attempted suicide cannot enter the priesthood and (b) a person who, while mentally normal, commits suicide cannot be buried in sacred ground nor with religious rites.

[2] St. Augustine bases his denial of suicide on four points: (a) *Non occides* [Thou shalt not kill] is an absolute law; (b) it is not possible to kill a guilty person; if the suicide is innocent, the sin is even greater; (c) the greatness and strength of the soul is in living, not in dying; and (d) to commit suicide in order to avoid committing a sin is an even greater sin, because it makes it impossible to repent. St. Thomas stated that suicide is a mortal sin against God who has given life and against justice and against charity.

[3] *Can. 985: 5.* Sunt irregulares ex delicto: 5. Qui se ipsos vel alios mutilaverunt vel sibi vitam adimere tentaverunt. *Can. 1240: par. I, 3.* Ecclesiastica sepultura privantur, nisi ante mortem aliqua dederint poenitentiae signa: 3. Qui se ipsi occiderint deliberato consilio. *Can. 1241.* Excluso ab ecclesiastica sepultura deneganda quodque sunt tum quaelibet Missa exsequialis, etiam anniversaria, tum alia publica officia funebra. *Can. 2339.* Qui ausi fuerint mandare seu cogere tradi ecclesiasticae sepulturae infideles, apostatas a fide, vel haereticos, schismaticos, aliosve sive excommunicatos, sive interdictos contra praescriptum can. 1240, par. I, contrahunt excommunicationem latae sententiae nemini reservatam; sponte vero sepulturam eisdem donantes, interdictum ab ingressu ecclesiae Ordinario reservatum. *Can. 2350: par. 2.* Qui in se ipsos manus intulerint, si quidem mors secuta sit, sepultura ecclesiastica priventur ad normam can. 1240, par. I, no. 3; secus, arceantur ab actibus legitimis ecclesiasticis et, si sint clerici, suspendantur ad tempus ab Ordinario definiendum, et a beneficiis aut officiis curam animarum interni vel externi fori adnexam habentibus removeantur.

It should be noted that, although the basic principle on which the law of the Church is based never changed, the practical application of the law has been somewhat lessened following the progress of psychiatric studies which consider many, if not all, suicides mentally abnormal. For example, suicide while in a state of mental abnormality is not subject to the penalty of exclusion from religious rites, and such deaths are not officially considered as suicides. Furthermore, this exemption is based upon a judgment about the mental condition of the deceased made by the priest himself. No expert opinion is required and no medical certificate is necessary. The decision is left entirely to the priest and, in case of doubt, he may presume mental abnormality and give sacred burial, provided there has been no great scandal and publicity. In a symposium held in 1949 by the Roman journalists, it was advocated that a minimum of publicity be given to suicide cases, in order to allow sacred burials in as many cases as possible.[4]

In Italy, the suicide rate has varied widely. At the beginning of the century it was less than 50 per million Italians. This rate rose to about 80 before World War I, dropped to between 60 and 70 during World War I, rose again to over 90 in the years 1924 to 1930, then slowly dropped below 40 per million during World War II. The phenomenon of the decrease in number of suicides during wars has been reported often. It seems to be a general rule and has evoked different interpretations. Italy apparently offers no exception to this rule. After World War II there was again a rise in the suicide rate, reaching 58 per million Italians in 1947, 63 in 1948, 66 in 1949, 57 in 1950, and 68 in 1951.[5]

It might be of interest to consider the rates of suicide in the different areas in Italy. For the latest available statistics, years 1947 to 1951, the distribution is as indicated in Table 8-1.

The decrease in the suicide rate as we move from north to south in Italy is evident. The northern rate is, on the average, 100 per cent higher than that in the south. The south of Italy is the area in which economic conditions are poorer, education is less adequate, and Catholicism, formally and otherwise, is stronger. As in the data from other countries, we find suicide associated with high income, high education, and low adherence to religion.

---

[4] It is interesting to note that Fascism, with a law passed on March 28, 1928, forbade publication in newspapers of data on suicide.

[5] These data are considered the most reliable, since they derive from reports on cause of death, which are filed with the Istituto Centrale di Statistica, and hence are not corrected on the basis of the priest's interpretation as to the mental state of the deceased (19).

TABLE 8-1

RATE OF SUICIDES PER MILLION INHABITANTS IN THE
DIFFERENT AREAS IN ITALY

Year	Northern Italy	Central Italy	Southern Italy	Sicily and Sardinia	All Italy
1947	84.75	57.50	46.80	65.00	58.00
1948	90.62	69.00	40.40	61.50	63.00
1949	101.50	59.00	48.40	49.50	66.00
1950	81.25	54.50	33.40	48.50	57.00
1951	106.00	68.00	39.60	55.00	68.00
Average for 5 years	92.82	61.60	41.72	55.90	62.40

The Catholic priest in the society of southern Italy is a major part of the society, an authority in himself, often more powerful than the civil authorities. Should we then accept Durkheim's view of the problem? A number of questions come to mind. How are we to separate economic causes of suicide from the religious factor? It is a widely accepted fact, and data from the state police records confirm it, that the reasons for suicide are more often economic in the north—bankruptcy, financial difficulties, and so forth—while in the south, emotional breakdown or family difficulties are more often responsible. Also, what is the relationship between education and suicide? We know very little about this point, and we can only guess with few facts as a basis.

Recent Italian researches on suicide are very scarce and mostly centered on the psychopathologic approach. Only two need be mentioned here. Catalano-Nobili and Cerquetelli (2), from the Neuropsychiatric Clinic of the University of Rome, examined records on suicides and interviewed those who attempted suicide in the Rome area. No importance is accorded by the authors to social factors and Catholicism is not considered. The cases are classified according to psychiatric diagnoses, and the entire problem is viewed in the frame of reference of mental hygiene.

The second study, by C. De Sanctis and G. Basini (4), is a socio-psychiatric research on juvenile (five to nineteen years) suicide cases. Again, the emphasis is on the neuropsychiatric aspects of suicide, considered as a result of conflict-full situations in the immediate environment of the subjects. No consideration is given to Catholicism as a factor.

Non-Catholic authors discuss the problem from different points of view. In a recent book, *Psychoanalysis and Prophylaxis of Suicide*, J. Flescher (9) presents the classic psychoanalytic point of view on suicide, approaching the problem from the psychodynamic standpoint.

George Simpson (16), in an introduction to a recent edition of Durkheim's book, raises a number of questions about the relationship between Catholicism and suicide. Are suicide data in Catholic countries accurately reported? What are the suicide rates among different Protestant sects? According to Simpson, Unitarians should have a very high rate and high church Episcopalians a very low rate. What exactly is the action of the Catholic Church according to Durkheim's conception; what are the common sentiments and beliefs to which he refers? Simpson holds that "Catholic sentiments and beliefs seek to relieve the individual of guilt, make all sins expiable, establish an intricate hierarchical system of father substitutes, and an ingenious, poetic image of the mother."

Apparently, the role of the Catholic faith in preventing suicide has not been widely studied at an individual level. All we have from the literature is a number of generalizations based on over-all statistical data. It is a field which calls for more adequate investigation.

Although there is doubtless some truth in the sociologic opinion on this problem, the manner in which Catholicism as a society prevents suicide is not so simple as Durkheim and Halbwachs seem to think. Suicide is one of the few sins for which there is no escape from eternal punishment. By its nature, it prevents any possibility of penance and safety for the soul. Another act with the same aspects is body cremation, which is indeed a rare thing among Catholics. Like suicide, cremation leaves no possibility for penance, and it is as strictly forbidden as suicide by the Catholic Church. How many Catholics have their bodies cremated? It might be of some interest to find out.

We may perhaps clarify the Catholic conception of such a problem by saying that the entire outlook of the Church is toward life, which must be lived in order to reach a more perfect life. This life-centered philosophy probably has an important connection with the deterrent effect of Catholicism on suicide. There is no possibility for the Catholic to rationalize suicide, except in a delirious way. When a truly Catholic person contemplates or commits suicide, he either is mentally sick or has given up religion. There are some instances in which belief in the hereafter does facilitate suicide in a Catholic person, but careful analysis of such cases almost always reveals the presence of serious insanity and delirium.

In one case which recently came under the observation of the author, a forty-four-year-old, very religious man killed himself by swallowing bits of broken glass. Near his body a Bible was found, with a long note in which he stated that he had had news from heaven, two years before, that he was to "meet the life of Christ," that his three-year-old son was his "angel," that God would give a sign to the priest who would conduct his burial, and so forth. It is clear that, in cases such as this, a religious delirium drives the subjects to suicide, and the problem of rationalizing suicide within the frame of reference of the Church does not exist.

There is another consideration which might help to explain the low number of suicides among Catholics. Not only is it true, as Simpson states, that Catholicism establishes "an intricate hierarchical system of father substitutes," but often these father substitutes take an active part in preventive psychotherapy for their "children."

Here, the reference is to Confession. Catholic authors reject the analogy between Confession and psychotherapy, but they do admit some effect of Confession in preventing mental disturbances. VanderVeldt and Odenwald (17) say that Confession may rid a person of his guilt feelings, act as a catharsis, and promote, in the examination of conscience that precedes Confession itself, some form of self-analysis at the conscious level. There is often a transference phenomenon between confessant and confessor, and Confession has some psychagogic (security-giving) elements. Complete analogy is, of course, impossible. Confession is a sacrament and belongs to the supernatural order, while psychotherapy is a method of healing.

Also, as White (18) points out, Confession is always at a conscious level, and "the ingredients of the sacrament of penance are neatly and definitely sorted out, formulated and tabulated; Confession requires concentration of the conscious memory, while analytic psychotherapy is based on the free flow of uncontrolled phantasy." White states: "The uncomfortable confessional box with its hard kneeler, and the couch or armchair of the analyst's office, admirably express and promote the two very different kinds of 'confession' for which each is appointed."

Yet, White suggests that "sacramental Confession, especially if practiced with regularity and with frank unflinching self-examination, may serve the ends, if not of psychotherapy, then at least of mental hygiene and prophylaxis." White quotes Jung, who stated in 1932 about his patients: "It is safe to say that every one of them fell ill because he had lost that which the living religions of every age had given to their followers, and none of them has been really healed who did not regain his religious outlook." To make the penitent regain his religious outlook, to rid him of guilt feelings, to act as a catharsis might well be one effect of Confession. The Catholic on the verge of a nervous breakdown, the Catholic who is slowly sinking into depression and social isolation, might be saved, more often than even the Catholic authors would claim, by Confession. This hypothesis might be investigated through careful interviewing of attempted suicides, with the collaboration of a number of researchers free from preconceived opinions about the role of religion. Various techniques are now being explored for the prevention of suicide. Among these may be mentioned the "Suicide Bureaus" (10) of the Salvation Army, the work of many mental clinics, the Emergency Clinic for Depression recently established in Stockholm, and the like. Have such means been available to the Catholic in the fatherly advice and in the guilt-resolving authority of the confessor? It is a problem that is worth investigation.

References

1. Altavilla, E., *Psicologia del suicidio*. Naples: Perrella, 1913.
2. Catalano-Nobili, C., and G. Cerquetelli, Il Suicidio: Studio statistico e psicopatologico. *Monografia della "Rassegna di Neuropsichiatria," Nocera Inferiore*, 1949.
3. Delmas, A., *Psychologie pathologique du suicide*. Paris: Librairie Felix Alcan, 1932.
4. De Sanctis, C., and G. Basini, Sulla dinamica del suicidio nell'età infanto-giovanile. *Infanzia Anormale*, 9: 696–722, 1954.
5. Deshaies, G., *Psychologie du suicide*. Paris: P.U.F., 1947.
6. Dublin, L. I., and B. Bunzel, *To Be or Not to Be*. New York: Random House, Inc., 1933.
7. Durkheim, É., *Suicide: A Study in Sociology*. London: Routledge and Kegan Paul, Ltd., 1952.
8. Ferri, E., *L'omicidio-suicidio*. Turin: U.T.E.T., 1925.
9. Flescher, J., *Psicoanalisi e profilassi del suicidio*. Rome: Scienza Moderna, 1948.
10. Gillin, J. L., *Social Pathology*, 3d ed. New York: Appleton-Century-Crofts, Inc., 1946.
11. Halbwachs, M., *Les Causes du suicide*. Paris: Librairie Felix Alcan, 1930.
12. Klineberg, O., *Social Psychology*, rev. ed. New York: Henry Holt and Company, Inc., 1954.
13. Menninger, K. A., *Man Against Himself*. New York: Harcourt, Brace and Company, Inc., 1938.
14. Morselli, E., *Il Suicidio*. Milan: Dumolard, 1879.
15. Palazzo, D., *Il Suicidio sotto l'aspetto fisiopatologico, sociale e giuridico*. Naples: Jovene, 1953.
16. Simpson, G., The Aetiology of Suicide. (Editor's introduction to Durkheim, É., *Suicide*). London: International Library of Social Reconstruction, Routledge and Kegan Paul, Ltd., 1952.

17. VanderVeldt, J. H., and R. Odenwald, *Psychiatry and Catholicism*. New York: The Blakiston Division, McGraw-Hill Book Company, Inc., 1952.

18. White, V., The Analyst and the Confessor. (In *God and the Unconscious*). London: Hagwill Press, 1952.

19. *Annuario Statistico Italiano,* serie V, vol. II, 1949–50; serie V, vol. III, 1951; serie V, vol. V, 1953; serie V, vol. VI, 1954–55. Rome: Istituto Poligrafico dello Stato.

9

Suicide and Law

HELEN SILVING

The approach of the law to the problem of suicide differs in method depending on the prevailing type of ethics. Absolute or "ontologic" ethics assumes an a priori position on this, as on any other, issue, whereas sociologic or utilitarian ethics demands that rules on suicide be related to scientific observation of the phenomenon of suicide, its causes and consequences, and the effectiveness of law as a means of preventing suicide.

ONTOLOGIC APPROACH TO SUICIDE

Ontologic ethics of suicide is importantly determined by religious views. But the influence of broad religious philosophies, as pantheism, pluralism, or monotheism, on attitudes toward suicide is believed to have been rather overestimated.[1] * Inconsistent attitudes toward death and suicide may be found in all these types of religious philosophy. In Buddhism, in which "the highest of all aims" is "the utter extinction of the illusion of personal identity—the utter annihilation of the ego ... the ultimate resolution of everything into nothing ... ,"[2] the killing of any form of life is strictly prohibited.[3] But instances of suicide in the course of religious practice are known to have occurred among certain Buddhist as well as Brahman sects.[4] That the approach of pluralistic religions to suicide is not uniform is evidenced by the Athenian prohibition of suicide,[5] as contrasted with the elevation of suicide to a method of punishment in the execution of Socrates. Plato and Aristotle [6] held suicide to be immoral, but the Stoics believed it proper to escape an undesirable life by flight into death. While monotheistic religions are generally opposed to suicide, there may be observed even in advanced stages of their dominance a peculiar discrepancy between the legal prohibition of suicide and its simultaneous social approval. The latter is expressed in customs imposing an outright duty of committing suicide (codes of honor).

* All footnotes are at the end of this chapter.

The Bible, perhaps in contrast to the Koran,[7] contains no prohibition of suicide. Exaltation of "suicide" in early Christian philosophy may be found in the calculated improvidence of martyrs and the enthusiasm for death on the part of ascetics, as well as in the glorification of suicide committed in defense of virtue. The Church adopted the prohibition of suicide at a rather late stage (Council of Arles, A.D. 452), justifying the prohibition on the ground that "whoever kills himself, thereby killing an innocent person, commits homicide." Apparently, suicide was conceived of as a sort of wrongful self-punishment. Later various efforts were made to rationalize this rather unique crime in which the criminal and the victim were combined in one person. Perhaps the most interesting among them is the argument that the duty of loving one's neighbor is predicated upon love of one's self, which, in turn, implies that we must love ourselves as we do our neighbors.[8] The Church, nevertheless, eventually adopted the extreme view, holding Judas Iscariot's betrayal of Christ a lesser sin than his later suicide. From permission to kill in defense of one's life, the inference was drawn that suicide is indeed more reprehensible than homicide.[9]

Further ambiguity was introduced into the law of Christian countries by the impact of Roman law. Owing to the mostly eclectic character of Roman philosophy and its dependence on inconsistent Greek sources, no clear-cut position was taken in Rome on the subject of suicide. But the basic attitude of the Romans was individualistic, and thus, of Cicero's various passages on suicide, that in which he paraphrased the Stoic view seems to have been most popular. He believed that where "God Himself has given a valid reason as He did . . . to Socrates and . . . to Cato, and often to many others, then of a surety your true wise man will joyfully pass forthwith from the darkness here into the light beyond." [10] It is controversial whether suicide was ever generally punishable in Roman law. It was unquestionably punishable where, owing to a man's special status, such as a *miles* [soldier] or a slave, the state or the master had a claim upon his life.[11] Punishment would also lie where the suicide was committed to avoid trial for crime, but in this instance the sanction was imposed upon that crime rather than upon the suicide.[12] Moreover, in those rare situations in which suicide itself was punishable, the obligation of life was conceived of as one not of the *jus naturale—quod natura omnia animalia docuit*—but as one of positive law.[13] Suicide was exempt from punishment where it was induced by "impatience of pain or sickness, some grief, or by another cause" (*impatientia doloris, aut morbi, luctusque alicuius, vel alia causa*) [14] or by "weariness of life . . . lunacy, or fear of dishonor" (*taedio vitae . . . aut furore, aut pudore*),[15] not, however, where it was committed "without cause," the reason advanced for making suicide a crime in such cases being that whoever does not spare himself would much less spare another.[16]

In the Christian doctrine the special duties of life assumed by the Roman law were expanded to a general obligation that every man owes to God and to the republic or the sovereign, and that obligation was sanctioned by excommunication of the suicide (Council of Toledo, 693 A.D.) and denial of a Christian burial.[17] But while no "just excuses" for suicide, as prevailing in the Roman law, are admitted in the Canon law, proof that the suicide was insane can be easily adduced.

The English common law of suicide was undoubtedly influenced by Christian religious views. But the origins of that law are traceable directly, that is, without the medium of the Canon law, to Roman sources. Bracton, obviously, "has been browsing on the leaves of Justinian's *Digest*." [18] In fact, he seems to have taken "practically all he has to say on the subject from the Roman law." Actually, the common law crime of suicide developed from the Roman rule providing for the punishment of suicide committed to avoid trial or conviction. Under the prevailing interpretation, in the English as in the Roman law, punishment was originally imposed not upon the act of suicide itself but rather upon another capital crime to which the suicide was related. Since in both laws, a man accused of a capital crime would not forfeit his estate until judgment was rendered, an accused or convicted person could save his estate for his heirs by committing suicide.[19] Hence the frequency of suicides in cases of conviction and the introduction into the law of a rebuttable presumption that suicide implies confession of the crime charged, carrying with it—in the absence of rebuttal—confiscation of property. That presumption was later omitted in the common law, and punishment related directly to the suicide rather than to the other crime which it was once presumed to evidence. The crime of suicide, which thus originated, was punishable at common law by denial of a Christian burial, sanctions imposed upon the corpse (burial in the highway with a stake driven through the body), and confiscation.

The crime of suicide at common law, however, is, notwithstanding its general character, no less obscure than its Roman law counterpart. Up to this day, we do not know what crime suicide constituted, whether a crime *sui generis* or a particular instance of murder, the better view being that it was the latter. Another interesting feature of that crime is the manner in which it was formulated. In the case of all other offenses, the common law defines the crime itself ("larceny is the felonious taking"; "murder is the unlawful killing"). But in suicide, not the crime but the criminal is defined: *"felo de se* is *he who kills."* Obviously, as was Christian doctrine, so was the common law struggling with the dilemma of a crime in which the aggressor and the object of aggression are united in one person.

Church influence is evident in those cases which classify suicide as murder, rationalizing this position on the ground of its being committed with premeditation and secretly,[20] but more particularly in passages such as "to kill himself, by which act he kills in presumption his own soul, is a greater offence than to kill another. . . ." [21] However, there are cases at common law which do not seem to be consistent with the Canon law view of suicide as murder.[22] Such early authorities notwithstanding, the English law has until the present time preserved the common law conception of suicide as a felony. While sanctions against the body and property of the suicide have been removed, so that suicide itself is no longer punishable, the attempt by a person deliberately to end his own life is still an attempt to commit a felony, though not an "attempt to commit murder" within the Offences against the Person Act of 1861 (24 and 25 Vict. c. 100). The maximum penalty for that offense is two years' imprisonment.

In the United States, the English common law on suicide was never accepted with all its implications. As stated in *Burnett v. People,*[23] "as we have never had a forfeiture of goods, or seen fit to define what character of burial our citizens shall enjoy, we have never regarded the English law as to suicide as applicable to the spirit of our institutions." Today, in rare cases, to be sure, attempted suicide is still a crime by virtue of express statutory provisions [24] or by virtue of general incorporation of the common law.[25] However, even where the crime of suicide has been expressly repudiated, as in New York, the legislator hastened to add into the language of the statute that, while not a crime, suicide is "a grave public wrong." [26]

The Canon law of suicide at one time influenced all continental European laws. In France, the *Établissements de Saint Louis* (Louis IX) of 1270 [27] declared the property of the suicide and his wife escheated to the lord. A custom of Brittany [28] provided that the suicide be hanged by his feet, dragged (through the streets) "as a murderer," and that his chattels be forfeited. A Criminal Ordinance of 1670 [29] required a criminal prosecution to be instituted "against his corpse or his memory." In Italy,[30] the *Costit. Piemontesi* of 1670 (IV, 34) required criminal proceedings to be instituted against the memory of anyone who, not being insane, committed "homicide against himself" (*omicida di sè medesimo*) and a sentence to be rendered that his corpse—and in the absence of a corpse, the effigy— be hanged on the gallows. The *Costit. Modenesi* (V, 4) provided for appointment of a relative as a representative of the suicide in his defense in similar proceedings. While Pietro Leopold of Toscana (1786) excluded suicide from the list of crimes, punishment of suicide may still be found in the Sardinian Code of 1839 (art. 585), which rendered the suicide's testament invalid and deprived him of an honorable burial. In Germany, for several centuries, the city hangman was given the right to all possessions found on the corpse of the suicide and around it, within a radius of the length of a spade.[31] Throughout the Middle Ages, suicides were punished by dishonorable interment. The reception of the Roman law (Italian version) [32] seems to have brought about some modifications. The *Constitutio Criminalis Carolina* of 1532 (art. 135) imposed confiscation only upon those who were deemed guilty of another capital crime that called for such punishment.[33] But the German common law preserved the sanction of dishonorable burial for suicides, subjecting attempted suicide to arbitrary punishment (Prussia, 1620). In Austria, the Criminal Code of Joseph II (1787) [34] still provided (§ 123) that the suicide be buried by the hangman and (§ 125) that attempted suicide be punished by imprisonment "until he [the suicide] be persuaded by education that self-preservation is a duty to God, the State and to himself, show complete repentance and may be expected to mend his ways." Where the suicide was committed to escape punishment for a crime, the same statute (§ 124) provided that, the crime being proven in accordance with law, the name of the suicide and description of the crime committed be affixed to the gallows and publicly proclaimed.

It may be appropriate to conclude this survey by quoting an often cited Order of the Day of Napoleon Bonaparte. In censuring a soldier who had committed suicide for reasons of love frustrations, the well-known soldier-legislator said: "A French soldier ought to show as much courage in facing the adversities and afflictions of life as he shows in facing the bullets of a battery. Whoever commits suicide is a coward; he is a soldier who deserts the battlefield before victory." [35]

However, Napoleon's dramatic pronouncement was not in harmony with the weight of the then current opinion in Europe. The apologists of suicide had long since been at work. Hume [36] vigorously fought the argument that suicide is sinful because it is an interference with the work of Providence, pointing out that almost every human action, however constructive, involves such interference. Montesquieu [37] stressed the absurdity of the assumption that a God of Love could wish to condemn man to receive a blessing which the latter experiences as oppressive. Beccaria compared the right to commit suicide to the right of emigration [38] and, significantly, argued that as there can be no wisdom in making the state a prison by prohibiting emigration, so there can be no merit in making suicide a crime. Suicide remained a favorite theme throughout the eighteenth and nineteenth centuries. Fichte's justification of suicide was considered most persuasive: "The decision to die is a demonstration in purest form of the sovereignty of idea over nature. In nature there is only a drive for self-preservation, and the decision to die is its very opposite." [39] To Schopenhauer [40] suicide appeared as a privilege of man over animal. No human right is more incontestable than man's right over his own person and his own life, and if he does not wish to live for his own benefit, it is exaggeration to require him to continue living as a mere machine for the benefit of others.

Diderot and Voltaire,[41] while not approving of suicide, supported Montesquieu's argument in favor of the secularization of the suicide problem. These writers of the Era of Enlightenment influenced French revolutionary leaders, and on January 1, 1790, the French National Assembly, upon motion of the famous Docteur Guillotin, repealed all sanctions against the body and the property of the suicide. Napoleon's own criminal code, the French Penal Code of 1810, does not mention suicide. The repeal of suicide legislation in France was imitated in other countries of continental Europe. However, the process was by no means a rapid one. Thus, in spite of the Voltairian approach of King Frederick the Great, Prussia did not repeal punishment for attempted suicide until 1796 (Prussian *Allgemeines Landrecht*, §§ 803–805), and in Catholic Austria sanctions imposed upon suicide were not abrogated until 1850.[42]

Thus, while attempted suicide is still punishable in England and in some jurisdictions of the United States, it has been generally immune from punishment since the second part of the nineteenth century in continental Europe. However, absence of sanctions for suicide does not eliminate the subject from the area of legal interest. In law, the act of suicide may still be relevant in adjudging harm done to others in the course of its commission and to the evaluation of acts of third parties who in one way or another contribute to it, the instigators and aiders of suicide. In the technical view of the law, their acts must be adjudged in context with the act of the so-called principal. Since in classical criminal jurisprudence the criminality of the act of the accomplice is generally predicated upon punishment or, at least, criminality of the act of the principal, immunity of suicide implied immunity of the instigator and the aider. This became a matter of grave concern in legal theory and practice. Separation of the conceptual tie between the act of the principal and that of the accomplice has been a major topic in the efforts at modernizing criminal law generally, and in attempting to demonstrate the absurdity of maintaining that tie, sociologically oriented jurists have often pointed to the law of suicide as a striking example.

The customs of primitive peoples are a useful source of information concerning the operation of the unconscious. For in them we often find rather clear evidence of psychologic processes which in civilized laws are more effectively disguised. If we succeed in working our way through the complex net of rationalizations that characterizes so-called "civilized," as distinct from primitive, law, we may find in its development a similarly fruitful source of knowledge. Our survey of the law of suicide from its early inceptions until the Era of Enlightenment and the rise of scientific law has brought out certain features which might be of interest to psychologists. As in the Trobriand community, described by Malinowski,[43] so in medieval Japanese and early Roman and English law, as well as in modern codes of honor, suicide is not a crime but rather a means of eradicating another crime.[44] In Socrates' day, indeed, suicide—then considered a crime—was an institutionalized method of punishment for another crime, a means of executing capital punishment. Freud has repeatedly emphasized that suicide in neurotics is regularly self-punishment for other, though perhaps imaginary, crimes of which the suicide feels guilty.[45] By his suicide, the accused in early law accomplished a social rehabilitation—he remained "innocent" and thus regained social respect. Psychoanalysis has shown that many neurotics entertain "hopeful illusions" that by committing suicide they will attain "forgiveness and reconciliation" as well as lost parental love.[46] The crimes for which the Roman and English suicides atoned were capital crimes—in early Roman law, mostly homicide.[47] Since after the suicide's death, the homicide could no longer be established, it was deemed at law never to have occurred. Thus, by his act, the suicide eliminated the homicide from the record, in a sense, substituting suicide for homicide. This later led to the definition of suicide as murder. The same relation between suicide and homicide is expressed—from the love angle—in the Christian rationalization of suicide as murder, in which neighborly love and self-love are interchanging. Freud has shown that suicide is often a substitute for a homicidal urge directed at an original love object.[48] Freud's view can, indeed, be best expressed in legal terms by saying that suicide is "murder."

Psychologically, it may be also important to note the character of the punishment imposed upon suicide throughout the ages. That punishment mostly consisted in a mutilation or dismemberment. As social mores became more refined, actual dismemberment of the corpse was replaced by a symbolical dismemberment, separation of the image from the body (hanging of the effigy) or of the memory or name from the individual (hanging of the name). Remnants of this conception of punishment may be observed in the recent New York decision holding that it is proper to clear the memory of the deceased suicide by showing that he was insane when he committed the act of self-destruction, meaning that he, as an individual or his memory, should not be identified with that act.[49] Since dismemberment as punishment for suicide occurs in various cultures, the choice of that punishment is hardly accidental. It is thus proper to ask what motives determine that choice and whether these motives are those of the group inflicting the punishment or merely social reflections of the suicide's own desires. Any answers to these questions the present writer might suggest would be entirely speculative. Suffice it to mention several bases for possible solutions. Dismemberment, as partial suicide, of course, best realizes the talion law. As shown in psychoanalytic literature, mutilation and dismemberment fantasies play an important role in the experiences of homicidal and suicidal patients.[50] Menninger mentions birth fantasies as possible source of the suicidal urge.[51] "Punishment" of the suicide by severance of parts of his body might be related to such fantasies of birth or rebirth.[52]

As noted by Freud, long before certain truths about the operation of the human psyche became cognitively accessible to psychology, they were intuitively felt and expressed by fiction writers.[53] In law, as in literature, volition and feeling play as great a role as reason, if not a greater one; things are often felt long before they are cognitively discovered. Of course, the fact that a law expresses a psychologic reality does not render it reasonable as legislation, that is, a wise rule of human conduct, for the law must direct human action by establishing reasonable social rules rather than express man's primitive demands or, as psychoanalysts would say, "the archaic superego."

SCIENTIFIC APPROACH TO THE LAW OF SUICIDE

In contrast to the "ontologic" or "classical" or "old" school of criminal jurisprudence, which posits that criminal legislation must incorporate absolute moral ideals, the positivistic or sociologic school believes that the supreme law is that of social *necessity*. It asserts that laws which are not based on sound scientific principles are doomed to be ineffective and are, therefore, devoid of meaning. According to this school, laws, to be sound, must not be deemed immutable, but rather they must be adapted to the variable conditions of time and place and follow "the laws of evolution, which apply to all natural phenomena, whether they belong to the physical or to the moral domain." [54] In planning rational law reform, this school, which originated in Italy, has utilized results of biologic, psychologic, sociologic, and economic research. In so doing, it produced a virtual revolution of legal thought, eventually threatening to disrupt the very notion of "law" itself. "Law" is traditionally conceived of as a system of norms of human conduct, containing rules which tell man what he ought and what he ought not to do. But the disciplines whose services the positivistic school has engaged view him as a *"homo phenomenon,"* an object of natural science acting in accordance with laws of causality which he cannot help following, rather than as a *"homo noumenon,"* a rational being free to direct his own actions. Since, in this view, man cannot act otherwise than he does act, punishment is both absurd and cruel. Accordingly, wise criminal legislation must rather aim at curing him and integrating him into society, at the same time protecting society against the dangers that are inherent in his personality. It may also provide motives—or counteracting causes—for desirable conduct. Criminal legislation must hence be replaced by criminology, and penal codes by codes of social defense. Retributive law must yield to preventive law. Under the impact of this theory, in Cuba, for example, the title of the criminal code was changed from "Penal Code" to "Code of Social Defense." However, while the appeal of the theory is increasing and an International Society of Social Defense actively supports the movement, considerable resistance may be expected from a source traditionally leading in criminal legislation, namely, German criminal legislation, which places an increasing stress on personal moral "guilt."

The annals of the movement of social defense are at the same time a history of the development of many natural sciences of man. These sciences have for obvious reasons shown a special interest in crises and failures of man's life, culminating in suicide. The Malthusian economic theory and, following it, the Marxian doctrine viewed suicide as a means of economic selection, ridding society of the weak and unadaptable, those unfit for the struggle of life. Lombroso's biologic doctrine views suicide as a result of biologic necessity. Having discovered certain biologic anomalies in autopsies of suicides, he suggested that as there are "born criminals," so there are also necessary suicides.[55] Durkheim,[56] in his classical treatise on suicide, made a thorough study of the sociologic causes of suicide. A number of psychiatrists, foremost among them Morselli,[57] studied its psychologic causes. These studies were supported by elaborate statistical data which brought about extremely interesting results. It has been found that, both geographically and chronologically, as the number of suicides increases, that of crimes decreases and vice versa. This was taken to demonstrate that there is what was termed a natural "antagonism" between crime and suicide, the mutual exclusiveness of homicide and suicide being based on firm causal laws. Before Freud, Corre defined suicide as "a sort of derivative of criminality directed at another person ... a solution adopted by unbalanced persons ... whereby they escape the urge to commit larceny or murder or render justice unto themselves.[58] Some writers, hesitantly to be sure, suggested that suicide is in a sense desirable, for it prevents crime, or that, at least, if a calamity is bound to occur, suicide is preferable to crime.

It is against this background that Enrico Ferri, the founder of the positivistic school, author of the celebrated *Sociologia criminale* (3d ed., 1892), and a man who has exercised a great influence upon American legal thought, took up the subject of the reform of the law of suicide. In a monograph entitled *L'Omicidio-suicidio* [Homicide-Suicide] (1883), he said: "Suicide is a misfortune, a deficiency which cannot be ascribed to the immoral intent of the individual who suffers it as a fate, either by force of a hereditary decree going back over several generations or owing to a diminished resistance of his fiber to the psychological hurricanes that at times ravage an entire life." [59]

However, so strong is the influence of established ideology upon the minds of men that in Ferri's theory of the law of suicide the causal, biologic, and psychologic explanation of the phenomenon is completely overshadowed by a formal, technical legal argument. The central idea of his reform project is the tenet of every man's "right" to dispose of his life.[60] This right, he alleged, flows from the fact that the law is not an abstract proposition but rather a *proportio hominis ad hominem* [a relationship between men], so that the notion of a man committing a crime against himself is absurd. Nor is the law, which is essentially a guide for the living, in Ferri's view, logically capable of punishing suicide, for man is subject to laws only *finchè vive,* that is, in the context of life.

In 1883, in continental Europe, of course, those who supported punishment for attempted suicide constituted a small minority. Except in the Canon law, punishment of suicide or attempted suicide had become history. The issue shifted to the problem of the proper treatment of instigators and aiders of suicide, particularly of survivors of suicide pacts, and the question of the responsibility to be imposed upon persons who, in attempting suicide, involuntarily cause harm to others.

As regards instigators and aiders, there was a growing feeling that the prevailing conceptualism of the classical school, according to which they share in the immunity of the suicide (he being the "principal"), is not in harmony with the general sense of justice. The relationship of the instigator and the aider to the act of suicide, it was felt, differs in kind from that of the suicide to his own destruction. The breach with the past was, nevertheless, accomplished indirectly, by rationalizing change as implied in preexisting ideas. Thus, while ultimately advocating special legislation for the punishment of instigators and aiders notwithstanding immunity of the suicide as principal,[61] Ferri proceeded from the immunity of accomplices as flowing from the suicide's "right" to dispose of his own life and his consequent "right" to consent to his own destruction. The immunity of the accomplice, however, as a logical consequence of the principal's "right," is, in Ferri's view, predicated upon absence of fraud and malice on the part of the accomplice, for fraud and malice traditionally vitiate consent. Thus, according to Ferri, the accomplice is immune only if his motives are not antisocial or antilegal.

With his characteristic acumen, Ferri noted that, motive being related to consent, the probability of a good motive is smaller in the case of the instigator, who induces the consent, than in that of the mere aider. He also pointed out that the difference between one who aids a suicide and one who actually performs the act of killing with the consent of the victim is frequently merely technical. Ferri thus raised the crucial problem of euthanasia, for which he demanded immunity, provided that its motives are good.

The rule suggested by Ferri has been since adopted in Switzerland. The Swiss Federal Criminal Code of 1937 (art. 115) provides that whoever instigates another to the commission of suicide or assists him therein is punishable provided that his action is caused by "selfish motives." Where the motives are altruistic, punishment will not lie. In several other countries, instigation and assistance in suicide are punishable as crimes *sui generis* (notwithstanding immunity of suicide and attempted suicide), motive being considered only, in the judge's discretion, in mitigation of punishment. In the United States, the laws of California, New York, Missouri, and Wisconsin recognize a specific offense of assisting suicide.

In general, however, world legislation on the subject of suicide is more widely split than on any other topic. Interestingly, France and Germany have preserved the principle of immunity of accomplices in suicide. The laws of the various jurisdictions in the United States range from granting complete immunity to imposing punishment for murder.[62] In England, the Royal Commission on Capital Punishment,[63] while not suggesting any change in the punishment of attempted suicide,[64] recommended enactment of a law whereby "any person who aids, abets, or instigates the suicide of another person should in future be guilty only of that offense and not of murder, and should be subject to a maximum sentence of imprisonment for life." For reasons which are not quite clear, the Royal Commission was particularly concerned with the harshness of the penalty at present imposed upon survivors of suicide pacts rather than with the general problem of punishment of assistance in suicide. Indeed, it devoted much thought to the question of evidence as to whether the survivor's own suicide attempt has been genuine, apparently assuming that an individual who himself commits suicide is less guilty of the death of his partner than a participant in another's suicide who does not himself honestly contemplate his own destruction. It also differentiated between cases in which "each of the two parties had tried to kill himself or herself and one had been unsuccessful" and cases "where the survivor of a suicide pact had actually killed the other party." The latter situation was not to be affected by the amendment; the survivor who "had actually killed the other party" and not merely assisted him in his suicide would remain subject to punishment for murder.

As may be seen, the law, in its present state, is far from "scientific." Ferri and his successors had initiated a most ambitious crusade for enactment of legislation which would reflect the wisdom gained by scientific inquiry. But on the subject of suicide, Ferri's own argument was anything but "sociologic," and until the present time, the reasoning of law reformers has remained rather "ontologic," as evidenced by the opinion of the Royal Commission on Capital Punishment.

CONCLUDING REMARKS

The law, which is an order of external human conduct, cannot possibly adjudge or even consider all the complex unconscious motivations which prompt action. As pointed out by Freud, "for the practical need of adjudging man's character, the action and the attitude consciously expressed in it are mostly sufficient." [65] When we move from the realm of evaluation to that of prevention, knowledge of unconscious motivations, provided that it reaches a certain degree of generalization, may be of great assistance to the legislator in his effort to formulate rules of preventive law. However, adoption of preventive rules, in spite of their great appeal, must be considered with utmost caution. We must never lose sight of the fact that these rules tend to interfere with human liberty. The legislator is thus confronted with the difficult task of striking a proper balance between two aims: prevention of undesirable acts and preservation of individual freedom. Legislative difficulties do not end here. The freedom of one individual may conflict with that of others. In the law of suicide and complicity in suicide all these difficulties are combined.

As shown by the fact that attempted suicide is a crime in only very few states and that even in these states prosecution is rarely instituted, moral censure of suicide today is not prevalent. But the problem of whether the law should impose punishment upon attempted suicide might conceivably be posed in terms of prevention. Does the law have power to prevent suicide? As pointed out as early as 1819 by Filangieri,[66] a decision to commit suicide cannot be affected by a threat of punishment. The question remains: Can a threat of punishment, perhaps, affect the unconscious processes which cause man to commit or attempt suicide? If the answer to this question is negative, punishment is senseless and, therefore, as stated by Beccaria,[67] "unjust and tyrannical." However, even should the answer to the question posed be an affirmative one, the present writer believes that the "personality" rights of man include the right to dispose of his own life— though this may not be a "right" in a technical legal sense—and that this right overrides the legislator's justifiable concern for the individual's survival. The assumption of a legal duty to live seems particularly objectionable in states which still maintain the institution of capital punishment.[68]

However, immunity of attempt itself, so far as it affects the actor's own life, should not be taken logically to include immunity from punishment for any harm caused by the act to another person. There can be no doubt that, under any law, suicide affords no excuse for harm caused to another either intentionally or by criminal negligence.[69] Nor did the Royal Commission on Capital Punishment—although it apparently thought that an honest intention to commit suicide brings the survivor of a suicide pact within a separate moral category—suggest the adoption of an exceptional rule for those attempting suicide. Intentional or criminally negligent harm to another, even though caused in the course of a suicide attempt, is and must remain punishable. The case of the accused who in the course of a suicide attempt has "accidentally" harmed another deserves separate consideration.[70] Our knowledge of the connection that exists between suicide and unconscious aggressive drives directed at other persons should serve as a warning. It is believed that judgment on the question whether such accidental causing of harm should be punishable ought to be postponed until further study of the question whether, by rendering man responsible for it, the law might not bring to man's consciousness the connection that exists in his unconscious processes between his suicidal and his aggressive drives, thus possibly preventing the occurrence of "accidents."

Similarly, with regard to assistance in, and instigation of, suicide, homicide upon request, and euthanasia, it might be desirable that legislators abide results of sociologic and psychologic studies of these acts. It is highly dubious, however, even from the standpoint of our present knowledge and moral feelings, that any of these acts should be punishable within the framework of the law of murder, for whatever their "unconscious" motivations may be, they are not "conscious" acts of murder.

NOTES

1. Masaryk, *Der Selbstmord als Sociale Massenerscheinung der modernen Civilisation* (1881), pp. 87 ff. From statistical data showing that in Protestant countries suicide occurs more frequently than in Catholic countries some writers have inferred that the character of religion has an important bearing on the phenomenon of suicide. See Morselli, *Suicide* (trans., 1882).

2. M. Williams, *Buddhism* (1889), p. 563.

3. Thus, according to the precepts for Buddhist monks, "Not only (*a*) killing a human being knowingly, but also (*b*) seeking out an assassin against a human being, (*c*) uttering the praises of death, (*d*) inciting another to self-destruction, and (*e*) according to the commentary of the Pātimokkha (Vin. iii, 73), abortion or the destruction of life in the womb, are to be regarded as crimes...." Tachibana, *The Ethics of Buddhism* (1926), p. 81.

4. Durkheim, *Le Suicide: Étude de sociologie* (new ed., 1930), pp. 241–243.

5. This prohibition was sanctioned by cutting off the hand of the suicide and prohibiting its burial together with the rest of the body. See Viazzi, *Suicidio* (*Istigazione o aiuto a*), in *Enciclopedia Giuridica Italiana* (ed. by Mancini, 1910), volume XV, p. 689.

6. Plato, *De legibus*, dialogue IX; Aristotle, *Nichomachean Ethics* 3.2.

7. *Sura* 4. Even this prohibition, however, is an implied rather than an express one. It may be interesting to note—as bearing on the question of the relation of religion to suicide—the results of statistical research recently made in Turkey by the University of Istanbul (*Enquête criminologique concernant 894 cas de suicide*. Université d'Istanbul, Institut de Droit Pénal et de Criminologie, 1954). Of a total number of 894 cases of suicide in certain selected communities, 853 cases involved Moslems. Of these, 4 were very observant, 20 observant, 370 strongly believing (*très croyants*), 235 believing (*croyants*), 18 slightly believing (*peu croyants*), 123 indifferent, and of the remaining 83 the degree of belief was unknown.

8. "Homo tenetur hominem amare, tamquam seipsum; ac proinde seipsum, tamquam alios homines." Heineccius (1681–1741), *Elementa iuris naturae et gentium* (3d ed., 1749), § 144.

9. Viazzi, *supra* 5, p. 690.

10. Cicero, *Tusculanarum disputationum* Liber I, Ch. xxx, § 74 (King trans. 1927), p. 87.

11. With regard to the suicide of a soldier see Justinian's *Digest* 48.19.38.12; with regard to that of a slave see *Digest* 15.1.9.7.

12. *Digest* 48.21.3.6.

13. Ulpian suggests in *Digest* 15.1.9.7 (*de peculio*) that *"naturaliter"* even slaves

were permitted to damage their own bodies or to commit suicide: *"licet enim etiam servis naturaliter in suum corpus saevire."*

14. *Digest* 48.19.38.12.

15. Hadrian's *Rescript*, see *Digest* 49.16.6.7.

16. *Supra* 14.

17. *Codex Bened.* XV (1917), Cans. 985, 1240, 1241, 2350, regarding sanctions imposed upon suicide by Canon law.

18. Mikell, Is suicide murder? *Columbia Law Review*, volume III (1903), p. 380.

19. The suicide of an accused or convicted person was viewed in Rome as a damage to the *fiscus*. See Carmignani, *Juris Criminalis Elementa* (5th ed., 1834), volume II, § 973.

20. *Hales v. Petit* (1562) Plowd. 261.

21. *Ibid.*

22. *Rex v. Warde, sub nom. Rex v. Warner* (1662), 1 Keb. 66, 548; 1 Lev. 8; *Reg. v. Burgess* (1862), Leigh & C. 258.

23. 204 Ill. 208, 68 N.E. 505, 510 (1903).

24. Revised Code of Washington (1951), § 9.80.020; North Dakota Revised Code (1943), § 12–3302.

25. *State v. Carney*, 69 N.J.L. 478, 55 Atl. 44 (1903); *State v. LaFayette*, 15 N.J.Mis.R. 115 (Camden County Court of Common Pleas, 1937).

26. New York Penal Law § 2301 (1944). In *Stiles v. Clifton Springs Sanitarium Co.*, 74 Fed. Supp. 907 (D.C.W.D. New York, 1947), the court held the personal representative of a suicide entitled to waive the latter's privilege against disclosure by doctors and nurses that he was mentally ill at the time of the act. The ground advanced by the court was that the physician-patient privilege protects patients against humiliation, embarrassment, and disgrace, but that disclosure that the suicide was insane would actually protect his memory, for it would show that he was not "a grave public offender" within the meaning of the New York statute.

27. *Les Établissements de Saint Louis* (ed. Viollet, 1881), volume II, book I, title 92. See also volume III, p. 51. But in 1254, the King permitted the heirs of *"une femme qui, à la verité, s'était suicidée, mais qui était folle"* to take the estate. See *Notes sur les établissements*, volume IV, p. 41, in which it is also reported that at one time leniency was exercised where a poor woman hanged herself from necessity or poverty, that, however, the woman was not permitted to have a Christian burial.

28. Title 22 of the *Coutumes de Bretagne* (ed. Vatar, 1737), art. 631.

29. See note to the cited article.

30. Manzini, *Trattato di diritto penale italiano* (new ed., 1951), volume VIII, note (4), pp. 94, 95.

31. Carpzov (1596–1666), *Responsa Juris Electoralia* (ed. Gleditsch, 1709), book VI, title 10, response 102.

32. Liszt-Schmidt, *Lehrbuch des Deutschen Strafrechts* (26th rev. ed., 1932), note (14), p. 219.

33. But in the event that the act was committed because of disease of the body, melancholia, weakness, insanity (erring mind), or similar lunacy (*blödigkeyten*), no confiscation would occur, any ancient custom, usage, or ordinance notwithstanding.

34. Kaiserl. Patent (nr. 611) of January 13, 1787.

35. Napoleon himself made an unsuccessful suicide attempt on April 12–13, 1814. Licurzi, *El suicido* (Cordoba, 1946) p. 213.

36. Hume, *On Suicide* (published posthumously; new ed., 1789).

.

37. Montesquieu, *Lettres Persanes* (ed. 1901), letter 76, p. 189.

38. Beccaria, *Dei delitti e delle pene* (1764; Calamandrei ed., 1945), § XXV. Beccaria pointed out that emigration is indeed more harmful than suicide, for the emigrant deprives the state of his property whereas the suicide leaves his property within the state.

39. Fichte, *System der Sittenlehre* (ed. 1798). But Fichte emphasized, on the other hand, the nobility of bearing an unwanted life. Such attitude, he said, is "sovereignty of idea over idea...triumph of the law governing ideas, the purest demonstration of morality."

40. Schopenhauer, *Parerga und Paralipomena* (ed. 1851), volume I, chap. 13.

41. Diderot, Suicide, *Dictionnaire Encyclopedique*. Voltaire, Du suicide, *Mélanges de litterature, d'histoire et de philosophie;* Du suicide, *Politique, Législation.*

42. Kaiserl. Patent vom 17.1 1850, RGB1. 24, art. XVI.

43. Malinowski, *Crime and Custom in Savage Society* (fourth impression, 1947), pp. 94–98.

44. The Japanese *hara-kiri* replaced capital punishment in instances involving the higher classes of society. When he committed it, the Japanese nobleman was deemed innocent and his family was spared dishonor and forfeiture of property. See Oberlaender, *Fremde Voelker* (1888). Mason, *The Meaning of Shinto* (1935), p. 127, thus describes the meaning of the medieval *hara-kiri:* "The disemboweling act, before an assembly, was to show that regardless of the material offense, the subjective divine soul would come forth from the body symbolically, to show publicly that it had not become contaminated." On suicide in atonement of the sins of others, see Scott, *The Foundations of Japan* (1922), p. 55.

Masaryk, *op. cit.*, p. 92, reports that in Iceland acquittal of a crime against the person could be secured only by showing that the accused had previously made an attempt upon his own life, for this was taken as proof of insanity.

45. Freud, Totem und Tabu, in *Gesammelte Werke* (Imago Publishing Company, 1940), volume IX, p. 185, note (3); Über die Psychogenese eines Falles von weiblicher Homosexualitaet, *ibid.*, volume XII (1947), pp. 289–290.

46. Fenichel, *The Psychoanalytical Theory of Neurosis* (1945), pp. 400, 401.

47. Capital punishment was imposed by the law of the Twelve Tables specifically upon one who *"occentavisset sive carmen condidisset,"* that is, committed homicide by singing a derisive song (Cicero, *De republica,* iv, x, xii), which was apparently assumed to have the magic power of bringing about death.

48. Freud, Bemerkungen über einen Fall von Zwangsneurose, *op. cit.*, volume VII, pp. 409 ff.; "Trauer und Melancholie," *ibid.*, volume X.

49. When a person commits suicide in a state of insanity, "the insanity...prevents the act from being in law the act of" that person. See *Beresford v. Royal Insurance Company* (1938), A.C. 586, p. 595 (per Lord Atkin).

50. Bromberg, A Psychological Study of Murder, *International Journal of Psychoanalysis*, volume XXXII (1951), p. 117. Melitta Schmideberg, A Note on Suicide, *ibid.*, vol. XVII (1936), p. 1, says: "Suicide always aims at hurting directly some loved person. It achieves this by...robbing them...unconsciously of a precious part of their body." N. D. C. Lewis, Studies on Suicide, *Psychoanalytic Review*, volume XX (1933), p. 241, shows that among American Negroes who rarely commit suicide mutilation is rather frequent.

51. Menninger, *Man Against Himself* (fourth printing, 1938), p. 79.

52. Such fantasies are undoubtedly present in sacrificial suicides. On the origins of religious suicides in human sacrifices for the appeasement of the anger of gods see Lasch, Religioeser Selbstmord und seine Beziehung zum Menschenopfer, *Globus*, volume LXXV (1899), p. 69. Lasch shows that the motive of appeasement was gradually replaced by the motive of rebirth.

53. Freud, Psychopathologie des Alltagslebens, *op. cit.*, volume I, pp. 107 ff.

54. Ferri, *L'Omicidio-suicidio* (1883), p. 8.

55. Lombroso, *L'Uomo delinquente* (3d ed., 1889), pp. 26 ff.

56. Durkheim, *op. cit.*

57. Morselli, *op. cit.*

58. Corre, *Les Criminels* (1889), p. 200.

59. In another context, Ferri formulated the causality of suicide in relation to that of insanity and of delinquency in the following terms: "When degeneration strikes intelligence, there is insanity; when it injures emotion, there is delinquency; when it affects the will, there is suicide." Cited in Momigliano, Suicidio, in *Enciclopedia Giuridica Italiana*, p. 670. But Ferri believed that the "antagonism" of suicide and crime is strictly limited to acts of killing and that there is no such antagonism between suicide and crimes other than homicide. See Ferri, Un Secolo di omicidii e di suicidii in Europa, *Bulletin de l'Institut International de Statistique*, 3ème Livraison (1926), p. 418.

60. The term "right," which is generally ambiguous, is particularly inappropriate in this context. That a person has a "right" to do something normally implies that others have a duty not to interfere with the exercise of such a right. In recent legislation, however, there is an increasing tendency to impose on certain persons a duty of preventing the suicide of others. On this see Silving, Euthanasia: A Study in Comparative Criminal Law, *University of Pennsylvania Law Review*, volume CIII (1954), p. 350.

61. The suggestion that complicity in suicide should be punishable as a crime *sui generis* was not new. For earlier laws making such complicity a separate offense and for recommendations to this effect see Liszt, *Toetung und Lebensgefaehrdung* (1905), pp. 135 ff.

62. On the present state of the law of complicity in suicide in the various countries see Silving, *op. cit.*

63. 1949–53, Report of the Commission, Cmd. 8932 (1953), pp. 59–63.

64. This was explained by lack of authority under the Terms of Reference; *ibid.*, p. 62.

65. Freud, Traumdeutung—Über den Traum, *op. cit.*, volume II, p. 626.

66. Filangieri, *La Scienza della legislazione* (1819), volume III, pp. 419–421.

67. Beccaria, *op. cit.*, p. 336.

68. It is particularly repugnant to the sense of justice that, in adjudging the act of suicide or any complicity therein, the law will not "take into consideration the fact that the suicide was under sentence of death, having but a few more hours to live." Wharton, *Law of Homicide* (3d ed., 1907), p. 69.

69. Perkins, The Law of Homicide, *Journal of Criminal Law and Criminology*, volume XXXVI (1946), p. 440.

70. As stated by Perkins, *ibid.*, "This has been held to be at least manslaughter, and perhaps murder, in Massachusetts, murder in South Carolina, and no crime at all, without additional facts, in Iowa."

PART II

Clinical Considerations

Psychotherapy of the Suicidal Patient*

LEONARD M. MOSS AND DONALD M. HAMILTON

(with Discussion by O. Spurgeon English)

To determine the factors responsible for the successful therapy of the seriously suicidal patient, an analysis of the case histories of 50 such patients treated at the New York Hospital, Westchester Division, between 1934 and 1953 was undertaken. There was no doubt of the intensity of the self-destructive drive in this group, and only by chance were the attempts unsuccessful.

One patient jumped overboard from a destroyer 30 miles from land into shark-infested waters. Another sustained a hemopneumothorax and lacerated liver when a knife, plunged into his chest, penetrated just below the pericardium. Several were revived by intensive medical treatment after ingestion of large amounts of sedative or after prolonged carbon monoxide inhalation. One patient survived a leap from a subway platform directly into the path of an oncoming train.

Our hospital population consists of patients considered acutely ill and potentially recoverable, who are above average in intelligence, education, and economic status. About one-fifth (20 to 25 per cent) of all admissions during the period under study were considered potentially suicidal. Of these, one-quarter made attempts during the present illness. About one-third of those who made attempts, or 2 per cent of all admissions, fulfilled the criteria for inclusion in this study. The twenty-year interval, 1934 to

* Reprinted, with permission, from the *American Journal of Psychiatry*, 1956, 112: 814–820. This material and the discussion were presented at the eleventh annual meeting of the American Psychiatric Association, Atlantic City, N.J., May 9–13, 1955.

1953, was selected so that the role of electroshock and other somatotherapies could be evaluated.

Follow-up periods ranged from two months to twenty years, averaging four years for all cases, five years for all surviving cases, and four months for those who committed suicide. Age ranged from nineteen to sixty-seven with an equal distribution in each decade, and the three major religions were represented.

All diagnostic categories of mental illness were included, but there was a higher percentage of psychoneurotics (22 per cent as against 10 per cent) and manic depressives (38 per cent as against 25 per cent) in our series as compared with the percentage distribution of the hospital population, and a lower percentage of schizophrenics (22 per cent as against 32 per cent).

Schizophrenic suicidal attempts seemed to differ from the others in that they exhibited generally bizarre or ambivalent features. The attempt usually occurred early in the illness when anxiety and bewilderment were prominent. This drive seemed to be diverted into impulsive combativeness or self-mutilation as the illness progressed, and as secondary psychotic manifestations such as delusions and hallucinations became more prominent. In only one case was the suicidal attempt in response to hallucination.

In evaluating the precipitating factors, there were no characteristic conflicts that gave rise to suicidal tendencies. The patients seemed to be struggling with conflicts common to other people of similar age and circumstances. The psychodynamics and symbolic significance of the suicidal attempt could be understood only in relation to the individual case.

In each instance, however, there seemed to be three coexisting unconscious or partially conscious determinants of the act of suicide: (a) A promise or hope of greater future satisfaction. This took the form of a permanent reunion in death with a lost loved one, the forcing of attention or satisfaction otherwise unobtainable from the present environment, or the pleasure of spite or revenge. (b) Hostility or rage directed toward important persons upon whom blame was placed for present frustrations, which because of guilt, fear, or anxiety became self-directed. (c) An expression of hopelessness and frustration—a relinquishing of any prospect of gaining necessary satisfactions from the present environment or reality situation.

These findings coincide with similar views already expressed by others. Bender and Schilder (1), discussing suicide in children, describe the suicidal attempt as an effort to gain increased love, a punishment against frustrating surroundings, and a happy, peaceful reunion with a loved object or person.

Bromberg and Schilder (2) found wishes to die frequent in children and suicidal fantasies common in normal adults. They conclude that the relationship between wishing oneself dead and a suicidal thought or attempt is quantitative rather than qualitative.

Zilboorg (8, 9, 10) considers suicide an archaic form of response to inner conflict, a psychobiologic phenomenon whose force is derived from the instinct for self-preservation, since through suicide man achieves fantasied immortality and an uninterrupted fulfillment of his hedonistic, or pleasure-seeking, ideals.

Thus, the suicidal fantasy is an effort at problem solving, albeit misdirected or unrealistic, an effort to gain satisfaction in a situation of great emotional stress.

THE DEATH TREND

The most outstanding and consistent feature in the background of our series was the occurrence of what we have considered the "death trend" in 95 per cent of all cases. This involves the death or loss under dramatic and often tragic circumstances of individuals closely related to the patient, generally parents, siblings, and mates. In 75 per cent of our cases, the deaths had taken place before the patient had completed adolescence. In the remaining 25 per cent, the "death trend" occurred later and precipitated the illness.

Sixty per cent had lost one or both parents in early life, the majority during puberty or early adolescence, the others in childhood or infancy. Forty per cent lost their fathers and 20 per cent, their mothers, during this period. In every case of paternal loss, however, the patient felt a removal of the mother's usual love and support brought about by a disruption of the home after the father's death. In some instances the altered economic status of the family necessitated the mother's working and sending the children to live with relatives or foster parents. In other instances the mother reacted to the death of her husband with bitterness, often becoming irritable with her children, or with immature self-centered reactions resulting in a demanding rather than a giving relationship with them.

Death of a parent before or during early childhood was frequently followed closely by premature and excessive sexual activity, sometimes of a homosexual or incestuous nature. This became a source of guilt feelings in later life, interfering with a mature heterosexual adjustment. The cases following are illustrations.

A patient lost her father at the age of two and was sent to live with a series of relatives while her mother worked. At seven, she had an incestuous relationship with an uncle and shortly thereafter a homosexual relationship with an older cousin. In adolescence, she was described as compulsively obedient and religious, hard-working and perfectionistic. At twenty, she took 5 grains of morphine intravenously when she felt there was no meaning to life, since she could not attract men.

At the age of ten, a young man lost his "adored" father. His mother became alcoholic shortly thereafter, and he, within a few months, had entered upon a homosexual relation with a man courting his mother. He attempted suicide by gas and by cutting his wrists in adult life when he felt rejected by a homosexual lover.

Palmer (5) reviewed background factors in 25 consecutive cases of attempted suicide and found 84 per cent suffered from the death or absence of a parent or sibling; 68 per cent lost a parent before the age of fourteen. Teicher's (6) findings support these statistics.

In over 60 per cent of our cases the death of someone close to the patient was an important precipitating factor in the present illness. Suicide in the immediate family was found among over 25 per cent.

Wall (7) and Jameison (3, 4), in reviewing the experience of this hospital with patients who subsequently committed suicide, found a suicide of considerable dynamic influence in the family histories of one-third of these patients; for example:

A 62-year old man had attempted suicide by a massive overdose of barbiturate. He had lost his wife by suicide when she learned she had an incurable brain cancer. Five years later, his only child died suddenly of a brain tumor, precipitating the suicidal attempt.

The "death trend" was significantly more frequent in the patients who made serious suicidal attempts than in either of two comparable control groups.

One control group consisted of 50 patients not considered potentially suicidal, whose age, marital status, diagnosis, and time of admission were similar to the cases studied. In a second group of 50 patients, all were considered potentially suicidal but none had made self-destructive attempts. The statistics in both control groups were similar.

The "death trend" was found in only 40 per cent of each control series as compared with 95 per cent of all seriously suicidal patients. Death of a parent before or during adolescence was four times as frequent in the seriously suicidal patient. Death as a precipitating factor in the present illness was twice as frequent. Suicide was rarely found in families of the control groups.

If one assumes that suicidal fantasies are possible forms of reacting to intense inner conflict and in some way represent problem-solving behavior, we may conclude from our study that the occurrence of the "death trend" in the patient's background would predispose him to act out self-destructive preoccupations. This may shed some light on why one individual with suicidal fantasies will act upon them with a suicidal attempt, while another, with similar fantasies, and equal emotional tension, will not.

REACTIVATION PHASE

Another significant and highly consistent finding was the characteristic reactivation of the suicidal drive in over 90 per cent of the patients. This occurred when the patient was considered markedly improved and had the opportunity to come into contact once more with the environment in which the illness began. The suicidal drive had therefore not completely subsided, even when the patient was considered convalescent and appeared to be relatively free from tension and anxiety.

Successful management of this reactivation is the most crucial aspect of psychotherapy. Since in our series only seriously suicidal patients were selected, therapy was often lifesaving. The place of this reactivation and its treatment will be discussed below.

The course of therapy was divisible into three separate phases—acute, convalescent, and recovery—each presenting characteristic problems in therapy.

Acute Phase

During this phase, therapy was directed toward adequate protection, relief of anxiety and hopelessness, and restoring satisfactory relationships with others. Hospitalization in itself removed the patient from the source of many of his stresses and afforded some relief from tension. Constant observation, necessarily invading every privacy, by a nursing staff who functioned as companions and not just as guards, was an absolute necessity with the seriously suicidal patient. In spite of the patient's expressed desire to be alone, he felt reassured by the presence of others. A well-organized program of hospital activities and physical and occupational therapies, lessened the opportunity for solitary and depressive ruminations.

Since the advent of somatotherapies, particularly electroconvulsive therapy (ECT), suicidal attempts by disturbed patients in this hospital are one-tenth as frequent. The acute phase has been significantly shortened and productive psychotherapy is begun earlier. Relatives are less discouraged by a prolonged disturbed period and are therefore more willing to cooperate in the therapeutic plan.

The physician, whose role was most intimate and personal, proved to be the most important single staff member in the successful therapy of these patients.

A suicidal attempt is a miscarried aggressive act directed toward an important figure in the patient's life. Most patients, therefore, reacted to having attempted suicide with fears of rejection or retaliation, or with feelings of guilt or hopeless unworthiness for having committed a "cowardly" or "sinful" act. Thus, the anxiety which preceded the suicidal attempt was increased by anxiety aroused by the attempt itself.

It is of vital importance, therefore, that the physician explain to the patient that the suicidal attempt was an effort to solve an overwhelming problem. Hope is held out that when the tensions and discomforts are decreased through treatment, and the patient's life situation reexamined, satisfactory solutions, other than suicide, may be discovered.

This therapeutic attitude helps bind the patient to the physician, tends to reduce guilt and fear of retaliation and rejection, and at the same time directs attention toward possibilities of future psychotherapy. It was found that a deep, probing approach was best postponed until the convalescent phase, when the degree of tension and anxiety was lessened. Patients in the acute stage were not ready to accept new solutions based on specific insights.

Face-saving maneuvers with the family or employers played an important role during this phase. Families and others important to the patient were coached on how to approach him. His employers, colleagues, and friends were frequently contacted and reassured about the significance of the illness, and if needed, employers were requested to send a letter to the patient stating his job would be available upon his leaving the hospital.

Convalescent Phase

This phase begins when the patient is relatively comfortable in the protected hospital setting and continues until he comes into contact with the environment in which the illness originated. This is a phase of active psychotherapy.

The physician best handled the suicidal drive by approaching it directly, by uncovering the anxiety involved in the precipitating situation—the unconscious psychodynamic meaning of the suicidal attempt and deeper unsatisfied personality needs and strivings. New solutions were then discussed.

Once the patient became more comfortable in the hospital, he tended to avoid painful problems by attempting prematurely to leave the protective atmosphere he still required. This "flight into reality" was a serious complication of therapy in 25 per cent of all cases, and was present in most. It usually occurred when the patient was beginning to face his conflicts, but before practical insight had been achieved. It represented resistance, often rationalized: "Now that I feel so much better, I'm sure I can handle my problems again." Cooperation of relatives in encouraging the patient to remain in therapy was vital. Their unconscious attitudes of rejection or hostility were often aroused at this time, and too often the patient was removed at this most inauspicious point.

Recovery Phase

The patient, now in contact with his original environment, attempted to cope with the previously frustrating situation. This precipitated a reactivation in 90 per cent of all cases and involved a calculated risk.

Four-fifths of all reactivations occurred while the patient was on a day or overnight visit. A small number were in response to events occurring after leaving the hospital, either by discharge or against advice. Suicidal gestures ranging from concealing weapons to successful attempts took place in 55 per cent of all reactivations. The remainder responded with either agitation and conscious suicidal preoccupation or symptoms reminiscent of those of the suicidal period but without conscious fantasies.

One patient commented, "I was amazed to find that after months of never having felt better in my life, I could experience a sudden return of those feelings I had when I cut my wrists." As a result of this return of symptoms, the vast majority required increased observation, somatotherapy, or curtailment of visiting privileges. This reactivation appears to be a consistent phenomenon which may represent a necessary aspect of the working-through process, usually leading to further insight rather than a relapse to previous levels of illness.

In cases in which a close therapeutic relationship existed and the meaning of the suicidal attempt was understood during the convalescent phase, the reactivation is most likely to involve more benign symptoms and there is much less danger of the renewed suicidal fantasies being acted out.

A patient often admitted a recurrence of such fantasies and stated that he would have acted on them if it were not for the feeling that he could not let the physician down. He usually came to the physician because of the rapport that existed, whereas during the original suicidal attempt he felt alone and deserted.

Not only should new techniques and solutions to the patient's problems be tentatively approached during the convalescent state, but the reactivation phase must be anticipated. The patient and his relatives must be adequately warned and prepared for a return of suicidal urges and symptoms.

FACTORS IN RECOVERY

Success in recovered cases was most often attributable to the therapist's active intervention in the patient's home environment. This should include helping relatives gain insight into possible feelings of rejection or hostility they may harbor toward the patient. They may have great difficulty in accepting the suicidal attempt itself, the patient's limitations, or the environmental changes necessary for the patient's future health. Often intensive psychotherapy is indicated for the relatives.

The therapist cannot function only as a mirror in which the patient's problems alone are reflected. Successful therapy requires that he involve himself deeply in the patient's personal life. This includes not only an awareness of the emotional, social, and cultural setting of the illness, and a workable therapeutic relationship, but equally important, an active therapeutic relationship with the patient's relatives, friends, and business associates.

When there is no clear understanding of the factors in the present illness, and when the therapeutic relationship is distant or casual, the patient remains a serious suicidal risk upon reentering his environment no matter what degree of clinical comfort and confidence he may show. Reactivation under these circumstances is most likely to have serious consequences.

An important problem of management is the relatives' discouragement upon reactivation of previous symptoms. It is then that they may unconsciously reject the patient by removing him from the necessary protective environment against the advice of the hospital. Two-thirds of those leaving without consent at the time of reactivation committed suicide. The last notes in the chart of one such case are quoted:

At the point when Mr. Z. became willing to discuss his feelings toward his wife more freely, he had a recurrence of agitation and depressed feelings, and urged his wife to remove him from the hospital. She did so much against our repeated warnings. At home she ridiculed his frequent expressions of insecurity. She arranged for him to go to a rifle range with her for practice even though he remained somewhat anxious and depressed. When he expressed discomfort and asked for the male nurse to be present, his wife belittled his dubious feelings. The patient then shot himself with his rifle.

We found consistently that recovery requires a major change in the life situation. Only three recovered patients returned to the same environment in which the illness arose without fundamental changes in the employment situation or personal relationships.

The most common changes, in order of frequency, were (a) changes in occupation or retirement; (b) significant improvement in the marital relationship; (c) emancipation from domineering and restricting parents; (d) breaking of unsuitable engagements; (e) changes in psychosexual orientation (six patients: three young adults matured to stable heterosexual interests, while three others accepted their homosexual orientation); (f) divorce of immature and sadistic mates (two patients) and marriage (two patients); (g) significant widening of social contacts, recreations, and hobbies.

Suicidal tendencies remain a serious problem until such alterations in the life situation develop as a probability for the patient and he gains a feeling of hope that new and more realistic satisfactions are possible. The reactivation usually arises when the patient comes into contact with the situation requiring change.

FOLLOW-UP

Each diagnostic category showed about the same percentage of recoveries and of suicides. The majority of recovered patients continued treatment for at least six months after leaving the hospital. The follow-up period varied between one and twenty years, and averaged six-and-one-half years.

Fifty per cent of our cases were considered recovered and 20 per cent much improved at the last follow-up. Four patients remained unimproved and permanently hospitalized. Eleven died by suicide; of these, 7 were removed from the hospital against advice during the acute phase or while in a period of reactivation in the convalescent phase. These deaths occurred within two to four months after removal from the hospital and represent casualties of the reactivation. Only 2 of the 11 committed suicide while still under therapy at this hospital, both while on temporary overnight visits; two died during the follow-up period after discharge.

Of the 37 patients considered recovered or much improved at the time of discharge, three had a recurrence of suicidal tendencies. One made suicidal gestures in an illness twelve-and-one-half years after hospitalization when disappointed in a love affair. She recovered, and, although depressed twice in the next six years, has made no further attempts. Another committed suicide four-and-one-half years later without premonitory signs of emotional illness. The third patient was a chronic suicidal problem who finally committed suicide nine months after the last of six hospitalizations, when his wife left him. None of these three patients had achieved workable or effective insight which would have enabled him to handle the return of his suicidal tendencies.

Six of the 37 originally considered to be successfully treated, with insight into their suicidal motivations and a change in their life situation, had subsequent psychiatric disorders; however, none of these made suicidal attempts, nor did they prove to be suicidal risks. Depression with retardation or symptoms of elation replaced the agitation found during the original illness. One became an alcoholic; the other five recovered after only a short period of illness.

It is interesting to note that the precipitating factors for these illnesses included the death of persons close to the patients. These losses would have served to reactivate suicidal preoccupations related to the "death trend" in the patients' backgrounds had the original therapy not been successful.

From this study, we conclude that the symptom of suicide can be successfully treated.

DISCUSSION (by O. Spurgeon English)

Suicide is statistically rated eleventh on the list of causes of death but is unquestionably much higher since the cause of death in these instances is frequently hidden. Incidentally, it may be of interest to note that suicide occurs twice as frequently in physicians as in all other males.

Some of the authors' figures tend to modify certain popularly held beliefs. It is shown that the religion of the patients does not prevent suicidal attempts, the incidence being approximately the same for Catholics, Jews, and Protestants; the highest percentage of suicides occurs in psychoneurotics and manic depressives even when compared with the low percentage of psychoneurotics that are hospitalized.

What the authors refer to as the "death trend" is, of course, very pertinent. The early loss of a parent—the father, in particular—results in so many cases in unfortunate personality development. This exposure to death has at least two important components. First, the fantasies provoked by the death of those libidinally invested combined with what might be called the suggestibility of death; and second, the marked effect of the emotional deprivation on the developing personality of the patient. The suggestibility of death has been described for years as resulting from the reading of books or newspaper accounts of suicide. The fear that psychic suggestion might play a role undoubtedly keeps many of our colleagues from discussing suicide with the patient lest the discussion itself have a complementary effect upon an idea already existing, but only germinally, in the patient's mind.

The emotional deprivation caused by loss of the father whether by suicide or otherwise is significant in many ways. To begin with, the love of the father is lost and, as is pointed out, the love of the mother may also be lost. This ties in with the great loss of self-esteem and the hostility so often found in the psychopathology of the suicidal patient. The authors make a strong point of meeting the patient's need for comfort and finding some solution to his "unsentimentality," which through the years his strong unconscious need for comfort and encouragement has kept hidden.

Two things at least have been emphasized which ought to have more widespread dissemination. One is the recognition that suicide, like war, is an attempted solution to an otherwise insoluble problem. Too many people still feel that a suicidal attempt is an incidental occurrence. The second is the fact that if the psychotherapy is not adequately carried out, there is a high risk of a further attempt at suicide during the reactivation phase, when the patient attempts going back to the original environment in which he became ill. It was rather startling to hear that four-fifths of these attempts were made during an overnight or day leave.

The treatment program utilized here indicates that, in orderly sequence, the physician should have the suicidal patient's emotional needs adequately taken care of—first, in the hospital by means of the staff acting as comforting, parental figures. This then should be carried into the environmental life of the patient in conjunction with psychotherapy. This paper may be proof of a growing trend in psychiatry (of which I personally approve) of dealing more adequately with extrinsic factors in the life of the patient and not relying so completely upon intrinsic factors only.

The changes necessary in order to bring about an adequate solution of the patient's emotional problems indicate the need for a high versatility on the physician's part in dealing with both extrinsic and intrinsic factors and point up how much psychopathology lies behind the suicidal act. Some of this psychopathology needs to be made conscious and to be integrated into the ego. Some of it needs environmental modification as well, because these patients tend to get involved in extremely frustrating situations. It has been said that suicide is preventable, and if the approach described here were more widely used, I believe we could soon bring suicide to a much lower place in the listing of causes of death.

References

1. Bender, L., and P. Schilder, Suicidal preoccupations and attempts in children. *American Journal of Orthopsychiatry,* 7: 225–234, 1937.
2. Bromberg, W., and P. Schilder, Death and dying: Comparative study of attitudes and mental reactions toward death and dying. *Psychoanalytic Review,* 20: 133–185, 1933.
3. Jameison, G. R., and J. H. Wall, Some psychiatric aspects of suicide. *Psychiatric Quarterly,* 7: 211–219, 1933.
4. Jameison, G. R., Suicide and mental disease: Clinical analyses of 100 cases. *Archives of Neurology and Psychiatry,* 36: 1–12, 1936.
5. Palmer, D. M., Factors in suicidal attempts: Review of 25 consecutive cases. *Journal of Nervous and Mental Disease,* 93: 421–442, 1941.
6. Teicher, J. D., Study in attempted suicide. *Journal of Nervous and Mental Disease,* 105: 283–298, 1947.
7. Wall, J. H., The psychiatric problem of suicide. *American Journal of Psychiatry,* 101: 404–406, 1944.
8. Zilboorg, G., Differential diagnostic types of suicide. *Archives of Neurology and Psychiatry,* 35: 270–291, 1936.
9. ——, Suicide among civilized and primitive races. *American Journal of Psychiatry,* 92: 1347–1369, 1936.
10. ——, Considerations on suicide, with particular reference to that of the young. *American Journal of Orthopsychiatry,* 7: 15–31, 1937.

II

Some Aspects of the Treatment
of the Potentially Suicidal Patient

ROBERT E. LITMAN

Psychiatrists recognize potentially suicidal patients by various objective clues such as self-destructive threats or fantasies, recent suicidal attempts, complaints of pain, suffering, and hopelessness, and physical signs of depression such as sleeplessness, anorexia, and weight loss. In addition, psychotherapists are sometimes alerted subjectively by their own intuition that the patient is suicidal.

Under favorable circumstances, some such patients can be treated successfully in office practice, although the task is difficult and complicated. This chapter presents some clinical experiences with suicidal patients. Two aspects are selected for discussion: (a) the initial psychiatric interview when suicidal intentions constitute the presenting complaint; and (b) suicidal crises which complicate psychotherapy that has already been under way for some time.

When a patient's wish to continue living balances precariously for a time against a strong wish to commit suicide, then relatively minor, often accidental, adverse environmental influences may be decisively fatal. For example, a salesman, age thirty-five, became despondent when his wife asked for a divorce to marry his best friend. The patient obtained sleeping tablets from his family physician, who recognized the depression and referred him to a psychiatrist. However, the patient canceled his appointment. One afternoon after conference with his wife's lawyer, the patient felt extremely depressed and acutely suicidal. He tried to see his brother, who was out of his office, and then his father, who was also out. He called the psychiatrist, who was busy in consultation. Finally, he called his wife at home, but her line was busy. Feeling completely isolated and estranged, he took the pills. After several hours the psychiatrist returned the patient's call, but there was no answer. Since it was now late afternoon, the psychiatrist called the home. The wife became concerned, went to her husband's office and found him there unconscious. The patient later reported that, had any of his calls been completed, he would not have taken the pills then. This example emphasizes how a series of fortuitous factors can be important in allowing a patient's suicidal wish to become a suicidal action, and equally accidental factors can prevent the suicidal action from becoming a suicidal death.

A general prerequisite condition for successful office psychotherapy with such a patient is that a psychotherapeutic relationship be established early and maintained consistently during the suicidal crisis, so that the patient is able to appeal for help and so that the therapist is able to perceive and respond to the appeal until the suicidal urges have abated. At moments of crisis, the psychiatrist must be able to throw his weight into the balance on the side of survival.

Ordinarily, in the first therapeutic interview with a new patient the psychiatrist feels no pressure with regard to time. He lets the patient unfold his story pretty much in his own way, while the psychiatrist waits for insight into the patient's personality and character before making some specific explanation or interpretation. When, however, strong suicidal urges are revealed at the first examination rather different tactics are called for. After taking a careful history of the onset and progress of the suicidal feeling, I usually express sympathy toward the patient's feeling of loneliness and painful depression and give a strong, positive, optimistic outlook with regard to treatment, without specifying in detail just what kind of treatment I have in mind. I feel justified in my optimism for I am reasonably confident that through one therapeutic agency or another, or a combination of several, the patient will be feeling much improved within a few weeks or months. In addition to psychotherapy and appropriate drugs, I think of such measures as environmental manipulation through interviews with friends and relatives, hospitalization when indicated, and, if necessary, electrical cerebral stimulation.

If the suicidal trend is severe, the patient should be seen daily. The patient's response to such an optimistic approach may be taken as a rough prognostic guide to the feasibility of office psychotherapy. The outlook is favorable when patients feel relieved after the first interview, with decreased tension and a slight lift in mood, and quickly form a dependent transference relationship to the therapist.

The following case illustrates this approach. A forty-eight-year-old associate professor at an Eastern school became depressed when an expected promotion was withheld. At the same time, his wife received a special award for research. The patient became suicidal when he learned that his promotion had probably been blocked by the very dean whom he most idealized. At faculty meetings the patient felt an almost uncontrollable urge to confess his (minor) academic sins and to resign. One suicidal attempt by gas in his apartment was prevented by his wife's unexpected return. The next day, he abruptly left town and came to Los Angeles, preoccupied with thoughts of suicide. Friends persuaded him to see a psychiatrist. I listened to his story and expressed sympathy for his frustration and confusion. I assured him that depressions of this type are always self-limited, the only danger being suicide. I predicted that with psychiatric treatment the depression could be lifted in one to three months. After that, of course, we would have the problem of trying to understand the personality factors which made him vulnerable to a depressive reaction. That second phase of the treatment might take many months or years. I arranged to see him the next day. The patient was tearfully grateful for the reassurance. That night he slept well for the first time in weeks. Because he was better each day I did not hospitalize him or further consider shock treatment. This was an excellent case for office psychotherapy. The patient appealed for help, it was offered him, and he accepted it gratefully. At the same time, friends were giving assistance. After three months the patient improved sufficiently to take a job in Los Angeles and later send for his wife. Still later, as the patient's treatment progressed, he had several periods of depression which were successfully interpreted as transference frustration reactions.

If the suicidal patient makes no emotional response to the therapist during the first few hours, the hazards of office psychotherapy are greatly increased. I prefer to hospitalize such patients for further evaluation, especially if there are indications pointing to schizophrenia, alcoholism, or impulsive psychopathic tendencies. For example, a thirty-five-year-old man came to the office with his wife. During his treatment with a psychiatrist in another city he had made two unsuccessful suicide attempts. The wife said she worried about him when he got a shifty, withdrawn look in his eyes. The patient himself blandly denied any suicidal wishes or suicidal thoughts. His face was immobile. He minimized the previous therapy and the previous suicide attempts with little affect. I said I knew he must be quite depressed and asked him to come back the next day but he refused to do so. He wanted treatment once a month, which I felt was not feasible. Three weeks later I learned that he was in treatment with a very competent psychiatrist once a week. Two weeks after that, several hours before his psychiatric appointment, in his wife's absence he neatly stuffed his nose and ears with cotton to avoid a mess and killed himself with a pistol. The psychiatrist had no indication of the suicidal intent. Another example: a forty-five-year-old divorcee had a history of alcoholism and promiscuous sexual behavior. The one stable and rewarding influence in her life was her work. She owned and managed a telephone exchange. When she first learned that her recent hoarseness was due to a malignant laryngeal tumor requiring a vocal cord resection, she became extremely depressed and talked of suicide. A psychiatrist recommended hospitalization, but she rebelled at the locked doors of the psychiatric ward and her relatives agreed with her. The psychiatrist somewhat reluctantly saw her as an office patient. Two nights before the scheduled operation, she got drunk on alcohol and committed suicide by drinking cleaning fluid. Experience teaches that schizophrenics, alcoholics, and impulsive psychopaths can be completely unpredictable with regard to suicide.

Occasionally the psychiatrist, hoping to establish a therapeutic relationship in time, may decide to take the risk of office psychotherapy even in those unpromising cases where the patient denies his need for help with indifference or even hostility to the therapist. One is tempted to take a chance when the patient is the only breadwinner for many dependents or when the patient is prominent in some social or political or business activity and feels that his career might be hurt by a record of psychiatric hospitalization. Sometimes the patient and family flatly refuse a recommendation of hospitalization. Then the therapist is advised to make it clear, preferably in writing, that the risk is acknowledged by all concerned. In such a situation I think it is essential that the patient have someone in the family or some friend to whom he is able to appeal for help during an acute short-lived suicidal crisis. The therapist can use this friend or relative as an ancillary therapist during dangerous periods in the treatment. If ambivalent feelings between the patient and the ancillary therapist threaten to complicate the situation further, it may become necessary to refer the relative or friend to another psychiatrist for support in his role as assistant therapist.

Sometimes the psychiatrist first meets his patient when the latter is in the hospital recovering from an unsuccessful attempt at suicide. One may then encounter what in another context has been called "the moment of truth," which should be seized with all possible decision and dispatch. Because of heightened apprehension and guilt, the patient, spouse, and key relatives and friends may reveal information and feelings which have eluded therapeutic efforts for years.

For example, a forty-year-old woman had been in psychotherapy for five years because of a street phobia and a fear of being alone. Finally, her husband began to hint that he was tired of her clinging. At the same time her therapist admitted that he was getting nowhere with her and suggested termination. She attempted suicide by taking a large number of sleeping capsules which she had been saving for some weeks. As she lay in a coma, her husband confessed to me the secret that several people had suspected but the patient had never mentioned to her therapist. The husband had been having an affair with the patient's sister, a steady visitor to the home, for six years. The patient's repression of this problem was responsible in large measure for her anxiety symptoms. This patient could not be treated in office practice because she could not return to face the truth at home. She required a long period of hospitalization.

In such cases, suicidal preoccupations and suicidal attempts announce a situation of emotional bankruptcy. Death appeals as a last resort to dependent persons who have alienated their relatives and exhausted their friends. Checking through their social relationships one finds no remaining assets. Such people usually have no special talents and no special interests. They have existed as emotional parasites and now the host has deserted them. My experience using office psychotherapy with such people has been unfavorable. Rehabilitation usually involves a relatively long period of in-patient, institutional care, even though such persons are not psychotic. If the patient is wealthy, this would mean a hospital such as the Menninger Clinic, Austen Riggs Center, or the like, preferably in some distant location. For patients of lesser financial resources, the local social agencies should be investigated. Patients often establish a strong dependent transference relationship to an institution, such as the Veterans Administration or the university clinic, and gain a source of confidence from this transference. Group therapy experience can help such patients develop more independent social techniques. On the other hand, such patients in individual office treatment are apt to go into a chronic suicidal crisis and make unending demands which strain the psychiatrist's patience and lead him finally to reject the patient. At best, this is another failure for the patient and, at worst, it means another suicidal attempt.

It sometimes happens that a good working therapeutic relationship established in the first interviews becomes dangerously attenuated in subsequent hours. This calls for renewed efforts from the therapist, as illustrated by the following case: A twenty-eight-year-old housewife reluctantly sought therapy at the urging of an old friend, a social worker. Without emotion the patient said that she had been depressed for a year and had saved about 30 sleeping capsules for her eventual suicide. She told of a deprived childhood at the hands of a rejecting mother and described how she had survived by growing tough, and had endured marriage by virtue of her husband's exceptional personality qualities which were directly opposite to hers. He was a retiring, sensitive, commercially successful painter who fled from any family strife to his art. The patient carried the brunt of family leadership. She had always taken great pride in her physical beauty, but her pregnancy one year before had ruined her figure. Without special emphasis, she mentioned that her child was probably mentally retarded. The therapist interrupted with exclamations of sympathy and thrust a box of tissue into the woman's surprised hands. She burst into tears and cried throughout the rest of the hour. Later she angrily protested that she had been tricked. But an emotional relationship had been established and the danger of suicide subsided. However, the patient did not give up her pills. Several months later, the feelings of utter hopelessness returned. Specialists had pronounced the baby hopelessly retarded. Plastic surgery on her breasts was unsuccessful and made her figure worse. Her only friend was out of town. The patient was indifferent to the therapist and preoccupied with thoughts of taking the pills. She dreamed of death. When she was late for an appointment, the therapist noted in himself anxiety and an urge to call her home for reassurance that she was not lying in a coma. The therapist did the following things: He told the patient he was worried about her and asked her to come for an extra hour. He called her husband and asked him to come out of his studio for a while to aid his wife. The husband was astonished to learn that the woman on whom he always leaned was having an emotional breakdown. He responded manfully to the therapist's appeal that for a change he should act as a protective parent toward his wife. She in turn was gratified by his response. The therapist got in touch with appropriate social agencies and encouraged the patient in plans for special placement for the child. With these activities, the patient's interest in therapy (and life) was renewed, and the suicidal urges decreased.

In any office psychotherapy, from the most superficial to the most intensive, an acute suicidal crisis precludes further progress until a more stable intrapsychic balance is achieved. Ideally the therapist will search for the various conscious and unconscious sources of the disturbance and explain the trouble to the patient. The interpretation of suicidal threats and fantasies as transference hostility toward the therapist can be overdone. Often these crises are desperate appeals for love and protection. When strong self-destructive urges appear as a phase of therapy, important and pertinent information is elicited by a careful self-examination on the part of the therapist for feelings of rejection toward the patient and covert wishes that the therapy were interrupted or terminated, which the patient takes as a death wish. In such an emergency, the use of consultation and supervision to check the therapist's countertransference is strongly recommended. This tends to relieve the therapist's anxiety and promote a more realistic appraisal of the situation with appropriate activity. At times explanations or interpretations in words are not suitable for the suicidal patient who has regressed to a paratactic form of logic and cannot understand ordinary communication. Interpretations are clearer when phrased as actions, for instance, increasing the frequency and length of the hours, or alerting relatives to the need for some special treatment of the patient, or taking the patient to a hospital. A consultant may be helpful in sharing the responsibility for such a drastic change in treatment as removing the patient to a hospital. It cannot be denied that such activity tends to increase the regressive dependent transference and may prolong the therapy. On the other hand, the therapist who is dealing with such deeply unconscious destructive feelings as those involved in suicide needs to have the feeling himself that the therapy is timeless, as the unconscious is timeless. Many of the suicidal crises occurring in therapy are precipitated by unconscious impatience in the therapist toward his patient or the patient's unconscious. Suicidal patients demand a great deal from the therapist in terms of time, effort, and responsibility. In return, the therapist should make sure that he has the time available and that he is paid a satisfactory fee. Two or three suicidal patients at one time are more than enough for any man's practice. The availability of excellent psychiatric hospital facilities for suicidal patients can ease the strain of therapy with such patients considerably.

The disadvantage of drugs, electric treatments, and hospitalization in general is that they provide essentially passive remedies for problems which often require active resolution. If patients are discharged abruptly from the hospital to return to their original conflicts the cycle of hopelessness and suicide may be repeated. The advantage of office psychotherapy is that it encourages the patient toward solving his problems himself, which promotes self-confidence and self-respect. Psychotherapy aims at changes in character, which are then reflected by changes in the patient's environment, leading to more satisfactions in life. Ideally, the hospital and the office provide complementary phases of the patient's treatment.

In summary, office psychotherapy of suicidal patients offers a greater reward for the patient but it carries an increased risk for, and imposes a special responsibility on, the psychiatrist. The risk is minimized when there is open emotional communication between the patient and the therapist. Office treatment is especially suitable for patients who form a dependent relationship toward the therapist early in treatment. However, extremely dependent or emotionally bankrupt patients may require the nurturing influence of a hospital or clinic for successful rehabilitation. The psychiatrist should be optimistic, patient, flexible, and resourceful. When confronted with a suicidal crisis, the therapist should carefully check his countertransference, preferably with the aid of a consultant. In suicidal emergencies, aid for the patient should be solicited without hesitation from appropriate relatives, friends, and social agencies. The hospital and the office can provide complementary phases in the successful treatment of suicidal patients.

12

The Suicidal Crisis in Psychotherapy

NORMAN L. FARBEROW

Probably no single event in the course of psychotherapy carries so much emotional impact and requires so much skill, knowledge, sensitivity, ability, and fortitude on the part of the therapist as a suicidal crisis in his patient. While the whole course of therapy constantly demands the right word or the best response from the therapist, this demand seems especially heightened by the drama of the suicidal crisis, where there is the suspense of a threat to kill or the immediacy of a gesture toward self-destruction. Often there is not even time to consider what has gone wrong in the therapy and why the crisis has developed. This is the time, instead, when the questions of what to do and how to do it crowd in: How serious is this impulse, should the patient be sent to the hospital without delay, and, if so, how should one get him there? What will stay his hand before he acts so that the crisis can be worked through; what words does he need? What happens if his psychotherapy is interrupted at this point? What will this crisis do to the future course of his therapy? The answers will vary, too, with whether the patient is being seen in private practice or in a clinic setting; with the therapist's willingness to undergo the emotional strain and the increased demands of this period; with the evaluation of the patient's ego strengths, his resiliency, the intensity and force of the suicidal urge; with the length of time in treatment, the rapport established, and the diagnosis of the patient.

It is true that no single course of action can be prescribed which would fit all cases. Probably, if any were to be suggested at all, the safest and surest one would be to place the patient within the protective walls of a hospital. But sometimes the most conservative approach is not the most productive one, and in some cases one is tempted to take the calculated risk of continuing to treat the patient in his present situation when the tensions and the conflicts immediately at hand can be worked through and understood. It is difficult to specify the factors that determine which cases will be helped by being sent to the hospital and which should continue in an outpatient therapy setting. As is so often the case, however, the determination of the best method of treatment cannot wait upon the exhaustive scientific examinations of the phenomenon under consideration. Service must be rendered while research goes on. Perhaps, however, by continued examination, appraisal, and review and by discussion, comparison, and sharing of experiences, the goal of prevention of the needless loss of life by self-destruction may be approached.

This chapter shares with the reader a detailed account of two therapy sessions for each of two veterans who were patients in a mental hygiene clinic. During their therapy suicidal crises occurred. (All identifying information has been removed in order to preserve anonymity.) It is important here to emphasize that these crises occurred after therapy had been in progress for some time—about three to four months. This chapter is limited to a discussion of suicidal crisis under these special conditions, that is, when it occurs in psychotherapy and when the therapy is already in process. Neither of these cases had come to therapy originally as a result of suicidal tendencies, but rather because of severe anxiety attacks, with symptoms which had not included suicidal tendencies. Had they come to the clinic with openly expressed suicidal feelings they would have been assigned to a medical therapist rather than to a nonmedical therapist, for it is the policy of the clinic (as well as the firm belief of the author) that such persons should immediately be assigned to a medical doctor where the legal responsibility for the life and health of the patient is already well defined. The clinic in which the author is employed provided regular psychiatric supervision and consultation for all its nonmedical therapists. This procedure is routine particularly for just such crises, so that there were frequent psychiatric consultations for the therapist during the trying periods described.

The cases were in two distinctly different diagnostic categories and the methods used in handling the crises were markedly different. In the first case, the approach was mainly interpretive, uncovering; in the second, it was mainly supportive and reassuring. These examples, of course, do not imply that the techniques employed in each of the cases are the best methods of handling suicidal crises in therapy. Rather, they are presented in order to provide the reader with a description of at least two of the many kinds of suicidal crises and to provoke interest in and discussion about this problem.

MR. S.

The patient was a 33-year-old white male who might be classified as an emotionally unstable, immature person with primarily obsessive-compulsive defenses. When he first came to the clinic, he was in the midst of an extreme anxiety attack amounting almost to panic. He was referred to the neuropsychiatric hospital where he spent approximately six months and then returned to the clinic. At the time of the reopening of his case, he was in the process of separating from his wife and one child, and he remained in a highly emotional, disturbed state for some time. He was making a marginal economic and social adjustment, living for some time in slums and skid row areas and rooming with friends from the hospital. He showed very little motivation toward seeking any kind of employment, and spent most of the time bemoaning the fact of his separation and impending divorce. He found little satisfaction in any of his personal relationships and showed considerable disturbance in his sexual functioning at the time.

Therapy was soon established on a twice-a-week basis, with the patient irregular in attendance, either missing his appointments or wandering in at some time other than his appointed hour. He was ambivalent about therapy, demanding, pleading for more time, and then not showing up for the extra sessions granted him. He showed marked mood swings, in one hour presenting a happy, cheerful front, and in the next, a swing to apathy and depression. Therapy proceeded on a limited insight level, with the focus of the discussion on the relationship between him and his wife, and with some references to the genetic sources of his difficulties in his past relationships with his mother.

At the time of the suicidal crisis the patient was receiving frequent notices from his wife's lawyers about arrangements for a divorce. The therapist had to be away from the office for three days, during which time it was arranged to have the patient tested. When the therapist returned, the patient was very depressed and announced he was returning to the hospital. However, he returned the next day and stated he had moved in with his parents. The next two sessions were filled with anger and bitterness toward his wife. Sessions 16 and 17 follow in detail. The patient announced that he had almost committed suicide the night before session 16.

Therapy Interview 16

The patient came in slowly. I could barely hear him because he spoke in an extremely low tone and in very brief sentences. He looked very depressed and apathetic. He said, "I have just one thing on my mind. I almost did it Friday night. I don't know why I stopped. I've really been sick these past few days, afraid to fall asleep. When I do, I have the most miserable dreams."

I asked what had happened to make it worse right now. He said, "The other night I went out with Jimmy and two other fellows." At this point, he began to talk a little louder. "I went to several bars and finally ended at one in our old neighborhood. I saw my father-in-law there with a strange woman. I didn't go over to him and he didn't come over to me. I always did suspect that he was playing around. We went to some other clubs, picked up one couple and went to a party. We took off from there and went to another party and finally left there around four or five o'clock. I had a lousy time. I slept most of the next day and watched TV a little. Then the idea got into my head and I felt that I really wanted to do it. I thought I might write some things just to get them off my mind. The pencil wouldn't keep up with my mind, there were too many things to say. I was going to take some stuff that I knew we had in the medicine chest. I thought, and thought, and thought all day, and just thought about my wife, about this guy, Joe, and how much I hated their guts. I think that night I dreamed I was beating up on him and I was thinking of so many different ways that I would like to. I guess I feel pretty bitter toward him and toward my wife. They stole the last possession I had."

I asked what this was and he said it was pride. I asked him to explain. He said, "Pride—that I was right and that others were wrong. Other people kept telling me that you can't trust a woman. I wanted to show them that they were wrong."

I said, "Why do you have to kill or hurt yourself because of that?" and he said, "She took the last thing that I had. There is nothing left to live for." I said, "You want to hurt her and the only way you can do this is through hurting yourself. You feel this is the only way that you can get at her." The patient protested. This wasn't true—he really didn't want to hurt her. He started all over again, "I've lost all my possessions," and so forth. "I can't even call on God."

I said, "You have been wanting to get back at her and hurt her and you have been telling me how you have been unable to. Maybe this is the way you feel you can hurt her." The patient disregarded me and said, "To think that it is me, me. I don't even ask, why me, any more. This is the kind of thing that you read about, or that you hear on the radio. I notice that I don't give a Goddam any more. I don't feel like fighting, I don't feel like anything else. There is nothing left to live for, just to come here, and I hate that because I know I have to leave."

The patient was talking louder, and with a little more vigor. I asked how he had felt on seeing his father-in-law. He said, "I was uncomfortable. I remember I started telling myself, 'That's where she got it,' but no, that's not the answer. I think I'm beyond sour grapes now."

I went back to my main point and said again, "The most important thing in the world for you was the feeling you wanted to get back at your wife, and **this is the way you felt you could do it best.**" Again the patient paid no attention and, instead, looked rather wistfully at me and asked if I had been in touch with his wife. I said I had not, and asked why he wanted me to be. He didn't answer for a while. Finally he said, "I know it's childish, wishful thinking, but I had the feeling that maybe you would make everything all right, maybe you would get us both back together again. But I know I don't have the feeling that things can be patched up. Because of this one thing, things can never be the same." He then continued, "I can't go on like this. I'm living in a void." Our time was up. I ended the session and made arrangements to see him the next day.

Therapy Interview 17

Patient came in late in the afternoon, looking better. He said he felt better today, he had had a long sleep. I asked why he felt better and he said, "I could share my troubles with someone." I said that wasn't all of the reason. The patient said, "I slept all day yesterday and worked around the yard. I spent some time with Jimmy, just talking. I got a little depressed at his house." I asked again what it was that made him feel better, since nothing had changed for him since yesterday. He said, "Sometime last night I changed. I must have had 50 different dreams. I started thinking that I wanted to snap out of it. I really don't know how it's changed. I don't think I feel any different about my wife or about Joe." I said, "How do you feel about yourself?" He said, "I don't want to die. I just want to get out of this void." I asked, "Was it anything that happened here yesterday?" He answered, "I feel, mainly, it was the unburdening. I wanted to tell someone. You were the only one I could talk to without feeling like a stupid ass. Not sympathetic, but understanding. Also, yesterday was the first time I ever realized exactly how I felt about my wife and about Joe. It must be good to cuss somebody out instead of mulling and mulling. There was no one else to talk to. I couldn't get any real satisfaction out of talking to Jimmy."

I asked, "What are your feelings toward your wife and toward Joe?" He said, "I really hate them. I hold her responsible for my present condition. I just can't seem to get proper satisfaction—she's dragging me down. I'm angry and I'm frustrated, and I have to fight the world as well as her. She wasn't helping me, she was only adding to my burden."

I said, "You felt if you could only hurt yourself, you would be hurting her, and in this way, you'd get back at her." He said, "I guess I felt guilty about feeling that way, but the strongest feeling that I had was the feeling that I couldn't hurt her. I wanted to be in the position to say 'no.' I made overtures toward her, hoping she'd come back and then I could reject her. I do know of one way now that I could hurt her, through her father. I just thought of it, but I don't like to hurt and I don't want to be hurt."

With this patient, interpretations were direct and pointed, with the focus on the dynamic of the patient's anger at his wife, his need to hurt her, and his method of accomplishing this, that is, by hurting himself. It is, of course, impossible to say how effective these interpretations were. At the time, the feeling was that they were not making much of an impression upon him, and yet, in session 17, he did return with his anger more appropriately directed at the external objects, his wife and her boy friend, Joe. It would still be difficult to evaluate how much of the subsequent behavior was due primarily to these interpretations, for in the effort to stem the tide of his self-aggressive feelings many other factors were introduced into the therapy: an immediate increase in sessions to five a week, lengthening of time as needed, increased therapist activity and participation in the discussion, and permission to call the therapist at any time the patient felt the need. The interest and concern of the therapist were undoubtedly powerful, if unmeasurable, influences in relieving the situation. The daily sessions were continued for about a week, when the intensity of the emotions around this crisis seemed to have subsided. Then the sessions were gradually spaced out until the former frequency of twice a week was reached.

Briefly, the further course of therapy was relatively uneventful, with the patient remaining in therapy for an additional thirty-three interviews, by which time he had found work and was seriously involved with a new girl friend.

MR. R.

This patient was a 28-year-old, white, married male who might be classified as conversion reaction in a basically schizoid personality. He had been in therapy at the clinic several times previously, one of these periods lasting over a year. One of his main complaints, which he felt had begun three years earlier after an operation on his ears, was a condition which he described as a "shaking of the neck." His previous therapists had described their treatment methods as conducted on a superficial basis with some minor attempts at insight and with the aim of strengthening his intellectual defenses. The patient was able to reduce his chronically high level of anxiety and partly to work through his fears concerning his feeling that he was not much of a man. His therapist also stated that though marked concern over homosexual interests was present, this area was avoided when some evidence of psychotic defenses started to appear. The patient was out of therapy for about a year and a half and then returned because of a severe anxiety attack centering around the responsibilities of a new baby, a new house, and the rush of added work in his seasonal job. The present course of therapy was instituted on a once-a-week basis and was conducted on a supportive level, with few interpretations except to repeat and to strengthen his intellectual defenses. The patient improved, and interruption was once again being considered when another seasonal trend in the patient's work caused an exacerbation of the patient's symptoms and an increase in anxiety which mounted almost to panic. The patient became obsessed with feelings of inadequacy in his work, entered into a deep, depressed period, and entertained serious suicidal thoughts. The following therapy sessions are practically verbatim reports of the two therapy hours which occurred at the onset of his agitated depression. This emotional disturbance actually persisted for about two months, during the early part of which he was seen practically every day and during which time there were frequent telephone calls at night to the therapist at his home.

Therapy Interview 12

I had not expected the patient at this hour. He came in as an emergency. He was very depressed, and to some slight extent, agitated. He started out saying, "I have been feeling terrible with headaches and pains that just continue in the back of my neck. I haven't been able to sleep for nights. I haven't been able to do the work. They [the patient's fellow workers] ask me a question and I can't answer. I was the same way at the trial when I got confused and didn't understand what they were asking me. [Patient had recently instituted civil suit for damages incurred in an automobile accident.] The doctor gave me some pills [APCs] but they didn't do any good.

"I had to go to the doctor for an operation on the tip of my penis. It's still spraying. The people at work are trying to snap me out of this. They know that I'm not feeling well. I don't even feel I have the right to feel sick. There's so much stuff at the office that I get confused." The patient began to cry, but regained his control quickly. He went on, "I went to a party, though I didn't want to go. I didn't enjoy myself. I quit smoking because I thought this would help me through the holiday. Maybe I was getting so tense because of smoking too much, but when I was at the trial and had to wait for the lawyer, I got so nervous I had to go down and get some smokes. The trial is over already. We had a trial just in front of the judge last Wednesday. He hasn't given his decision. Tuesday night we were at the lawyer's and Wednesday I was on the witness stand, under cross-examination, for two or three hours." I asked how this had gone and how he had felt. He said, "I felt fairly good. I became afraid that my neck was going to be held responsible for the numbness that I had been having in my hand. My lawyer told me little things to say that weren't exactly the truth, and I either forgot them, or else I felt I couldn't tell any untruth while there on the stand."

I asked how the operation had gone. He said, "I really didn't want to take all that time, but my 'stream-line' was so bad that it sprayed all over. I had to sit on the toilet in order to take a leak."

He said, "I get self-conscious," and I asked what it was that made him feel this way. He said, "It's my short penis, my big nose, and when I walk, I bounce along. It's my blond eyebrows and my light beard." I asked what these, put together, meant he was afraid of, and he said he was afraid of life. I asked what it was, specifically, he was afraid of, and he replied, "Probably I'm afraid I'm not man enough, but I don't want to believe that.

"Lately, I've lost all my sexual drive with my wife. I've heard that this means a guy's going to have a nervous breakdown." I told him this was not true. I stated it was possible to have a lot of anxiety and still be able to function. I also told him that people frequently lose their sex drive when they are very anxious. He said he had thought of committing suicide, and I told him I was glad he had come in to see me first, and was talking about it with me. He went on, "I'm so anxious, I can't hear the questions that other people ask me. I feel guilty because another fellow is doing my work."

Arrangements were made to see him the next day.

Therapy Interview 13

The patient came in very slowly. "I didn't go to work today because I've been feeling very bad. I think I'm going crazy. Is there something I can do about it? Maybe I ought to go to the hospital." I asked what was making him feel bad and he said, "These pains in my head and this tension. It's as if bands are pulled real tight around my head. I can't sleep and I can't eat. I can't do my job, I can't go to the store, I can't do anything. I know I'm worse than before. When I went to see the doctor, I was afraid to sit in the reception room. I've been making my wife nervous, moping around the house. I was really going to commit suicide today. First, I took all my pills and then I went for a long ride up the Boulevard. I was going to get a hose but couldn't find any. I went to the drugstore and got a quart of beer and a scratch pad to write my wife a note. I parked on a deserted street and started writing the note and then my pen ran out of ink. I had to laugh. I drank some more of the beer and felt a little bit better, and then felt that I just didn't have the guts to go through with it. When I went home, my wife gave me a list of things to get in the store, and I took some films into the drugstore. Afterwards, the lady across the street came over and played with the kids."

I asked what the reason was for this wanting to kill himself. He said, "It was my shattered childhood. I didn't have a father to instill any confidence. I want my wife to remarry to someone who likes children. Then the thought came that no one likes a child as much as his own folks. When I kissed my wife and child good-bye this morning, I really hated to go. Then I thought, 'I've got to hang around to take care of my boy and of my wife.' " He began to cry again. "When I was young I had asthma and I was oversensitive. The war worried me a lot. Being cooped up in that house for five days,[1] I couldn't

---

[1] In combat, the patient was trapped for five days in no man's land.

eat or sleep. I can't relax, I can't concentrate, I'm thinking only of myself."
I asked what it was right now that made everything seem so terrible. He
said, "I can't do my job, I'm a failure." To him, this meant that he was a
complete failure, and I pointed out how he was seeing everything in black
and white, and that he was feeling that if he couldn't do his job, he was
worthless. He said he felt like an outcast. I pointed out all of the things that
he had been able to do—how well he actually had been able to function despite
the tension he had been feeling. I mentioned his house, his wife, his child,
his job, but the patient was unconvinced. "At work, even if you're half dead,
you're supposed to go in at this time. Other times I can call in if I'm sick
and it's okay, but I'm afraid of what others will think now.

"I can't feel friendly or be friendly to others. I have to wait and see if
they like me first." I said he felt people had to like him and if they didn't,
they'd hate him. It was an all-or-none process, just like the other thing.

He talked about his operation for circumcision when he was young. Dr. C.
had said, "I've never seen one like that before." The patient thought he was
referring to how small his penis was. When he came home after the operation,
his folks went out. He got sick, and the lady next door had to come in to
change the dressing for him. "I got out of bed too soon and started swimming
too soon. My stepfather punished me once by making me stand on a stool
naked and raising the window shade far enough so that my sexual organ was
exposed to the outside. He took me out of bed one night when I was only
half asleep because I didn't do the dishes right. He was always tearing me
down, always belittling me. At camp one summer the boys were swimming and
took off their trunks. One fellow pointed to my genital and said, 'Look at
the way it's shrunk up.' "

I asked what this meant to him, and he said, "It means I'm less stable."
I wondered what this referred to. He said he and a girl were swimming one
day and she swam between his legs. As she came up she said to him, "Get
that stabilizer out of the way." I asked what "stable" meant for him and he
said it meant being a more solid individual.

I said he was wondering if perhaps he were a woman, or like a woman.
The patient denied this vehemently, and I told him his inability to work at
this point did not mean that he was a woman.

As I ended the session, the patient said he still felt anxious and said he
thought perhaps I should send him to the hospital. I replied that we could
always send him to the hospital later if he needed it and that, though I recognized how strong his feelings were and how bad he felt, we would talk about
it here and try to understand what was making him feel so bad. I told him
I felt confident in his strength to pull through this period of strain. He could
call me at any time, day or night, if he wished. I also reassured him directly,
telling him these things would pass and that he would get better. I pointed
out how he had felt bad in the past and it had always gotten better. I made
an appointment to see him the next day.

The therapy that followed with Mr. R. in the next week and a half consisted of almost daily sessions and numerous telephone calls from him. The interviews were much the same, with the activity of the therapist directed at offering support and reassurance. During this time the seasonal rush in the patient's employment passed and the pressure which the patient had felt was considerably lessened. However, the guilt feelings remained strong; he felt he had let his fellow employees down, and he assumed they were looking down on him. These feelings were relieved partly by some intellectual discussion of his fears. He was encouraged to talk over his feelings and his fears with his wife and was surprised to find she accepted him even though he had admitted his fears to her. The patient's depression lasted approximately two months, with the last month indicating steady relief of his feelings. Therapy was gradually reduced to the former once-a-week basis. The telephone calls ceased without further comment. The patient was seen for about two more months, during which time he seemed to have become stabilized, both emotionally and vocationally. At the time of termination, the patient stated that the therapist had made one very significant comment to him during his depression. This was the statement that the therapist had confidence in the patient's ability to stand the strain of that period.

The calculated risk is much more apparent in this case than with Mr. S. This patient, in contrast to Mr. S., had a much more tenuous ego organization and poorer defenses, which indicated a psychotic substructure. These signs are significant as danger signals in suicidal tendencies because of the added difficulty in the prediction and control of psychotics. Moreover, the patient himself had asked for the sanctuary of the hospital, and the way was open for the most obvious and recommended procedure without the usual accompanying difficulties of convincing the patient, conferring with relatives, arranging with the hospital, and the like. Nevertheless, there were factors that seemed to warrant taking the chance of outpatient therapy. A review of the patient's past history revealed assets which could be counted on. Despite the evidence of some psychotic substructure, the patient showed a considerable—even surprising, in the light of his family history—amount of ego strength. He had finished high school, had been a good athlete—a star in some sports (even though it was compensatory behavior)—and had worked consistently since the war. He had gone through a difficult stretch of war service, experiencing a great amount of combat without an emotional breakdown requiring hospitalization. He had married and was raising a family. On the negative side were the indications of psychotic functioning, the history of a short period in a mental hospital since the service, and the seriousness, as well as the tenacity, of the depressive feelings. A strong factor in the decision not to hospitalize him was the feeling of the therapist that to accede to the patient's request for hospitalization was to agree that he was weak, ineffectual, and inadequate. It was exactly this feeling which was being combated in his therapy. Another important consideration was that if sent to the hospital the patient could no longer be seen by his therapist, and therapy would be interrupted for an indefinite period of time.

There are at least four important conclusions which emerge from the consideration of the experiences of both the patients and the therapist in these two cases.

(1) In both cases, treatment to meet the emergencies was changed by greatly increasing the activity of the therapist. This included increasing the frequency of the meetings, lengthening the time of each meeting if possible, inviting and being available for telephone calls at any time, day or night, and participating more in the discussions in each session. All this activity was designed to give the patient a feeling of sincere concern and interest by the therapist in his welfare.

(2) Commitment to the hospital must be evaluated by the therapist from the points of view of the two people most immediately involved, first, the patient, whose safety and health must at all times be the primary consideration, and second, the therapist. Thus, hospitalization may have several meanings to the patient, even diametrically opposed ones. The patient may obtain a feeling of security and comfort, knowing that he is being protected from the terrible conflicts which may be raging inside him; or he may be disappointed and crushed, feeling that his therapist, too, does not consider him strong enough to cope with his feelings. The therapist must weigh these and any other feelings he may sense in the patient, such as those of rejection and abandonment, as probable reactions to such a move. For the therapist, commitment to the hospital involves the interruption of therapy and the alteration, and frequently the relinquishing, of the therapeutic plans for the patient. The therapist must search his own motivations thoroughly for any narcissistic and omnipotent feelings which may be influencing his judgment of the status of the patient before he makes a decision to continue his therapy with the patient or to hospitalize him.

(3) One of the most important factors influencing the decision of the therapist is his own willingness and ability to undergo the emotional strain during the period of the suicidal crisis. This includes accepting the increased demands on his time and attention, the intrusion into his private

life, and the requirement that he be available at all times. The therapist must be willing to accept the tension of not knowing what might be happening while his patient is out of sight and sound. He must be able to bear the weighty responsibility if his calculation of the risk was in error and his patient does succeed in taking his own life.

(4) Inasmuch as in the suicidal crisis there is always the possibility, no matter how remote, that the patient may succeed in taking his own life, it is especially important for the nonmedical therapist that the medical profession be a part of the total treatment picture.

13

The Recognition and Treatment
of Suicide in Children

MARSHALL D. SCHECHTER

The purpose of this chapter is to describe from a psychoanalytic point of view some of the pathologic states in children (including adolescents up to eighteen years of age) that lead to suicide or suicidal equivalents and to suggest treatment programs for these conditions. Although this chapter is written primarily to present and to discuss clinical experience with the states described, some theoretical premises are included inasmuch as suicide in children is so relatively uncommon. The material in the chapter is divided into three sections that deal with (a) some theoretical formulations and a description of the concept of suicidal equivalents, (b) different diagnostic categories of suicidal children, with illustrative case material from hospital, agency, and private practice, and (c) some treatment suggestions based on the formulations as they appear in the chapter.

THEORETICAL DISCUSSION

The dynamics of depression have been well described (7, 10, 13). In general, in adults, these descriptions have stated that, when an individual's hostility cannot be expressed outwardly, it is turned against the introjected objects, which—because they are a part of the self—results in the attempted or actual destruction of the self. Depressions in children have also been described clinically (20, 22, 23, 24, 25). While the same dynamic of hostility directed against a formerly loved, but now hated, introjected object is hypothesized, these descriptions have also stressed the factor of the extreme dependence of the child on the parent, his love object. Thus, whenever children feel the threat of the loss of a love object, they not only develop feelings of rage toward the frustrating object, but feelings of helplessness and of worthlessness as well (2). This results in, and is equivalent to, a depression. Actually, these states of affective tension occur in a lesser degree rather frequently during childhood. To deal with these affective states, children learn to utilize a number of defense mechanisms, especially those developed in their personal history and those emphasized in their environment (2, 8). It is when the degree of tension is extremely high and the defense mechanisms break down or become ineffective that suicide or suicidal equivalents may appear.

Inasmuch as the child is still so dependent upon his love objects for gratifications and as the process of identification has not been completed, turning of the hostility against and destroying the introjects within himself is too painful and too frightening. But another important factor is that the child's size and ego status also militate against the use of specific instruments of destruction. Thus, children rarely commit suicide, or even make overt suicidal attempts or threats, but rather express their self-destructive feelings in other ways. These may be called "suicidal equivalents," that is, attenuated attacks on the introjected object which result in depressions, "accidental" injuries (30), antisocial acts, and the like—all of which have the potentiality for ending in the destruction of the individual. These partial attacks on the self should be treated with the same caution as the more direct, overt self-destructive act in the adult. In the adolescent the impulses can more easily take the form of overt suicidal acts because of the lessened dependence on the love object (accompanied by the heightened emotional stresses of reawakened oedipal conflicts) and also because he is now a person physically more capable of hurting himself (30). In addition, in the actions of the suicidal child can be seen not only the hostility against the frustrating parents turned inward, but also the desperate attempts at regaining contact with the lost gratifying love object. In other words, the suicidal act also represents a type of restitutional phenomenon. It is in this psychoanalytic framework—the attack of the introjected object and the attempts to recover it as a love object—that we can best understand some of the suicides or suicidal equivalents of children.

CLINICAL MATERIAL

This section presents different diagnostic categories of suicidal children with illustrative case material drawn from hospital records, agency files, and the author's own private practice. It is important to note that thoughts of death at one's own hand do occur in the normal. Especially is this true in the common childhood fantasy of dying as a means of punishing parents,

"I'll kill myself or get killed, and then they'll be sorry they treated me this way." The elements of hostility as well as the masochism can readily be seen in these children.

Henry, a normal boy of seven, had been playing with a girl and a boy of the same age. There was no previous history of psychologic difficulty except a short period of anxiety a year before at the death of a relative. The girl evidenced some preference for the other boy. Henry was overheard to remark, "I think I'll run out in the street and get killed by a car."

When aggression, or perhaps better, motor activity, is inhibited in the very young child, the result can be a turning inward of the aggression with consequent resultant self-destructive tendencies (1). The following is presented as a possible analogue to the dynamics of depression.

Wilbur, the son of a physician, at one year of age was given Denis Browne splints [1] for congenital club feet. Up to this age, the parents reported no difficulty in his development or any other signs of congenital deformities. The child had exhibited a number of autoerotic activities, including sucking his thumb and rocking occasionally. He had just begun to walk and was getting a tremendous joy out of the muscular activity that this entailed. He had also given up the bottle. Teething was painful and prolonged. He was a warm and affectionate child of kind, accepting, and understanding parents. Shortly after the application of the splints, which were used just in the night, the child began to rock violently and then bang his head on the headboard of the bed. This was within the first two weeks of wearing the splints. Following the establishment of head banging in the bed at night, the child began to bang his head on any hard object whenever he was frustrated, as well as to hit himself whenever he was naughty or angry. The parents were advised to give up the Denis Browne splints and to pick him up each time that the head banging began. Another suggestion made at this time was to give the child something hard to bite on in order to ease him over the teething period. After following these suggestions for one month, the parents reported a remission of the symptom of head banging and after four months reported that the child no longer hit himself when angry.

Depressive Reactions Following Death of a Parent

As Spitz has shown in his papers on anaclitic depression (22, 23, 24), the child's reaction to the death (or removal) of a parent is severe and intense (15). This is true at any age but is especially marked in the pre-

---

[1] The Denis Browne splint is a splint for the correction of a club foot deformity. It keeps the two feet separate by a steel bar and coordinates the movements of the two feet.

oedipal period. There is a tendency to identify himself with the departed object (21, 29)—which also occurs in the older age groups—often with a loss of many ego functions. Zilboorg (30) has suggested that the death of a parent occurring early in a child's life predetermines suicidal tendencies later in life. These children look and act like old people [see the discussion of marasmus by Spitz (25)].

When Bill was 13 months old his mother was killed in an automobile accident. For the entire span of Bill's life, his father had been in a sanatorium. Bill was the youngest of three boys and at the time of his mother's death had just begun to talk. His mother had remained at home with him constantly until he was six months old, when it became necessary for her to seek employment. From age six months on, therefore, and certainly after his mother's death, the child had a constant stream of changing housekeepers, none of whom remained longer than three months. His father was discharged from the sanatorium at the time of his wife's death. However, he, too, shortly went back to work, leaving Bill in the hands of various housekeepers and maids. During the first six months of life Bill was considered bright, alert, happy, and contented. However, he lost his ability to speak at the time of his mother's death and became morose and withdrawn. His physique changed from active and wiry to lethargic and potbellied. His expression was always sad and preoccupied. It was difficult to make contact with him. Over long stretches of time, though he was with many people including members of his family, he was never seen to smile. At 27 months he gave the appearance of being retarded. Treatment was recommended but not undertaken.

Tommy was three when he was first seen. He too, like Bill, the boy mentioned above, was withdrawn, potbellied and sad-looking. Tommy's father had died when he was nine months old, at which time his mother went into a severe depression which lasted for almost a year. She reported that immediately after his father's death, Tommy's outgoing and happy personality seemed to change, and she even felt that each evening when the father was wont to come home, Tommy could be seen looking for him and showed disappointment when he did not arrive. Tommy was placed in a foster home when he was about twenty months of age, where he did relatively well, beginning to speak and to develop some relationships with the foster parents. In his second year, some difficulty developed with the foster father, so that the contacts between Tommy and the foster father were decreased. This precipitated the morose, depressed appearance described. It also resulted in his giving up speech completely, for all intents and purposes. In treatment, Tommy's games consisted of crashing and banging various trucks and trains together with no verbal or even facial expression. This continued for many hours until, under his breath, with his back turned, vocalizations could be heard. His body became intensely taut, as he reached a crescendo in the play, and occasionally the formed word of "bang" or "I crash you" could be heard distinctly. These actions were interpreted as suggesting the amount of anger that he had toward his mother and his feeling of loss with the death of his father. With treatment based on these interpretations his behavior promptly began to change. Speech returned not only in the therapy but outside also, and his whole physical appearance returned to normal. All this was aided by giving his mother insight into his problems, especially his hostility to her, so that she could be warmer and closer to him.

Sven's father died when he was four. They were extremely close because the father's illness had kept him at home the entire year before his death. The boy was referred for consultation while in a hospital for correction of a congenital atrophy of his right arm. At this time he was six. In the interview with him, he spoke glowingly of his father's Norwegian background and there was an ever-present wish to join him in the Valhalla that had been so beautifully described for the boy. The anxiety that was present was mainly related to his fear of separation from his mother.

Ted was seen at the request of an agency because, in the three days prior to the consultation, he had not stirred from bed and refused to eat (11, 18). He was eight years old and living with foster parents. The acute symptoms developed after a visit from his father had been canceled. His mother had died two years previously and he was placed by the agency in a home with excellent foster parents with whom he related well. An older brother was placed in a residential home for children and did fairly well there. The boys visited with each other frequently and the father visited with one or the other son. At times both boys went together with their father on visiting days. When his father was not able to come on his promised day, Ted went into an acute depression and actively sought death as a punishment for his father and as a means of pressuring his father and the agency into reestablishment of his home (and also, perhaps, unconsciously trying to force return of his mother). Certainly the affect was a revival of that which he experienced after his mother's death (2). Treatment consisted of increasing the visiting opportunities with father and brother, and also increasing the foster mother's attention to his needs. He was seen very frequently by one of the agency's staff psychiatrists, who formed a close relationship with him and interpreted to him his grief and hostility. He soon began to eat and before long returned to his normal activities.

Hysterical Reactions

Adolescents particularly are prone to act out various impulses in an impetuous, precipitous way. Especially when angered, their deeds may be seen to contain not only their anger directed against the environment but the punishment for their acts as well. In these suicidal children may be seen not only the attempt to fulfill aggressive, hostile impulses and super-ego prohibitions, but also the return of omnipotent, magical means of avoiding punishment by escaping through death (17).

Mary, 14, had always had difficulties with peer relationships. She had also felt defeated in her oedipal struggles by a domineering and aggressive mother. She had aggressively used her withdrawal as a defense and as a weapon against authority. One day, her mother had refused to allow her to do something she wished, and, in the resulting argument, had spoken disparagingly of her. When alone, Mary took a bottle of aspirin and then announced to her mother she was going to die. The suicidal attempt was performed partly out of spite, but also occurred because of the feeling of worthlessness in comparison with her sophisticated mother (2).

A number of diabetic children, on learning of their illness and its physical reactions, would use it to threaten their environment if any gratification was withheld (16). As a result they were frequently seen either in coma or in acidosis, both of which could be interpreted as a threat to their own life. Hospitalization was often necessary, with a treatment program geared to forming a close bond to the psychiatrist upon whom the patient could become dependent and the transference could be worked out (4).

Anxiety States and Compulsion Neuroses

During adolescence there is a recrudescence of the oedipal problems which sometimes results in a reinstitution of obsessive compulsive defenses which, however, decompensate during periods of stress. When this occurs there is a flooding of the personality with instinctual tension and anxiety that is manifested in connection with a fear of loss of control or in regard to overwhelming of the ego by the id impulses. At these times, suicidal thoughts and actions can occur.

Betty, age 16, had just started dating. Her relationship with her mother had always been infantile and filled with demands. When her mother suggested that she cut down on the amount of dating that she was doing, she responded with anger. At this particular time the mother also insisted on some dental treatment which was painful and prolonged. Suddenly, the girl found herself having destructive thoughts and feelings toward her mother which became so overpowering that she feared leaving her mother out of sight, as well as being in her presence. She was preoccupied with this type of ideational content and, because it stimulated so much anxiety within her, she was simultaneously concerned with doing away with herself so as to prevent ·committing horrendous acts. Immediate hospitalization was advised, but for a week none could be found that the parents deemed suitable. The girl was given Thorazine (75 mg. per day) and seen daily for a number of weeks as an outpatient. The acute problem abated as she spoke of her overly dependent relationship with her mother and her growing sexual feelings toward all men. These included thoughts of her father and brother. She was very aware of the conflict within herself and was soon able to see how her feelings toward her mother were filled with ambivalence. The medication was used for only two and one-half weeks and then discontinued. She was seen five times a week for three weeks and then less frequently for the next two months. Her mother called two years later to report continued progress in all spheres, especially socially, with no recurrence of the original symptoms.

Helen, age 13, became fearful of the attitudes of the teachers and other pupils shortly after return to school following a severe and lengthy throat infection. Each day became a torment filled with anticipated criticisms from the teachers and rejection by her classmates. Her school work had always been above average. Two other times she had experienced unhappy events which resulted in fear of going to school. When she was six, her father abruptly left her mother, and the girl was so upset she didn't attend school for nine months. She returned to school only after her father returned home. When Helen was 11, one of her acquaintances was killed by a sexual pervert on the way to a party the patient also attended. At this time, too, she had great fear in going to school, but did continue regularly, and the fear gradually abated. Her parents sought psychiatric help for the current episode that had none of the extremely traumatic impact of the previous occasions. The physician felt that with increased firmness on the part of the parents and the school, she would again be able to overcome her anxiety. Her response to this pressure was an increase in anxiety culminating in slashing her wrists. When this was not accepted as evident proof of her fear of leaving home and attending school, she obtained the keys to the family car and drove it into a tree. After consultation with the therapist, her parents agreed to permit her to remain at home (where she did all her school work with dispatch) and to attend outpatient therapy as frequently as possible. The parents were advised as to the potential danger of keeping her as an outpatient but they felt this was preferable to hospitalization.

Joan, age 16, was presented for consultation because of barbiturate addiction, obesity, and petty thievery. She was constantly getting into fights with both mother and father but in general demonstrated her depression in her constant need for reassurance from the mother. She had a younger brother about whom she had overt incestuous fantasies. The difficulty began when she was 13 years of age, shortly after establishing the addiction to barbiturates which was part of an attempt to cure her obesity. She began to take amphetamine drugs, once taking so much that she had to be hospitalized. Retrospectively, it could be seen that much of her behavior was due to her being flooded by her incestuous feelings for her brother, which in turn were the outgrowth of the unresolved oedipal feelings toward her father.

Character Neuroses

At times, warding off depression can result in antisocial or delinquent activity. But when the repressed returns into consciousness, the self-destructive aspect of the abnormal behavior becomes clear.

Bob was born in Australia and he and his parents had moved to this country in the early part of 1950. He seemingly got along well the first few years, but then began acting out, in a long series of antisocial activities. Despite very superior intellect he was failing in school and it was observed that he seemed to lack energy in performance of any of his duties. His general mood was one of depression and he was unable to say anything nice about himself, knowing constantly that the antisocial activity was wrong. He was 17 at the time of referral, at which time the depressive qualities were especially noted and treatment was urgently recommended, but was refused. Repeated difficulties occurred, each one of them becoming more severe, as he tended to involve himself with the law. A short while after the initial consultation, the agency, through which he was originally seen, learned that he had killed himself driving 95 miles an hour, trying to avoid being picked up for speeding by the police.

Jerry, too, acted out antisocially during his adolescent period. A short episode will be reported in connection with his problems. He was first seen when he was 12, rather sporadically at that time, but more intensively at age 14. He reported that preceding each of the delinquent acts, whether stealing or speeding in his automobile, he would experience a deep and all-pervasive depressive feeling. The delinquent act could be seen to be an expression of defense against this depression, a means of attempting to deny his impotence by feeling omnipotent, and to reestablish magic means of avoiding feeling inferior. Following one of the hours in which he spoke with tremendous feeling about his depressions, he was seen driving his car away from the office, swerving into the oncoming line of traffic, only to avoid it at the last moment. In the subsequent hours, when he was confronted with this activity, he mentioned that he felt extremely depressed when he left and that something accidentally fell from the seat of his car which he bent down to pick up. In this case, placement away from home was recommended as soon as his pathologic relationship with his mother could be identified. In treatment he could see his attempts to force his mother into gratifying his wishes by the constant threat of self-injury (26, 27, 28).

Perversions

Many cases which have been attributed to "accidental" death have been cases involving transvestites. As part of the pathology of the perversion, many of these people not only dress themselves in female garments, but also bind themselves with ropes and chains around their limbs as well as the neck. Death of these boys has occurred during the period in which they apparently are struggling against the bonds as part of the acting out of their fantasy. The dynamics of the transvestite have been described elsewhere (6). The fantasy includes an identification with the female and a passive submission in a sexual act to an aggressor. Death therefore can be seen in these particular boys as a suicide in which the act itself represents the final submission to the all-powerful male figure (2).

Joe was 12 at the time that his parents discovered his tendencies to dress in female clothing. They attempted many different approaches, from exhortation and injunction to psychiatric treatment—all to no avail. Finally because of a very difficult home situation, he was placed in a private boarding school for a period of a year. On his return home during a summer vacation, the parents were pleased to notice no recurrence of the symptoms. However, when away from the city on a vacation, they left him alone in the motel for approximately an hour. On their return they found him dressed in his older sister's clothing, bound hand and foot to a chair with one of the ropes tautly around his neck. He was semiconscious and required the aid of the fire department to bring him completely back to consciousness. Briefly, this boy's history revealed a constant comparison between himself and his older, very attractive sister. He suffered from a mild form of cerebral palsy, resulting in difficulties in motor coordination. His defects only increased the amount of dislike that the boy's father had for him. The sister not only was attractive but was talented in many different areas. As Joe grew older, his wish to be a girl remained in the form of open comparisons between himself and his sister, as well as in stating that girls have a better deal than boys. He had acne at a relatively early age and would insist upon the father's expressing the comedones and pustules every night. The frequent arguments at home were stimulated and provoked by him and would result in the father's severely attacking him both verbally and physically. During the period away from home, there was no evidence of dressing in female clothing. Since this was the case, placement away from home was again recommended by another physician. On return home following the last episode of school placement, this child was again seen to dress in female clothes and bind himself when alone. His mother feared a repetition of the previous episode and called for consultation. The boy was a withdrawn and hostile youngster who identified mainly with the mother and sister and repeatedly demonstrated his female identification, constantly provoking his father. He was seen intensively for a period of a year, and the self-destructive elements, as especially seen in his sadomasochistic relationship with his father, were noted and interpreted.

Psychoses

Psychotic children also at times commit suicide. Their suicide has many different aspects; one of the facets can be seen in the following case:

Paul was 14 when he was first referred for treatment. He was referred primarily because of a difficulty in getting to school on time. Many obsessive-compulsive defenses were noted. However, shortly after the first month of contact, he began talking about creatures from another planet who were sent to this earth to observe him. As he spoke about his past and present, it could be seen that he used primary-process thinking most often. He reported a persistent fantasy: He was alone on top of a peninsular high cliff. The feeling of desolation, isolation, and loneliness was very frightening. He attempted to combat this feeling by becoming hostilely attached to a number of different people, but each time that he did this he felt that he was being swallowed up. He described himself as a chameleon. During a period in which the loss of ego boundaries was particularly evident (5), he began to talk in an affectless way about doing away with himself. Coupled with this was the threat of killing his siblings and parents. Immediate hospitalization was advised as well as placement on Thorazine (75 mg. per day). Facilities for adolescent boys are limited. His parents and responsible relatives were advised as to his condition and he was constantly watched. The father had some firearms and he removed them from the home. The Thorazine was increased (to 150 mg. per day) until placement was found. Unfortunately, this was out of the city. When last heard from, he was still on sedation and refused to come home for a visit.

TREATMENT

The handling of suicides or suicidal equivalents in children is based entirely on the concept of actual or threatened loss of the love object. The child's act is considered to be not just an attack on this object but also an attempt to regain it. The depressive elements in all cases are outstanding. Therefore, irrespective of the diagnostic category the case presents, treatment consists of strengthening object relationships (20).

Intensive psychotherapy on an outpatient basis can be established. In this therapy, not only is there a need to make a quick and firm relationship with the therapist, who must be most giving, but also, as soon as possible, to give interpretations so that the child can understand his motivations. At times the hospital or foster home placement must be called upon as a means of removing the child from the frustrating environment and also as an aid in preventing the child from attacking himself. Sedatives and tranquilizing drugs can be used to allay the anxiety and/or depression sufficiently so that the relationship with the therapist can take place. The parents as well as others in the environment must not only be advised as to the danger in the situation but must be included in the attempt to gratify some of the instinctual needs of the child. Those in charge of the patient should have explained to them what feelings the child is attempting to express in his actions (2). Even intellectual insights into some of the dynamics can be of help.

Despite the frequency with which depression occurs, electroconvulsive therapy is not used, as this cannot be of value in increasing the chances of the therapist to form adequate object relationships with the patient. Other physicians can be of help in supporting and explaining the situation to the parents as well as in controlling any physical concomitants in the child. If any doubt exists as to the diagnosis or treatment plan, consultation should be sought (3, 5, 7, 14, 19, 29, 30).

Suicide in children has multiple motivations, but the primary dynamic reason is the real or threatened loss of a love object. Treatment consists primarily of reestablishing adequate rewarding and gratifying object relationships.

References

1. Bender, L., and P. Schilder, Aggressiveness in children. *Genetic Psychology Monographs,* 18: 410–526, 1936.
2. Bibring, E., The mechanism of depression. (In Greenacre, P. [Ed.], *Affective Disorders.*) New York: International Universities Press, Inc., 1953.
3. Despert, J. L., Suicide and depression in children. *Nervous Child,* 41: 378–389, 1954.
4. Deutsch, F., *The Psychosomatic Concept in Psychoanalysis.* New York: International Universities Press, Inc., 1953.
5. Erickson, E. H., The problem of ego identity. *Journal of the American Psychoanalytic Association,* 4: 56–121, 1956.
6. Fenichel, O., *The Psychoanalytic Theory of Neurosis.* New York: W. W. Norton & Company, Inc., 1945.
7. ———, The psychology of transvestism. *International Journal of Psychoanalysis,* 11: 211–227, 1930.
8. Fowler, C., Suicide as a symptom of neurotic conflict in children. *Smith College Studies in Social Work,* 19, no. 2, 1943.
9. Freud, Anna, Psychoanalysis and education. (In *Psychoanalytic Study of the Child,* volume IX.) New York: International Universities Press, Inc., 1954.
10. Freud, S., Mourning and melancholia. (In *Collected Papers,* volume IV.) London: Hogarth Press, Ltd., 1925.
11. Gero, G., An equivalent of depression: anorexia. (In Greenacre, P. [Ed.], *Affective Disorders.*) New York: International Universities Press, 1953.
12. Greenacre, P. (Ed.), *Affective Disorders.* New York: International Universities Press, Inc., 1953.

13. Jacobson, E., Depression: the Oedipus complex in the development of depressive mechanisms. *Psychoanalytic Quarterly*, 12: 541–560, 1943.

14. Kanner, L., *Child Psychiatry*. Springfield, Ill.: Charles C. Thomas, 1948.

15. Keeler, W. R., Children's reaction to the death of a parent. (In Hoch, P. H., and J. Zubin [Eds.], *Depression*.) New York: Grune & Stratton, Inc., 1954.

16. Mason, P., Suicide in adolescents. *Psychoanalytic Review*, 41: 48–54, 1954.

17. Menninger, K. A., Psychoanalytic aspects of suicide. *International Journal of Psychoanalysis*, 14: 376–390, 1933.

18. Milner, M., A suicidal symptom in a child of three. *International Journal of Psychoanalysis*, 25: 53–61, 1944.

19. Powers, D., Youthful suicide attempts. *Northwest Medicine*, 53: 1001–1002, 1954.

20. Rochlin, G., Loss and restitution. (In *Psychoanalytic Study of the Child*, volume VIII.) New York: International Universities Press, Inc., 1953.

21. Schilder, P., and D. Wechsler, The attitudes of children toward death. *Journal of Genetic Psychology*, 45: 406–451, 1934.

22. Spitz, R. A., Hospitalism: An inquiry into the genesis of psychotic conditions in early childhood. (In *Psychoanalytic Study of the Child*, volume I.) New York: International Universities Press, Inc., 1945.

23. ———, Hospitalism: A follow-up report on investigation described in volume I, 1945. (In *Psychoanalytic Study of the Child*, volume II.) New York: International Universities Press, Inc., 1946.

24. ———, Anaclitic depression: An inquiry into the genesis of psychotic conditions in early childhood. (In *Psychoanalytic Study of the Child*, volume II.) New York: International Universities Press, Inc., 1946.

25. ———, Physiologic aspects of infantile depression. (In Hoch, P. H., and J. Zubin [Eds.], *Depression*.) New York: Grune & Stratton, Inc., 1954.

26. Stearns, A. W., Cases of probable suicide in young persons without obvious motivation. *Journal of the Maine Medical Association*, 43: 16–23, 1953.

27. ———, Accident or suicide? *Journal of the Maine Medical Association*, 46: 313–320, 336–337, 1955.

28. Sterba, E., The school boy suicide in André Gide's novel 'The Counterfeiters.' *American Imago*, 8: 307–320, 1951.

29. Zilboorg, G., Suicide among civilized and primitive races. *American Journal of Psychiatry*, 92: 1347–1369, 1936.

30. ———, Considerations on suicide with particular reference to that of the young. *American Journal of Orthopsychiatry*, 7: 15–31, 1937.

14

Suicide in Old Age

I. R. C. BATCHELOR

If the layman were asked to guess if suicide is common in old age, probably he would answer no. Old people, he might argue, are not given to rash and violent actions but are typically overcautious and conservative; and he would remember the many old people he had known who had clung so tenaciously to the tatters of their lives. Yet the facts are that, in many countries of Western civilization, suicide is relatively more common in the higher age groups, and with the exception of extreme old age, it becomes a progressively more frequent reaction both in men and women as they grow older. Male and female attempted suicide and suicide rates vary according to the culture in which the individual lives, but there appears to be a general tendency in old age for male rates for suicidal acts to be higher. As the proportion of old people in our communities becomes larger, suicide among them is likely to become an increasing medical and social problem (8).

What are the reasons for this association of suicide with old age? According to the theory of the four humors, which was developed in classical antiquity and accepted for centuries, melancholy belonged to autumn and evening and the threshold of old age, which is crossed about the sixtieth year. Medical writings on suicide have recorded the *taedium vitae* which may overcome the old person as he struggles with physical discomforts and disablement, his feelings of futility in idleness, and his loneliness amidst accumulating sorrows and the shadow of incapacity and death. Recent investigations of mental illness after the age of sixty have reemphasized the close link between depressive illness and old age, and recent psychiatric studies of cases of attempted suicide have also demonstrated the significance of depressive illness as the common setting of suicidal acts in this age group. At all ages, both individual and social factors contribute to the

143

genesis of suicide. In old age, individual factors are the more important, and mental illness of a clearly recognizable kind plays a leading role.

It is probable that in old age attempted suicides and suicides fall into clinical groups which, if not identical, are very closely allied. In old age, a suicidal attempt is rarely a gesture or threat; it is usually a suicide which has failed for reasons other than the seriousness and determination of the actor. The study of attempted suicides in old age can therefore give us much information about the problem of suicide itself. The description which follows is based on this assumption. There are a number of important points about which there is still uncertainty and which must be elucidated by further studies, for example, the significance of social isolation and loneliness in this group, the nature of the acute confusional reactions, and the incidence of organic psychoses. However, two independent investigations of a series of cases of attempted suicide after the age of sixty (3, 5), carried out in Scotland and the United States, have reported findings which are so alike that we may feel some confidence that the main lines of the picture can now be correctly drawn.

FAMILY AND PREVIOUS PERSONAL HISTORIES

There was a family history of psychiatric abnormalities in the majority, and in 17 per cent of a series of 40 cases there was a family history of suicidal acts. An apparent familial manic-depressive trait is commonly important.

Suicidal old people rarely come from the erratic, delinquent, socially mobile elements in the population. Most of them have had satisfactory work records. But it is perhaps only about a quarter who have been unequivocably stable. One may expect at least half to have had previous mental illnesses, usually depressive in character, and there may be a history of suicidal attempt in a previous illness. Those who have not been mentally ill previously often show personality traits which limit social adaptation—undue sensitivity and shyness, dependency, egocentricity and restricted interests, anxiety, and hypochondriasis are frequently reported by relatives. In the Edinburgh series (3), social adaptation was considered defective in one-half of the cases, who had kept outside social groupings and had had few friends; while one-quarter of the whole group had not married. Further investigation of the previous personalities of this suicidal group is required, however, since, in the St. Louis series, O'Neal and her colleagues (5) considered that there was little or nothing exceptional in the previous personal histories of their patients.

A broken home in childhood seems to play a significant part in many suicidal attempts (4), but more particularly in the case of young—and especially psychopathic—individuals than in old people.

REACTION TYPES

In old age, the great majority of suicidal people are suffering from psychoses—they could be certified as of unsound mind—and fall into two clinical groups: the depressive states and the organic dementias. Whatever the reaction type, it is probable that all are depressed.

The majority are suffering from depressions, usually from the depressive phase of manic-depressive psychosis. Their illnesses are typical symptomatically. Depression, insomnia, tension, and agitation are almost always present together. The individual usually is not markedly retarded but may feel muddled. Hypochondriacal bodily complaints are centered often on the head or alimentary tract and often are frankly delusional; the individual may state, for example, that his head or abdomen will burst as a result of the internal pressure which he feels. Delusions of poverty may be expressed. A nameless dread may assail the patient, so that he is afraid to be left alone. Fears of having contracted a fatal physical illness, or of insanity, are common, and the threat of admission to a mental hospital is not infrequently the immediate precipitant of a suicidal attempt. There may be ideas of reference and in a small number of cases there are auditory hallucinations. Only a minority make overt suicidal threats.

The minority of suicidal old people are suffering from the typical organic psychoses of the senium—cerebral arteriosclerosis or senile dementia. Sainsbury (7) reported senile and arteriosclerotic psychoses in 10 per cent of 409 suicides of various ages (an unexpectedly high incidence), while among attempted suicides after the age of sixty, O'Neal and others (5) found 26 per cent and Batchelor and Napier (3) 10 per cent falling into these categories. Probably in most of these cases the dementia is not gross and there is a marked affective component; in some cases one in fact would be justified in diagnosing a concurrent depressive illness. There may be a history of a previous attack of depression. In all cases, sufficient affect and volition must have been retained to allow the individual to feel despair and to follow its promptings.

A small number of old people attempt suicide when confused. This confusion is usually of acute onset and is transient. Probably, it is most often organically determined—a delirium due to intoxication, cerebral anemia, metabolic disorder, or vitamin deficiency. In a few cases it appears to be psychogenic—such as a sudden panic reaction in a setting of despair and bewilderment which leads to clouding of consciousness and disorientation.

In the cases of this type which we have seen, there was no definite evidence of physical illness and the confusion cleared to reveal a profound depression.

Suicide in old age is also attempted by a few people who fall into other reaction types more commonly found among younger suicides.

PHYSICAL ILLNESS AND ITS EFFECTS

Although the majority of suicidal old people are suffering from significant physical illness or disability at the times of their self-injury, physical illness is the major precipitating factor probably only in the minority of cases. It is of course to be expected in this age group that degenerative diseases, particularly of the cardiovascular and nervous systems, will be commonly found. The latter directly diminish control over conduct, while physical illness elsewhere may also weaken inhibitions by causing fatigue and by diminishing the general resistance of the individual to stress. Physical illness may also initiate brooding and introspection, bringing the old person to a harsh realization of his frailty or the threat of permanent invalidism and dependence. Some old people dread helplessness more than death. Many old people after their suicidal attempts say that they had with great distress suddenly "felt their age," or felt "done." It seems that if this painful self-awareness is abrupt, it is more likely to be intolerable. Commonly, dysfunctions due to the wearing out of the body become the foci for depressive hypochondriacal delusions and fears.

OTHER PRECIPITATING FACTORS AND MOTIVES

The most important determining factor for suicide in old age is the mental illness from which the old person usually is suffering at this time. This illness cannot however be separated from the circumstances of his life and his emotional reactions to these circumstances. Where a suicidal act has occurred in the setting of a depressive psychosis, one may say that it would not have happened had the illness not developed; however, the mental illness in itself is not often a sufficient explanation of suicide, and one should scrutinize the individual situation in every case to try to discover the particular causes of unhappiness which have driven the person to such an issue. In younger people, suicidal attempts are often precipitated by obvious external events, such as quarrels or demands for settlement of debt; hate and evasion are prominent motives. In old age the situations are different, suicide is rarely an immediate response to a crude frustration, and precipitating factors and motives tend to be less easily identifiable because they are more subtle.

Among the attempted suicides recently investigated in Scotland (3), feelings of loneliness, of being a burden on others, or of being unwanted were found in 23 out of 40 cases. These feelings were communicated to the doctor or were expressed in suicide notes. All those individuals who had been living alone or in a lodginghouse spoke of their loneliness, but those who had been living with a spouse did not. Loneliness was also complained of by some of the old people who might have seemed superficially sufficiently integrated in the community, since they had been living with their offspring; they had been or felt rejected by these younger people, or unable to keep their pace. These findings match those of Sainsbury (7), who, in a detailed examination of suicides in London, found a significant correlation of suicide rates with rates for social isolation, and came to the conclusion that social isolation provides a consistent explanation of the high incidence of suicide found in a wide variety of social groups—the aged, unemployed, and divorced, and among immigrants. On the other hand, O'Neal and her associates found that only three of their nineteen subjects gave loneliness as a reason for suicide attempts; and in each of these cases the loneliness had resulted from the death of a loved one. The importance of loneliness is therefore an aspect that requires further investigation.

There is no doubt that the loss of a loved one may be an important precipitating factor. In old age, the death of the spouse is particularly hard to bear, and the wish to become reunited with the spouse may override the wish to live. Identification with, or the hope of rejoining, a dead person is a factor in perhaps as many as a quarter of all suicidal attempts, both in youth and in old age.

Other social factors which may be significant in certain cases are retirement (in males) from employment, changed domestic circumstances, and financial anxieties. Sainsbury has noted that during World War II in England, when elderly men were able to obtain useful employment, the suicide rate among them fell more than that of younger men. In investigating cases of attempted suicide, one also finds a few cases in which retirement has clearly been an immediate factor in precipitating breakdown by causing feelings of uselessness and lack of purpose. Changes of home and district and removal from friends and associations are often poorly tolerated in old age. Those who have lost much in social status, financially or otherwise, particularly if the blow has been sudden and unexpected, are more likely to commit suicide than those who have always been used to little.

Alcohol may, by releasing inhibitions, precipitate a suicidal attempt in old age by an individual who may or may not have previously taken alcohol in excess. The amount of alcohol consumed is usually not sufficient to produce amnesia. In old age alcohol is less commonly a factor in suicidal attempts than it is with younger, temperamentally unstable people (1).

Among the deeper motivations of suicidal acts in old age, as at all ages, one finds the emotions of hate, fear, and guilt. Perhaps because suicide in old age is not often closely connected with some particular personal relationship which has become disturbed and caused the release of intense ambivalent feelings, hatred of another person (turned against the self) is a less common factor in these acts than it is in younger age groups. Nor, rather surprisingly, does guilt commonly appear to be a prominent motive, although depression is the usual reaction type. Fears often seem to be derived from the other symptoms of the patient's illness, although they may of course have deeper origins.

It must be emphasized that the etiology of these acts is multiple, and that our knowledge of their dynamics is in many individual cases only partial and superficial.

THE SUICIDAL ACTS

Although many old people take overdoses of hypnotic drugs, other poisons, or gas, the majority who kill themselves employ more active methods such as cutting, drowning, leaping, strangling, or shooting. This trend is revealed also in their abortive attempts, wherein violent methods are more commonly employed than they are by younger people. The suicidal attempts of old people are nearly always genuine and are usually admitted, and of those few who deny their suicidal intentions most admit to recent feelings of hopelessness. The minority of these attempts are impulsive; many have been contemplated and brooded over (often silently) for weeks or months. One suicidal attempt may be followed by a later one in the same illness.

PROPHYLAXIS AND TREATMENT

The prophylaxis of suicide depends on our knowledge of the causes of suicide in a particular group or country and on our being able either to prevent these causes or to treat them effectively if they have arisen. We now know enough about the etiology of suicide in old age to be able to make some practical suggestions about prophylaxis, which has both social and medical aspects.

We know that old people are more apt to suffer mental breakdown if they are not socially integrated in the community and if they do not feel useful, valued, and loved. We should therefore encourage old people to continue in their occupations for as long as possible—and we must make this administratively possible. Family ties should be kept close; for the lonely, social clubs should be provided, especially in our cities; we should see that retirement and leisure can be happily used; in every way we should foster in the community an understanding of the psychologic needs of old people and of the social role they should play as transmitters of the culture's traditions. The old person who feels that he is a burden upon his relatives is likely to want to relieve them of that burden by his death.

Those whose mental health has been preserved in earlier years are less likely to become suicidal in old age. Those with a history of previous depression will require special care, since a further attack in old age is likely to be not so well tolerated as previously. Any depression or other psychotic illness with depression as a symptom must be treated promptly with full awareness of the suicidal risk. Any suicidal talk by an old person should be considered as a warning of a suicidal attempt. Neither must physical illness be forgotten in this connection, since its debilitating or toxic effects, and the fears which may accompany it, can precipitate mental breakdown.

When an old person has attempted suicide, the self-injury usually requires urgent medical or surgical treatment. In addition, in every case, a thorough and unhurried investigation of the whole situation is essential; the patient's mental and physical status and his social environment must all be assessed. It is most convenient therefore to admit the old person initially to a general hospital. He need not stay there long after his injuries have been treated, but while he is there sedation and protection from further self-injury are essential. During this time a meticulous physical examination must be carried out, as well as any laboratory investigations which may be indicated. Energetic treatment of cardiac or renal failure, of diabetes mellitus, or of vitamin deficiency may result, particularly in those cases with clouding of consciousness, in a marked improvement in the mental state. The latter requires, of course, equally careful investigation, and if possible the opinion of a psychiatrist should be obtained in every case. A psychiatric social worker should report on the home background. It is only after all these data have been collected that suitable plans can be made for the old person's future. In the majority of cases, mental hospital treatment is indicated, and the patient will often accept this voluntarily. Discharge should be to the care of relatives or friends, or to a hostel; some continuing contact with the doctor and social worker is often helpful, whether or not inpatient psychiatric treatment has been required. A suicidal old person should never be quickly discharged from the hospital in the facile belief that what he has done was really a mistake or that having learnt a lesson he will not try it again. His psychic wounds must be healed as well as his physical ones, if his life is to be properly safeguarded. Electric convulsion therapy, modified by the use of the anesthetic thiopental and the muscle-relaxant succinylcholine chloride, permits the treatment of depressions in old age which, without this aid, might prove much more prolonged and dangerous.

PROGNOSIS

When suicide is attempted by an old person suffering from an organic dementia or from a personality deviation of long standing, the prognosis is of course invariably bad—deterioration will be progressive. On the other hand, an acute confusional state carries usually a much better prognosis, at any rate in the shorter term.

Of those in this age group who attempt suicide while suffering from depressions, about 60 per cent recover from their illnesses and return home, and some resume gainful employment. The relapse rate is high, however, and perhaps one-fifth will have further depressions within the next two years. Furthermore, a considerable number die soon of physical illness.

Both American and British studies (2, 5) suggest that of those who attempt suicide in old age, around 12 per cent will commit suicide within two years. This suicide rate is several times higher than one finds in the follow-up of young adults who have attempted suicide. The rigidity of old age shows itself also plainly in the suicidal pattern. The ultimate suicidal act tends to be carried out in the same setting of depressive illness, for the same motives, and in the same way as the earlier attempt.

One may state that usually a suicidal attempt by a mentally ill old person indicates a favorable rather than an unfavorable prognosis for that illness. The long-term prognosis then depends considerably on the old person's physical state, on the promptitude with which a relapse into depressive illness is recognized, and on the efficiency with which that relapse is treated.

References

1. Batchelor, I. R. C., Alcoholism and attempted suicide. *Journal of Mental Science,* 100: 451–461, 1954.
2. ———, Management and prognosis of suicidal attempts in old age. *Geriatrics,* 10: 291–293, 1955.
3. ——— and M. B. Napier, Attempted suicide in old age. *British Medical Journal,* 2: 1186–1190, 1953.

4. ———— and ————, Broken homes and attempted suicide. *British Journal of Delinquency,* 4: 99–108, 1953.
5. O'Neal, P., E. Robins, and E. H. Schmidt, A psychiatric study of attempted suicide in persons over sixty years of age. *Archives of Neurology and Psychiatry,* 75: 275–284, 1956.
6. Roth, M., and J. D. Morrissey, Problems in the diagnosis and classification of mental disorder in old age. *Journal of Mental Science,* 98: 66–80, 1952.
7. Sainsbury, P., *Suicide in London.* London: Chapman & Hall, Ltd., 1955.
8. Swinscow, D., Some suicide statistics. *British Medical Journal,* 1: 1417–1423, 1951.

15

Suicide in a General Hospital

SEYMOUR POLLACK

This chapter is concerned with the problem of suicide in a general medical and surgical hospital. An analysis was made of the clinical records of 11 hospitalized patients who committed suicide while under medical care and observation. The purpose here is to suggest possible clues which physicians in a general hospital setting may use to recognize potential suicidal risks.

Although there have been many studies of attempted suicide in the general population, with elaborate statistical and epidemiologic analysis of the data, there have been relatively few studies of suicide committed within the hospital setting. Recently, clinical evaluations of suicide attempts have been made in order to guide therapy and clinical management of patients after their recovery, to evaluate the seriousness of the suicidal risk, and to suggest an approach which might reduce the suicidal possibility after patients have been discharged. The follow-up study by Schmidt, O'Neal, and Robins (3) of attempted suicide in 109 patients admitted during five months in 1953 to the St. Louis City Hospital emphasized that two-thirds of their patients were psychiatric casualties. They noted significant distinguishing features between two groups: those patients with a serious suicidal risk and those in a nonserious suicidal risk group. Patients with a diagnosis of either manic-depressive depression or dementia were considered serious suicidal risks, whereas patients with psychopathic personality or chronic alcoholism were considered to be slight (nonserious) suicide risks. It was emphasized that significant findings helpful in differentiating patients with serious risk from those with nonserious risk were readily obtained while taking a history and observing the patient. Also significant was the conclusion that special psychiatric techniques and training were not needed for this evaluation, but some clinical knowledge of psychiatric

152

disease was indispensable for a proper evaluation of suicide risk in these patients.

A few suicides occur within psychiatric facilities in spite of the most protective surveillance. A recent study by Banen (1) analyzed the records of psychiatric patients at the Bedford (Massachusetts) Veterans Administration Neuropsychiatric Hospital at the time of their suicide. In the twenty-five-year period between 1928 and 1953 there were only 23 successful suicide attempts by the psychiatric hospital population. Of these 23 patients, 12 were on furlough or on pass from the hospital when they committed suicide, and only 11 patients were actually under observation in the neuropsychiatric hospital at the time of their death. An analysis of the clinical histories of these 11 hospitalized cases of suicide while under psychiatric observation revealed the inherent difficulties, even under optimal neuropsychiatric hospital conditions, in evaluating the suicidal risk. The difficulties in forecasting and preventing suicide attempts despite the most careful precautionary measures were discussed.

A more recent study by Levy and Southcombe (2) revealed that 58 suicides were committed in a state mental hospital in the 58 years covered by the study, during which time 15,199 neuropsychiatric patients were admitted for care and treatment. The suicide rate for this hospitalized group of psychiatrically disturbed patients ranged from 42 per 10,000 admissions in the years 1891 to 1936 to 32 per 10,000 admissions in the years 1936 to 1949. During this latter period electric shock treatment was instituted and freely used. The authors concluded, however, that the suicide rate for younger hospitalized patients changed very little after the introduction of shock therapy. Decrease in the suicide rate noted in the older hospitalized patients after the introduction of shock therapy did not appear related to the influence of shock treatment, because this form of treatment was infrequently used in the older age group.

Increasing attention has been called to the need of the nonpsychiatric physician to become more intimately acquainted with the psychiatric problems in medical practice, the subtle signs and symptoms of psychiatric pathology, hidden depressions, borderline psychoses, and so forth, and to the need to incorporate a psychiatric history and evaluation with the routine history and examination. The present study is concerned with the typical approach of the (nonpsychiatric) physician who has gathered a minimum of social and psychiatric history and who deals with his patients' medical and surgical problems largely by means of a clinical approach. From this study it is possible to emphasize those clinical features significant for possible suicide in the (general medical) hospitalized patient which the nonpsychiatric physician might have used for evaluation of the suicide hazard. It is true that a relatively small percentage of successful suicide attempts are made by hospitalized patients with organic syndromes or by patients with sufficiently severe physical disease to warrant hospitalization. But inasmuch as all such patients were under observation and treatment by physicians and hospital staff before the suicide attempt, certain questions can be raised by a review of the clinical records. What clinical conditions seen in general medical and surgical practice showed a high suicide risk? What clinical signs of suicide hazard appeared significant in this group of hospitalized patients? What difficulties appeared in the evaluation of emotional disturbances in the "nonpsychiatric" patients in the general hospital? How can the (nonpsychiatric) physician become more acquainted with the psychiatric problems of general medical practice as applied to the suicide problem? To try to answer these questions an analysis was made of suicides committed in a general hospital setting in which clinical records were available.

This study concerned itself with a detailed analysis of the clinical records of the eleven cases of successful suicide attempts committed by general medical and surgical patients during the five-year period from December, 1948, to December, 1953. In the hospital concerned, a Veterans Administration teaching hospital with close medical school affiliations, the total medical care, supervision, and treatment of patients is comparable to other grade A teaching hospitals. Suicide precautionary measures are instituted at the slightest suspicion of suicidal intent detected by the staff.

There are no "psychiatric beds" in this hospital, and no patients admitted for treatment are initially designated as "psychiatric patients." After admission, all seriously emotionally disturbed patients are immediately transferred to the adjoining neuropsychiatric hospital for special care, observation, and treatment. Psychiatric patients requiring medical or surgical care are not admitted to this general hospital but are admitted directly (along with all other psychiatric patients) to the adjoining neuropsychiatric facility. This is stressed in order to emphasize that the patients in this study were "nonpsychiatric patients" and, therefore, were comparable (except for their veteran status) to other general hospital patients.

Review of the case material showed that while patients were in the general hospital, depressed feelings and psychotic disturbances could develop or increase; bizarre reactions to continued or increased pain and suffering might develop; fear of suffering or of death might become manifest or increase; or the patients' state of consciousness might become sufficiently clouded to impair awareness and understanding of their surroundings and behavior. It is apparent that all such changes occurring in the general hospital setting could increase the possibility of suicide risk, and recognition of these changes would suggest that precautionary measures be taken. Immediately following his admission, the patient's emotional and mental status was often minimally disturbed, there were no frankly psychiatric or bizarre symptoms, and the emotional or mental status did not openly suggest a suicidal tendency or hazard. But sometimes, even on admission, there were suggestive signs of psychiatric disturbance which were noted in the record but were not correctly interpreted. An increased index of suspicion of suicide would help direct clinical attention to these signs and possibly lead to the institution of precautions against suicide.

Following are brief clinical studies of the eleven cases (all male) of suicide committed by hospitalized patients in a general medical and surgical hospital with presumptive (psychiatric) diagnoses based on subsequent evaluation of the history and clinical material.

Case 1

A 54-year-old Caucasian, Protestant, married, unemployed, admitted for treatment of epigastric pain and severe anemia. History and diagnosis of bleeding peptic ulcer, also diagnosis of hypertension, convulsive seizures, and cerebral arteriosclerosis. Previous NP (neuropsychiatric) history of organic psychosis with confusion state and convulsive syndrome. Following admission, patient showed signs of mild mental deterioration. Suicidal risk was not considered and no precautions were taken. Responded favorably to medical treatment until the thirty-third hospital day when he committed suicide by jumping from the fourth floor to ground. Suicidal act not observed. Presumed basis for suicide was a psychotic confusion state possibly related to a convulsive seizure.

Case 2

A 36-year-old Negro, Catholic, married, student, admitted for treatment of hemoptysis. History of chronic bronchitis with diagnosis of bronchiectasis. NP history revealed chronic, severe alcoholism. Following admission no significant psychiatric signs noted until shortly before suicidal act when sudden unprovoked anger and peculiar behavior were noted by neighboring patients. Suicide risk not considered and no precautions taken. Patient committed suicide on second hospital day by jumping from fourth floor window. Presumed basis for suicide was alcoholic (toxic) psychosis.

Case 3

A 44-year-old Caucasian, Protestant, divorced, student, admitted for treatment of upper respiratory infection. History and diagnosis of chronic bronchitis and bronchial asthma. Previous NP history and diagnosis of chronic alcoholism, psychosis with alcoholism and barbiturate intoxication, and schizoid personality. Following admission, patient appeared anxious, nervous, and tremulous. Nocturnally he appeared agitated with confusion, showed disorientation, hallucinations, and paranoid ideas, but during the day he showed clear sensorium without agitation or signs of psychosis. Suicide risk not considered and no precautions taken. Upper respiratory infection responded favorably to medical treatment until third hospital day when patient committed suicide by jumping from fourth floor window. Presumed basis for suicide was alcoholic psychosis.

Case 4

A 54-year-old Caucasian, no religion, divorced, unemployed, admitted for elective herniorrhaphy. Diagnosis of recent bilateral inguinal hernias and hypertension. No NP or alcoholic history. Following admission, patient showed emotional depression with strong guilt feelings, self-depreciatory and self-punitive ideas and attitudes. Suicide risk not considered and no precautions taken. Hospital course uneventful with patient awaiting surgery until tenth hospital day when he committed suicide by jumping from fourth floor washroom window. Presumed basis for suicide was involutional depression.

Case 5

A 26-year-old Negro, Protestant, single, aircraft worker, admitted for treatment of abdominal complaints. History and diagnosis of recurrent subacute pancreatitis. NP history negative except for history of chronic alcoholism and recent heavy alcoholism. Following admission, patient described as nocturnally agitated, delirious, and confused, but during the day he showed clear sensorium without psychosis. Suicide risk not considered and no precautions taken. Responded favorably to conservative medical treatment until fourth hospital day when he committed suicide by jumping from third floor window. Presumed basis for suicide was alcoholic psychosis.

Case 6

A 60-year-old Caucasian, Protestant, married, retired postal clerk, admitted for treatment of severe cardiac dyspnea and chest pain. Diagnosis of rheumatic and arteriosclerotic heart disease with cardiac decompensation. No NP history. Following admission patient appeared emotionally depressed and anxious about possibility of death, hyperreactive to his physical illness, and overly concerned about relatively insignificant items of hospital care. Suicide risk not considered and no precautions taken. He showed steady downhill physical course with auricular fibrillation and pulmonary edema not responding to medical management; on day before death appeared to be improving physically when on sixtieth hospital day he committed suicide by jumping from fifth floor window. Presumed basis for suicide was depression related to poor health.

Case 7

A 63-year-old Caucasian, Protestant, married, unemployed, admitted in coma for treatment of suspected acute barbiturate intoxication. Six-year history of general ill health, and diagnosis of generalized arteriosclerosis and arteriosclerotic heart disease. NP history of nervousness; varied somatic complaints unconfirmed by physical examination. A previous psychiatric diagnosis of hypochondriacal syndrome. At time of admission, the case was diagnosed as suspected attempted suicide with barbiturates. Barbiturate ingestion denied by patient and not confirmed by laboratory studies. Following admission patient was unresponsive for the first four days and subsequently improved physically but was emotionally depressed, withdrawn, and uncommunicative; patient appeared unhappy about lack of success in suicide attempt; on the fifth day he expressed delusional paranoid ideas with bizarre behavior. Suicide risk noted by doctors but not considered high. There was no further suicide intent observed following admission; on last day, suicide precautions were recommended with additional observation and bed rails, but on sixth hospital day patient committed suicide by jumping from fourth floor window. Presumed basis for suicide was psychotic depression.

Case 8

A 48-year-old Caucasian, unknown religion, single, aircraft worker, admitted for treatment of hypertensive encephalopathy. NP history of hypertension with gradual mental changes. Recently more severe mental and personality changes noted with emotional depression and schizoid behavior accompanying the clinical signs of encephalopathy. Following admission, patient showed progressively increasing personality disorder with development on fifth hospital day of agitated depression, preoccupation with intense guilt feeling about early sex behavior, and guilty fear of having developed venereal disease; patient associated his encephalopathy to VD. Suicide risk observed with increasing awareness of patient's suicide threat on seventh hospital day. Suicide precautions recommended with additional observation and emergency psychiatric consultation requested on seventh hospital day, shortly before patient's suicide, which was executed by jumping from fifth floor bathroom window. Presumed basis for suicide was psychotic agitated depression, probably related to chronic brain syndrome with hypertensive encephalopathy.

Case 9

A 61-year-old Caucasian, Catholic, married, unemployed, admitted for treatment of severe asthma. History and diagnosis of chronic bronchial asthma treated at hospital without sustained improvement. NP history of excitable "hysterical" behavior and emotional instability with marked fear of death and exaggerated reaction to the physical signs and symptoms of illness. Following his admission, the patient's physical condition remained unchanged but was not considered critical. Suicide risk not considered and no suicide precautions taken. On day of suicide, the patient called his family to describe his unrelieved complaints and to tell them he was dying. Early in the morning on the seventh hospital day the patient was seen praying by his bedside. Patient appeared more excitable and "hysterical." He committed suicide in ward washroom by lacerating neck and exsanguinating. Presumed basis for suicide was emotionally unstable personality with anxiety reaction and depression secondary to physical disease.

Case 10

A 64-year-old Caucasian, Protestant, divorced, unemployed, admitted for treatment of chronic respiratory disorder. History and diagnosis of chronic bronchitis and compensatory emphysema; also diagnosis of CNS (central nervous system) lues, late, with cranial nerve involvement, generalized arteriosclerosis, and inactive tuberculosis. NP history of anxiety reaction with depression, hyperventilation, and "hysterical" hyperreaction to physical difficulties. Following admission patient developed pneumonitis which responded favorably to antibiotic therapy. Suicide risk not considered and no suicide precautions taken. Nocturnal agitated confusion state with nocturnal disorientation noted from second hospital day, but patient appeared clear during day, demonstrating excessive and exaggerated physical complaints. Physically improving on the fifth hospital day, when patient committed suicide by jumping from fourth floor window. Presumed basis for suicide was psychotic confusion state related to cerebral arteriosclerosis and toxic state.

Case 11

A 65-year-old Caucasian, Protestant, married, retired carpenter, admitted for terminal care of metastatic cancer. Seven months history of malignancy with surgery five months before entry. Diagnosis of bronchogenic carcinoma with metastasis. No NP history on previous admissions except for report of patient's "mental aberrations" while he was taking ACTH therapy in previous hospital. No suicide intent noted and no suicide precautions taken. Following admission patient appeared more upset about inability to obtain relief from increasingly distressing dyspnea. On evening of second hospital day patient committed suicide by jumping from fifth floor window. Presumed basis for suicide was depression as reaction to extreme pain and physical disability.

In this series, all of the patients were male veterans with a wide range of age (from twenty-six to sixty-five), different racial extractions (nine Caucasian, two Negro), religious affiliations (six Protestant, three Catholic, one no religion, and one unknown), marital status (six married, three divorced, and two single), and occupational status (five unemployed, two retired, two aircraft workers, and two students).

Clinical features of the suicide patients also appeared significant. On admission, no patient (with the exception of Case 7, who was admitted with a diagnosis of suspected acute barbiturate intoxication) carried a psychiatric diagnosis, and no case during any period of hospitalization received a diagnosis of psychosis. Varied medical diagnoses were present: chronic respiratory conditions were present in four cases (Cases 2, 3, 10, 11) and arteriosclerosis was present in three (Cases 1, 6, 10)—conditions probably correlated with the high percentage of these medical disabilities seen in the selected geriatric population at the veterans hospital. All the patients had medical problems requiring evaluation and treatment in a general hospital setting, but only one (Case 11) could have been considered so critically ill before his suicide that he would have died shortly of his physical disease. Significantly, three-fourths of the patients were responding favorably to medical treatment and management until their deaths by suicide. Three cases (Cases 6, 9, 11) appeared nonpsychotic but showed increasing agitation with some depression related to the progress of their illness. They showed extremely strong emotional reactions to pain and disability as they continued in the hospital setting without getting relief from distressing physical symptoms. Although fear of death was present, and in two openly expressed, their agitation appeared more specifically related to the distressing physical disabilities than to the fear of death. The patients' fear of death was no deterrent to the final suicide. In all three of these patients the most distressing physical symptom was severe dyspnea from respiratory or cardiac disease; and all three, with a relatively long history of respiratory or cardiac disease, were sixty years of age or older, and retired or unemployed. All these factors would tend to lead to the same consequence, increasing unpleasant emotions with tension and agitation finally reaching an unbearable level. The specific tension-producing quality of severe dyspnea may have been of qualitative as well as quantitative importance in these patients.

The technique of suicide in all cases except one (Case 9) was jumping from a hospital window on the ward or in the bathroom or from an open ramp to the ground, four or five floors below. Death occurred immediately or almost immediately as a consequence of multiple traumatic injuries. The one patient hospitalized on the first floor committed suicide by cutting his throat.

It was noted that although nine of the eleven patients had a significant neuropsychiatric history (all but Cases 4 and 6), in only one was this history significant with respect to suicide risk (Case 7, admitted with a diagnosis of attempted suicide with barbiturates). The psychiatric histories obtained by the medical staff did not appear to have been correlated with the patients' clinical psychiatric pictures developed during hospitalization.

In the available psychiatric histories there was nothing (except in Case 7) that could have alerted the physician to a specific suicide hazard. Signs of acute brain syndrome with delirious reactions were present in seven patients (Cases 1, 2, 3, 5, 7, 8, 10), with signs in one (Case 1) probably related to a convulsive syndrome. The three patients under the age of fifty years (ages twenty-six, thirty-six, forty-four) gave a history of severe chronic alcoholism; and in these cases (Cases 2, 3, 5) an investigation of the doctors' histories, progress notes, and nurses' notes, describing the patients' mental and emotional states following admission, gave the definite impression that all three were suffering from alcoholic psychoses at the time of suicide. A clinical history of chronic brain syndrome and signs of acute or chronic brain syndrome with psychosis were present in four additional cases (Cases 1, 7, 8, 10) and allowed retrospective diagnoses of psychotic confusion states with superimposed acute toxic signs.

Diurnal variations in sensorium with nocturnal confusion, obvious disorientation, and psychotic reactions, characteristic of organic and toxic psychotic states, were noted in three cases (Cases 3, 5, 10). These observations were not made by the physicians to whom the patients' sensorium appeared clear during the day, but were clearly described in the night nurses' notes. Only one case (Case 4) showed definite signs of a functional psychotic reaction with agitated depression, marked guilt feelings, and self-depreciation, which were noted in the chart but to which little, if any, significance was attached.

The remaining three cases (Cases 6, 9, 11), all over sixty years of age, showed obvious and marked signs of emotional disturbance related to the physical disease and their distressing physical symptoms, but no definite clinical signs of psychosis could be inferred from the patients' clinical picture. Case 6 showed suspicious signs of an underlying psychotic reaction associated with a chronic brain syndrome, but because these were not sufficiently pronounced nor described with sufficient clarity in the notes, this patient was included with the nonpsychotic group. These patients showed marked emotional instability and tension with anxiety and depression, which appeared secondary to the physical disease. However, only one patient (Case 11) showed serious enough physical disease, with severe physical pain and disability (severe dyspnea and pain due to obstructive bronchogenic carcinoma with metastasis), to make the suicide appear related to the severe pain alone.

Only one patient showed no significant psychiatric signs at least twenty-four hours before the suicide; and this patient (Case 2) showed sudden, unprovoked anger and peculiar behavior on the ward, noted by his ward mates, immediately prior to his suicide. All of the other patients showed definite signs of serious emotional disturbance at least twenty-four hours, and many forty-eight hours or longer, before they committed suicide. These signs were of mental deterioration, marked anxiety, agitation and depression, toxic confusion with disorientation, hallucinations and delusions, intense guilt feelings about alleged early sex activities, marked preoccupation with physical symptoms and physical disability, marked self-depreciation, ideas of unworthiness, paranoid ideas, and continuous excessive dramatic demands for help and treatment. Because these signs of severe emotional disturbance and psychoses were not properly interpreted, there was no awareness of the possible suicide hazard in nine of the eleven cases. In two cases (Cases 7 and 8) signs of psychiatric disturbance were not considered significant of high or immediate suicide hazard and no stringent precautionary measures were instituted. In Case 7, the only case admitted for treatment of an attempted suicide, there were no definite precautions taken even though the patient appeared depressed, uncommunicative, and very angry about his failure in the attempted suicide. Psychiatric consultation was requested in only one of the eleven cases. In Case 8, the patient's behavior was considered sufficiently bizarre just before the suicide to prompt the physician to make a request for a psychiatric consultation and to recommend suicide precautions, but this patient committed suicide before either was carried out.

There were no specific psychiatric signs which could be cited as significant of suicide hazard, but the relationship between suicide risk and psychosis was apparent. The high suicide hazard for psychotic individuals has been stressed in many previously reported studies. This suicide risk may be even higher for those psychotic individuals who also have severe physical illnesses requiring hospital care with confinement and drug (especially barbiturate) treatment, or for those physically ill patients who develop psychotic reactions during the course of their illness and their hospitalization.

An evaluation of the limited neuropsychiatric histories revealed that behavior significant of neuropsychiatric disorder (including chronic alcoholism) was present in nine of the eleven cases, but the neuropsychiatric history was of little value for the evaluation of suicide risk. What was more significant was the impression that the suicide hazard in these hospitalized patients could be evaluated almost solely from the patients' clinical picture. Obvious psychiatric signs of severe emotional disturbance appeared at least twenty-four hours before the suicide in ten of the eleven patients, with seven of these ten showing frankly psychotic behavior during this time. Retrospective analysis of the clinical case records indicated that eight of the eleven patients who committed suicide had unrecognized psychoses: seven with organic psychotic reactions and one with an involutional psychotic reaction. Of the seven with organic psychoses, four had organic confusion states with psychotic depressive reactions associated with chronic brain syndromes, and three showed toxic psychotic reactions associated with their acute and chronic alcoholism.

There are many general hospital patients with neuropsychiatric histories who show serious personality problems or signs of emotional disturbance without psychosis. In attempting to highlight the clinical features characteristic of the few nonpsychotic patients in this study who committed suicide, the following constellation appeared indicative of a high suicide hazard: chronic progressive physical disability—especially severe dyspnea unimproved by treatment—in individuals sixty years of age or older showing long-standing hypochondriacal or "hysterical" reactions which reached a new high in intensity, coupled with an increasing depressive reaction, a feeling of hopelessness, and possibly the expression of a suicide idea or wish.

It may be concluded from the examination of these eleven clinical case histories of patients who committed suicide during their hospitalization in a general medical and surgical hospital that a suicide hazard exists in some patients seen by the hospital staff. Most patients in this series showed unrecognized psychoses associated with organic brain syndromes with confusion states and toxic psychotic reactions manifested at least twenty-four hours before the suicide. The evaluation of the patients' clinical picture brought to light no specific features significant of a high suicide risk beyond the general correlation between suicide hazard and psychosis. It may be concluded that the older male with a physical disability plus an organic psychotic reaction should be considered a suicide risk and precautions should be undertaken. It is not necessary that such patients in the general hospital be transferred to a neuropsychiatric facility for these precautions, but it is believed that suicide precautions should be considered as part of the total medical approach to these patients during their acutely disturbed state. It appears that the psychotic state with its suicide hazard can best be evaluated from the clinical picture of the toxic psychotic reaction and organic confusion state. The psychotic reactions were characterized by fluctuating confusion and disorientation, hallucinations and delusions— particularly of paranoid nature—agitated depression with self-depreciatory and self-punitive ideas and attitudes, and exaggerated guilt feelings, especially about early sexual behavior. The suicide patient who did not appear clinically psychotic showed a constellation of clinical features which also may be related to an increased suicide risk. He was an older male patient with chronic respiratory disability and severe dyspnea who showed increasing agitation and depression related to his lack of clinical improvement in the general hospital setting with accepted medical treatment, who showed increasing and exaggerated concern over insignificant items of his physical condition, and who made increasing complaints and demands for help, which he felt either were ignored or were considered hopeless and futile. None of the patients in this series of cases was considered psychiatrically ill or a suicide risk on admission or during his hospitalization, except for two patients whose disturbances were recognized before the suicide but not soon enough for institution of adequate suicide precautions. This emphasizes the increased need for psychiatric orientation in the nonpsychiatric staff physician. His difficulty in recognizing psychiatric syndromes may be related to a lack of psychiatric orientation and background with difficulty in recognizing psychiatric conditions (particularly psychotic states) outside of the accepted neuropsychiatric setting. Problems in evaluation of psychosis and suicide hazard in the general hospital probably resulted from a number of factors: (a) patients in a general hospital were not generally considered psychotic unless constantly, grossly, and visibly disturbed in behavior; (b) there appeared to be an unfamiliarity with the clinical picture of organic confusion states and the toxic psychotic reactions associated with alcoholism; (c) the suicide hazard had not been closely identified with organic psychosis by the nonpsychiatric physician, who showed a low index of suspicion of suicide in general hospital patients; and (d) psychiatric orientation among nonpsychiatric physicians generally appeared to be low.

References

1. Banen, D. M., Suicide by psychotics. *Bedford Research,* 4: 1–8, 1953.
2. Levy, S., and R. H. Southcombe, Suicide in a state hospital for the mentally ill. *Journal of Nervous and Mental Diseases.* 117: 504–514, 1953.
3. Schmidt, E. H., P. O'Neal, and E. Robins, Evaluation of suicide attempts as guide to therapy. *Journal of the American Medical Association,* 155: 549–557, 1954.

16

Observations on Attempted Suicide

NORMAN TABACHNICK

The clinical data reported in this chapter were gathered as part of a larger project on suicide conducted by Drs. Edwin Shneidman and Norman Farberow, and supported by funds from the United States Public Health Service. This part of the investigation represents an attempt to obtain data from persons in the *community* who have attempted suicide, as contrasted to the group who are more readily seen in neuropsychiatric hospitals. The patients comprised a group of about 60 individuals who had made suicidal attempts, the majority of whom were studied for a short period, but ten of whom to date were studied intensively with an attempt made to gather pertinent facts regarding the suicidal attempt, the previous history of the individual, and his dynamic personality make-up. The majority of these patients came from the medical wards of the Los Angeles County General Hospital, where they were admitted (in 1955 and 1956) on the basis of their need for treatment for an orally ingested drug or poison. (The fact that the subjects of this report attempted suicide via the oral route may be of considerable importance in determining the kind of data elicited from them, and it may be that the observations and conclusions apply only to patients who attempt suicide in this way.) The patients were interviewed shortly after admission to the hospital, or in the case of those who had been rendered unconscious or unable to communicate by reason of the effects of the drug or poison, after they were able to talk again. In the method of clinical investigation used, it was first necessary to establish rapport with the patients and then to have them freely associate to material that was centered around the suicidal attempt and around other significant areas in their lives. This procedure was supplemented by direct and specific questioning where this seemed valuable. Clinical observations on each case were, in addition, checked on a questionnaire consisting of 225 items of personality description.

It should be stressed that this particular report is a clinical study, not a statistical one, and that the observations and conclusions are necessarily empirical and intuitive.

The following observations refer to the apparent patterns of disturbance in early childhood in the suicidal persons, the precipitating sources of the suicidal attempts, and the motives of the suicidal acts.

The major dynamic factor which seemed quite striking was a recurring pattern of disturbance in early childhood in relationship to the mother or mother surrogate. Almost every patient examined seemed to show a significant kind of difficulty with the mother or the mothering and giving aspects of significant parental figures. The kind of relationship was different in various subjects within the group, but in general a feeling of rejection seemed to be important. The rejection occurred in different ways. In some situations the patient was deprived of the mother for long or short periods of time. An example of this kind was Case 1, that of a middle-aged woman, who in talking about her childhood experiences recalled being sent on frequent vacations by her mother. The mother overtly protested her love over and over again, but almost every summer the patient would be sent away for long periods of time without her mother. At other times when the mother seemed preoccupied with her own problems, the patient was left to live with friends or relatives. Also, she remembered that the mother in some ways would make demands on her—the mother would be ill, go to bed with sick headaches, and request the patient to take care of herself for the day or two the headache lasted. An important element in the personality of this woman was that she felt that it had always been impossible for her to express anger or dissatisfaction with her mother.

To other patients, the mother was seen predominantly as a dominant, controlling figure who was good to the patient but who exacted a price for her attention. This price was that anger or dissatisfaction with the mother never be expressed and that the child be continually obedient. Such was Case 2, a young man whose mother was the dominating parent in the family. She was a competent woman who controlled the lives of her children and her husband and also was an important figure in local social and political circles. There was an opportunity to see and to interview this mother who clearly demonstrated that she wanted her children always to do everything she said and never to have opinions of their own. The patient remembered that much of this continued during his entire life. He also remembered never being able openly to defy his mother and that he had constant moderate feelings of depression and inferiority.

In other cases, the mother was seen as a person who was incapable of giving real affection, through selfishness or emotional difficulties of her own. Case 9, a middle-aged woman who had made several suicide attempts during the past few years, was of this type. Her mother was described as selfish, mean, and petty; a woman who was interested only in her own status and, from the patient's point of view, used her husband and her children as steppingstones in her own drive for personal prestige. The patient recalled many events in which the mother seemed to be fearful and jealous of the love of the father and others for her children. Almost nothing that the mother ever did was seen by this patient as having other than a selfish motivation.

There was one instance, Case 7, in which there was some question of the mother's being the main culprit. Case 7 was a young man who made a suicide attempt at the age of twenty-three. His father had died when he was four or five years old, and the patient's mother remarried when he was six. The second father and the mother were both described as being fair, but in addition the father was spoken of as "strict." Although he denied feelings of rejection about this, the patient brought out the point that both mother and father had other preferred siblings and indicated that this had fostered his resentment. The question in this case is whether the mother or the father was the main source of rejection. On the whole it seems that both were, and it is perhaps significant that this patient made his suicidal attempt after considering divorce from his wife, to whom he had been married just one week. One of the reasons given for divorce was the feeling that his wife was not paying enough attention to him and was in fact going out with other men!

There were variations of these feelings and many times the mother was seen as possessing a mixture of undesirable attributes, but the total of the feeling toward the mother, in almost every instance, was that for some reason she had not been able or had been unwilling to give enough to the patient.

There seemed to be a common factor in the precipitating cause of the suicidal attempts. Here again, one notes a striking relationship to a mother figure. The suicide attempts, almost uniformly, were reactions to criticism by the mother or by a mothering figure. A variation of this as a precipitating cause was desertion by a mothering figure. Some examples of these types of precipitating events follow: First, there is the suicidal attempt precipitated by criticism by the actual mother. Such an example is Case 2. This is the young man referred to previously, whose entire life and training had been overseen and controlled by a dominating mother. In general he had never had great occasion to argue with her, but previous to his suicidal attempt, he had fallen in love with a girl of whom his mother disapproved. He became angry and depressed at his mother's unwillingness to approve of his intended marriage to the girl, and for a time he solved his problem by joining the army. When he returned, however, his positive feelings toward the girl and his feelings of resentment toward his mother became stronger. It was at this point that he made the suicide attempt. He described the pain which he experienced at his mother's opposition to the marriage as being quite intolerable and one of the hardest situations with which he had ever had to deal.

An example of desertion by a mother substitute is seen in Case 3. He was an inhibited elderly man whose health had been failing for some time so that he became dependent on his wife. The economic situation became such that the wife was forced to consider placing the patient in a rest home while she went out to work. It was at this point that the patient made his suicide attempt.

Another variation of this kind of precipitating event is the criticism by a mother substitute. Such was Case 6, a middle-aged woman who did not know her real parents but had been raised predominantly by a foster father. Her main feeling toward her own husband was that he, too, was a mothering individual. Because of differences in their cultural backgrounds, this patient found herself drawn to company other than her husband's. Her husband was willing to accept this situation for a period of time but finally became critical of her because of her social activities. It was then that the patient made a suicidal attempt.

The last group of clinical observations refer to the motives of the suicidal attempt. What was the patient actually trying to achieve? In what way did the suicidal act attempt to restore some equilibrium to a disordered mental economy? Here again a variety of factors was observed, and again it was difficult to say that any one factor was paramount in a single case. In the following abstracts an attempt will be made to point out what seemed to be the predominant motives for the suicidal attempts.

In Case 2, referred to previously, it seemed that the most important motive for the suicide was a need for punishment. The patient had been attempting to escape his anger toward his mother for some years; finally, this escape was no longer possible, and it was necessary for him to see that he was angry toward her. He was unable to tolerate this feeling and attempted to deal with it by running away, this time taking a trip to Mexico; yet this was not successful and finally he felt hopeless, as if he were left all alone. At this point he made his suicidal attempt. It would seem that what was really operative here was an attempt to get back into the good graces of his mother by "castrating" himself (by attempting to kill himself), and in this way to expiate his guilt.

In other cases there was a kind of symbolic killing of the hateful object. Such seemed to be true in Case 1, the middle-aged woman whose mate assumed many of the features of a mother. This patient's husband had died two years prior to the suicide attempt. Shortly after his death, she began a relationship with another man which paralleled in many ways her relationship to her husband; the man was protective and giving, the patient could ask for whatever she wanted and it was given her by her mate. However, after about a year of this kind of life, there was some retreat on the part of the second man, and he was no longer as sheltering as he had been. The patient's depression at this point became more severe and, finally, in a fit of unexpressed rage, she ingested some pills in an attempt to get rid of the bad "mother." There is considerable evidence to indicate that this woman actually became the same kind of person as her own mother; there was a good deal of evidence of identification with the mother. It is interesting to note that the mother had died by committing suicide.

In the cases that have been studied, there is a recurrence of certain themes which suggest that the patients involved suffered important traumas in the oral stage of their psychodynamic development. Repeatedly, the patients' mothers (in the patients' memories of them) seemed to be overtly or subtly hostile toward the patient. Attitudes of rejection, domination, and strictness often appeared to be present. Some of the patients as children were deprived of their mothers for shorter or longer periods. In addition to this there was a feeling of rejection on the part of the children toward mother surrogates.

The question should be raised as to how closely these feelings of the patients approach reality. It is tempting and easy to take them at face value, but we should perhaps be somewhat more cautious. The patients were for the most part passive (markedly so), and while it is true that passivity often results from maternal rejection, it is equally true that this is not the only cause; the passive individual has a distortion in his own innate tendency to see the external world as rejecting. Another source of potential difficulty in trying to establish the actual state of events is that the passive individual, because of his excessive demands, can often bring about the type of rejection which he fantasies. There are other possibilities for the production of passivity besides maternal rejection; for example, overindulgence, in terms of giving, and the resultant decrease in the active drives. One procedure which would shed much light on many of these questions would be a study of the mothers of patients who make suicidal attempts.

The patients' motives for their suicidal attempts seem to be consistent with the dynamic diagnoses of passive, orally traumatized individuals. Masochistic elements, identification with feared and hated objects, with subsequent attempts to hurt them symbolically by self-destruction, were common. Again in keeping with the masochistic orientation, one can see the attempt to win the love of the object toward whom ambivalent feelings are held through punishing and abasing oneself. Finally, guilt and anxiety over anger often seem to be extreme in the period immediately preceding the suicidal attempt. In regard to these points, it might be fitting to attempt to apply Freud's final theory of instincts, in which he proposed the thesis that beyond all activity of living matter lies an attempt to return to a state of peace, of oneness with the universe (1, 2). Suicide has often been set forth as a manifestation of such a tendency. The cases described in this chapter offered evidence that could easily fit into this theory. There was often great anxiety and agitation which lay behind a feeling of resignation and hopelessness on the part of the patients. It seemed to them that suicide offered an attractive solution to their difficulties and an end to the unrest which many had experienced for long periods. It is tempting to offer this speculation—that what many of these people attempted was a return to a state of oneness with, or sheltering by, an unambivalent, oral mother.

References

1. Freud, S., *Beyond the Pleasure Principle*. London: Hogarth Press, Ltd., 1948.
2. ———, Mourning and Melancholia. (In *Collected Papers*, volume IV.) London: Hogarth Press, Ltd., 1948.

17

Psychologic and Social Work Clues to Suicide in a Schizophrenic Patient

EDWIN S. SHNEIDMAN AND DORTHEA M. LANE

If one may group all persons who are imminently suicidal into those who are not psychotic and those who are—in contradiction to a long-held, widespread belief that all people who commit suicide are psychotic— then one sees that, while the task of predicting the suicide of a non-psychotic individual is an immensely difficult one, the task of predicting the suicide of a psychotic individual is even more complicated. Indeed, to predict the psychotic's suicide would ultimately involve the effective understanding of the nature, etiology, and remediation of the psychosis itself. Study of such cases, however, where the suicidal tendencies are openly displayed among the symptoms of the mental illness, may yield much significant understanding of the suicidal act and practical suggestions for its prevention.

With this in mind, this chapter presents a case of a psychotic person, specifically a paranoid schizophrenic whose illness included suicidal ideation and declaration of suicidal intent. The subject was a twenty-five-year-old hospitalized male—here called Henry White—who committed suicide while on a pass from a neuropsychiatric hospital. The materials for the chapter were taken primarily from the hospital records and include excerpts from the hospital admission notes, the doctor's progress notes, the nurses' notes, and a newspaper clipping. In addition, the social work report and the psychologic test protocols, of special importance in this case, as well as some comments about them, are presented.

ADMISSION

When the patient first appeared at the neuropsychiatric hospital for admission, he was interviewed by the admitting psychiatrist, who wrote the following admission note:

January 18: This 25-year-old white, single, Catholic male was brought to the general medical hospital by his family because of nervousness. He was transferred the same day to the neuropsychiatric hospital for observation and treatment.

Present Illness

Patient's parents state that onset was immediately upon his return home from the service. He was shy, withdrawn, and more seclusive than he had been as a youngster. He became exceedingly interested in religion, was preoccupied with thoughts about hell, and he occasionally swung from a mood of depression to a state of elation. He persisted in talking about suicide rather frequently; however, the family never took him seriously. The patient made several inadequate attempts at suicide, after which he gradually became more seclusive and depressed and, at times, freely hallucinated. On admission, the patient stated that his anxiety and nervousness had dated from difficulties with his father, who frequently beat him and threatened to send him to reform school, accusing the patient of consorting with gangsters, prostitutes, and drunks. He further stated he had a persecution complex, but that he was good and religious. He did not want to work; "brushing my teeth is enough." When interviewed, he complained that he heard voices from the spiritual world and that God was against him. He believed that there was no use living and he would be better off dead.

Physical Examination

Height, 70 in.; weight, 160 lb.; blood pressure, 130/80. Physical examination essentially negative and within normal limits.

Neurologic Examination

Gait and station normal. Deep tendon reflexes slightly hyperactive. No abnormal physical signs or reflexes elicited.

Laboratory Reports

Blood: RBC, 4,190,000; WBC, 9,800; hemoglobin, 84% (13.1 gm.); neutrophils, 54% (49 segs, 5 stabs); lymphocytes, 41%; monocytes, 2%;

eosinophils, 3%; CI, 0.98. Urine: 3+ mucus; rare RBC; 1 WBC per HPF. Blood serum determinations within normal limits. Spine X-ray normal. ECG normal. EEG impression: "cortical abnormality both parietal areas but maximal in the right anterior temporal area; consistent with psychomotor equivalent epilepsy."

Mental Examination

Patient is a dull, grim-looking young man whose clothing is unkempt and deranged. He is verbose, coherent, but not always relevant. He has flight of ideas, ideas of reference, and feelings of insecurity. His contact with his immediate environment is borderline—patient describes his condition as: "I consider this is a dream. This is hellish—fear, torment." He has some somatic complaints referable to his throat and stomach. His emotional responses and mood are not consistently appropriate. During the interview, patient states that within the last two years he has had 16 homosexual relationships and has lost all interest in women. He states that within the past few months he has had numerous nightmares. These consist of herds of animals chasing him and biting him. He really feels the pain of the bite and yells out in anguish. Insight is completely lacking by the patient. He is oriented, emotionally flat, depressed, and extremely verbose. He says that he hears voices from the spirit world telling him to commit suicide, but there is no painless way to commit suicide. During the last interview the patient stated that he had ceased to hear voices and no longer felt as though everyone was "out to get him."

Diagnosis

Schizophrenic reaction, mixed type with paranoid features, manifested by seclusiveness, auditory hallucinations, ideas of reference and of persecution.

SOCIAL WORK REPORT

A social study was received on the patient January 22, four days after he was admitted. The following is an excerpt from the report:

Source of Information

Informants were patient's father and mother who were interviewed separately on the same day.

The mother was a tall, well-dressed, middle-aged woman who at first seemed quite self-assured. Her self-assurance seemed but a recently acquired protective mantle. In speaking there was still a trace of her foreign background. Her emotions were very close to the surface and she wept quite frequently and throughout most of the interview. She had relatively good insight into her son's relationship with his father, but insight into her own relationship with the patient was lacking.

The father was an extremely dominating individual. His need to master every situation was so strong that it almost became a real entity. Underneath the businesslike veneer one readily saw insecurity and the wretchedly pathetic fear eating at this man. He was a person who seemed to expect everything to succeed for him—a person who would find success in all his endeavors, be they music, art, business, or children. It was in this last area that he was not succeeding. His insecurity about discussing his son's situation was best exemplified by the following statement he made on first meeting the social worker: "If I had been in your shoes, I would have handled these interviews exactly the way you did. I would have seen the mother first and would have gotten the sob story, and then I would have seen the father to get the facts."

Birth and Early Development

The patient was born in Chicago; birth and early development were quite normal, and he was seldom ill. He was an only child. According to the parents, the early developmental years were quite uneventful. It appeared to the social worker, however, that the patient was probably overlooked by the father during a good deal of the time and was left very much to himself. His mother was undoubtedly the person closest to him during these years and a very strong attachment developed between them.

Education

The patient started school at the age of 5 and completed 2 years of high school at the age of 16.

Health

The patient enjoyed good health most of his life. He was injured once in an accident during childhood and suffered fractures of an arm and leg, according to the informants.

Interpersonal Relationship Adjustment Prior to Service

The patient was very close to his mother but seemed unable to form a close relationship to his father. The father was a very busy person, whose business activities ostensibly kept him from participating in the normal father-son activities. He was the primary disciplinarian of the family, being overly strict, and setting standards higher than the patient could meet. Later when the father realized that he had been too severe he tried to win the boy over with gifts. The patient did not make friends easily, and he was rather seclusive as a youth. He found it difficult to share his feelings with others, and turned to the outdoors, becoming quite an enthusiast over nature lore. However, the patient made a good adjustment in summer camps and enjoyed these experiences as a child. Little recognition was given at the time to the patient's problems and accomplishments. He seemed even at this early date to have "placed his father on a pedestal." He seemed always endeavoring to impress his father.

Military History

At the age of 16, patient ran away from home and enlisted in the navy, but was "discovered" and returned within a few months. As soon as he became 18, he enlisted in the army. His parents believed it would "make a man of him." The family knew little of his service adjustment—in fact, touched most lightly on this area. They were definite in stating that he had changed markedly while in the service. While in the service he was placed under observation in a neuropsychiatric ward. The patient was discharged from the service after less than a year with a medical disability for nervousness.

Post-service Adjustment

The change in the patient was noticeable immediately upon his return home. He was shy, withdrawn, and more seclusive than ever. He seemed fearful of people and he frequently spoke of suicide. Although the patient and father had not been close before, there was now a high barrier. The patient seemed especially fearful of girls and he behaved quite strangely when they came around to visit. He would either run and hide and have to be called by his parents, or he would become exceedingly entertaining and keep it up so that his guest was both exhausted and bored. He became exceedingly interested in religion and seemed to derive considerable help from Christian Science writings. He was preoccupied at this time with hell and constantly wanted his father's assurances that this well-known place could not exist. He was very moody and swung from elation to depression frequently.

The patient persisted in talking about suicide rather frequently. However, the family never took him seriously. He made one attempt, by choking himself, but even this was not thought to be serious by the family. The father pointed out that they were pretty sick and tired of hearing him threaten to take his life. At one time the patient's father told him that if he wanted to commit suicide, he would help him. He then opened a window and dragged the patient to it, telling him that if he wanted to jump he could jump right now. The patient became very terrified and put up a struggle which only served to further convince the family that he was bluffing.

The patient also spoke at great length about his past life, enumerating all of the unhappy experiences he had as a child. He seemed to dwell on these things at great length which was quite contrary to his previous behavior and attitude.

The patient's father endeavored to secure medical care for his son and took him to a psychiatrist. The father was emphatic in assuring the worker that no evidence of "bisexuality" had ever been found although a great number of psychologic tests were given. The father apparently anticipated a question regarding the patient's sexual adjustment and met it by this very defensive statement. It was noted that both the mother and father were either completely unaware of any sexual deviation of their son or they were so fearful of what they did know about it that they were unable to accept it. The latter is felt to be nearer the truth. During one of these psychiatric visits the patient was given a sodium amytal interview, and the father reported to the worker that no evidence was found that the patient was afraid of his father.

Summary

Neither parent has much insight into the illness of the patient nor into their own part in this illness. All their fears and bitter experiences are focused around this young man who is their son. Little cooperation of a real give-and-take sort can ever be expected from these people as they are too rigidly involved to give any real help. They will probably always be demanding of others in an effort to fulfill their own needs. As long as their own needs are met, they will carry through treatment plans recommended for this patient.

When the time comes for the patient to be discharged, it would seem advisable for him to have little personal contact with his parents as the same process which led to his present illness will probably be repeated.

Comment

This social study emphasizes the fact that there were clues pointing to the need for help even earlier than the present hospitalization. Particularly outstanding is the patient's degree of unhappiness before the age of 16 when he showed enough strength to try to break with his family by running away and enlisting. At this time, as indicated by his good summer camp adjustment, he probably could have used psychiatric treatment to his advantage.

The question of integrating the contribution of the psychiatric social worker in the management of the patient is raised because of the statement in the Summary about the traumatic effect on the patient of the family's rejection. There is no indication that the patient was given an opportunity for outside social relationships other than with family members. A psychiatric social worker could, for instance, offer help to the parents in relation to their feelings on the patient's progress in the hospital.

It would have been appropriate for the social worker in this case to tell the family to take the patient's threats seriously and to give them support in the validity of their concern for him. This might have lessened their insistence on taking him "on pass." In the absence of continuing notes, it is not possible to determine the continuing role of the social worker. It is clear, however, that the social worker was convinced of the damaging effect of the parents on the patient for a long time.

The role that the psychiatric social worker can assume in treatment—by service to relatives on behalf of the patient—should be considered and used more extensively.

DOCTOR'S PROGRESS NOTES

The patient's progress and course in the hospital are indicated by excerpts from the following doctor's notes:

1/18   This 25-year-old white male admitted. See admission note. Impression: Schizophrenic reaction, mixed type with paranoid features and hyperactive element.

1/19   Shock staff.

1/20   Complains he hears voices from the spiritual world and that God is against him. Thinks there is no use in living and that he would be better off dead. Transfer to Ward C for observation.

1/21   Wants shock treatment to kill fright, nightmares, fears, headaches. Patient is verbose, coherent, but not always relevant. He has ideas of influence—feelings of insecurity. His contact with immediate environment is borderline. He considers "this" is a dream. This is "hellish—fears, torment." He also has somatic complaints referable to his throat and stomach. Has feelings of guilt—but is trying to project them out. Emotional response is not appropriate. "When he sees patients blowing their top, he feels like doing it also—after all he is in same ship they're are." Thinking is concrete. In last 2 years had 16 homosexual relations. Lost all interest in women. His nightmares consist of herds of animals chasing him and biting him. He really feels the pain of the bite and yells out. Insight lacking. He feels only EST [electroshock therapy] can help him, and if he does not get it— he is being deprived of his rights. *Impression:* Schizophrenia. Paranoid.

1/23 Some underlying persecutory feelings are in the process of being established.

1/24 Parents were interviewed for a few minutes. They wanted to know why EST had not been started. The father gave me the impression he was domineering, cold, narcissistic, and rejecting figure to the patient. Mother appeared overprotective and very submissive.

PSYCHOLOGIC TEST PROTOCOLS
AND INTERPRETATIVE COMMENTS

On January 25, a week after the patient's entry into the hospital, and while on the suicide observation ward, he was administered psychologic tests.

The following are selections from Henry White's Make a Picture Story (MAPS) test protocol. The MAPS test is similar to the Thematic Apperception Test (TAT).[1] The MAPS test was administered to this patient in a quiet examining room on the ward; the rapport was good and the patient was cooperative.

In the following excerpt, the verbatim responses to the Living room and Bridge backgrounds are reproduced.

Living room. (Selected Figure M-8, the priest.)

This is a priest and these people were all talking in here and he was just coming in the door and he heard from the neighbors, they were having an open discussion, this family and the neighbors told the priest. What it is all about, is that the girl has been having trouble in school and the father has been having trouble in his business and they've been frustrated by their beliefs. So the father has been having headaches, been nervous and jumpy in his office, been making mistakes—little girl that goes to school has been having nightmares about school.

---

[1] Descriptions of both the TAT and the MAPS test, as well as several methods of test interpretation, are presented in Edwin S. Shneidman [Ed.], *Thematic Test Analysis* (New York: Grune & Stratton, Inc., 1951). In the TAT, pictures (typically showing two or three people together) are shown to the subject who then is asked to make up a dramatic story, telling who the characters are, what they are thinking and feeling, and how the situation turns out. In the MAPS test, the background pictures and the figures are separate and the subject has to select one or more from among 67 cut-out human-like figures (male, female, legendary, children, etc.) and place them on background pictures (bedroom, camp, forest, medical scene, etc.) and then tell a story of the situation that he himself has in part created.

So this priest figures, well, knowing the truth as he does, he decides to call on the family, pay them a friendly visit and straighten them out. He knocks on the door, door's open and he's standing there. He's approached by the father who is very irritated at the present moment, because they're in the midst of a discussion. The argument didn't go his way. So he tells the priest to keep his nose out of what doesn't concern him. He figures the problem's personal. The mother says, "Wait a minute, John, he looks sincere, you haven't even heard him yet." The priest says he came to help, not to hinder. From then on in he solves their problem for them, and the man comes around to his way of thinking. He accepts the priest too, he wants to know what is truth. More than anything else, it's his crying need for the truth that lets him stay. He's dependent on it. It helps him meet a crisis. He's strong from spiritual nourishment, and God sends the priest. [What might the title be?] How the Neighborhood Priest Came to Answer Truth. He solves all their problems for them, proving that without religion you can't succeed.

Comment

The primary feature of this story is the strongly religious theme. Certainly religiosity, per se, does not indicate pathology, but in this case, what is reflected is the patient's need to know truth, to allay his guilts, to have a repository for his dependencies. Many authorities feel that firm religious belief is often a deterrent to suicide, while weak religious ties or vacillating religious beliefs are much more frequently seen as a concomitant—not necessarily the cause—of suicide. Paradoxically, the belief in a life after death or in the hereafter, which is found in many religions, may also correlate positively with suicide, because if one believes in a life after death, then death is not the end.

Bridge. (Selected Figure N-6, a dejected looking male.)

This is the best story I ever told in my life. He's very mentally depressed, he's a self-pity victim. This is the George Washington Bridge in New York City, and he's in a mental depression. He figured he got a raw deal from life. He's an isolationist. He leaves his home and thinks, I'm going to find a priest. He's not going to tell the priest he's going to jump off the bridge. He'd made up his mind before to jump off the bridge. [Here the patient stops and asks the examiner to read back to him what has been written so far.] He's going to seek counsel from the priest. He doesn't eat any lunch, he wants to drink on an empty stomach. He's afraid of people stopping him from jumping off. He finds a bar away off from the bridge. He's afraid of people reading his thoughts. Afraid they'll stop him. He has a guilt complex. Feels he's already committed the murder in his own mind. Dejected, nervous, upset, scared stiff. He gets off the bus, he figures he'll have to spend the money for liquor. So he buys the most expensive cigar in the store. He's afraid if he buys something cheap, he'll receive the greater condemnation.

Afraid if he doesn't give money to the poor he'll be punished for all his sins. He leaves enough to get three or four drinks under his belt. Then he thinks, well, what am I going to do now, he needs a cigarette. He has a pack in his pocket. He smokes one and gives the pack away. He's all through with his drink at the bar. Cheap, powerful stuff. He leaves the bar and walks out, kind of cockeyed. He imagines he's Christ, that he's also murdering Christ.[2] He walks up to the bridge. He won't take the short cut, he takes the devious way, so no one will spot him. He actually makes things twice as suspicious. He thinks someone is following him. He's afraid his father might show up and stop him, or brother might drive by and recognize him. He starts to run. He's pursued by his mind. He starts running up the ramp. He looks back, trips, and falls, and hurts himself real bad. Picks himself up and starts walking again. He hurt his knee and walks with a limp. He figures the left hand side is no good because he's right handed and has to jump off the right side. He's suspicious, superstitious. If he doesn't jump off the right side, he wouldn't die. He crosses the street to the right and almost gets killed by a car. The fenders hit him on the leg, gives him a shock. Like a shock. He's in a state of actual terror. He's something to be pitied because he's frustrated by fear. He's not the master. He gets on the right. By this time it's 4:00 in the afternoon. Daylight saving time. He brought his prayer book with him. He sees all these benches and realizes he's tired. He sits down, gets out his religious book and searches the scriptures. Starts praying. He preaches to the world but they can't hear him. He gets up and says I've got to cut this short, the longer you wait the harder it seems. He walks over, still feeling his liquor, still full of self-pity, now he's up ready to jump off. Says, "Gee whiz, this is quite a drop," and his mind answers him, "Yes, it is." And he has quite a battle with himself. Says he's got to stop now, I've invested money in this, I've given away my cigarettes, spent my last money for drink and all that. Keeps goading himself, thinking how his girl friend broke faith with him. He grabs the railing, gets up on it and with a mighty heave of energy he makes it. He's on the rail. Says he's not going to dive, he's going to jump. Like a dope he says some prayers and some cars come along and some guys come along and he doesn't even hear them. Somebody

[2] This statement by the patient, as well as his previous statement in this same story ("Feels he's already committed the murder in his own mind"), amount almost to a declaration that he is willing to excise the intolerable aspects of himself, *even though it kills him*—and indicate that he somehow equates suicide with (self) murder. One is reminded again (see Chap. 4, The Logic of Suicide) of the duality of the self-image. In this same vein, Arieti, building on Freud and Sullivan, in his discussion of the development of a delusional state (in terms of introjection, assimilation, and projection) states that "... this process of externalization of the *you*, which occurs in the paranoid form of schizophrenia, is almost the opposite of what happens in psychotic depression. In psychotic depression the self-devaluating *you* is totally incorporated and the *I* is eliminated. The *I* needs to be eliminated to such a point that the patient may commit suicide." (Silvano Arieti, Some aspects of the psychopathology of schizophrenia. *American Journal of Psychotherapy*, 8: 396–414, 1954.)

touches him in the shoulder, and a voice says something, and he connects them, says they must be together. He jumped, he was about this far over and a pair of capable hands caught him under the armpits. They asked him all kinds of questions. He was humiliated and insulted. He was convinced he was the son of God. Didn't think humans could interfere with him. Drove him off the bridge, sent him to the hospital, put him in a ward there. Then he was taken out and taken to court and there was a sergeant sitting there, pompous, behind a desk, and the sergeant says, "Don't you know you had no right to try to kill yourself," and I say "I am a law unto myself." I got him around to my way of thinking actually. But it didn't work.

Comment

Along with its openly suicidal theme, this story is an excellent example of schizophrenic language and thought. Note for example, after he implies that he is lonely, his tangential association, "He's an isolationist." Note also the paranoid-like thought, "He's afraid of people reading his mind," and "He's pursued by his mind." This includes the statement, ". . . Feels he has already committed the murder in his own mind"—an indication of his equating his killing himself with his killing of another; and "He imagines he's Christ, that he's also murdering Christ." Here it is evident that he is willing to expunge the troublesome aspects of himself even though it costs him his life. The open illogicality of the following sequence is clear: "He figures he'll have to spend the money for liquor, so he buys the most expensive cigar in the store." He also uses the characteristically schizophrenic alliteration in his phrase, "He's suspicious, superstitious." He shows the inappropriate attention to picayune detail which gives the entire production an inappropriate flavor: "By this time it's 4:00 in the afternoon. Daylight saving time." Clearly this is a test protocol of a schizophrenic subject with religious delusional themes. It illustrates not only the "paleologic" thinking of the schizophrenic but also the "catalogic" ideation of the suicide.

For the schizophrenic suicide, the question of management is essentially that of watchful protection. So long as an individual has religious or guilt-laden delusions or so long as he receives persecutory hallucinatory stimuli, he is potentially an unpredictable suicidal risk (just as he is superficially unpredictable in other ways) and the prevention of suicide must be correlated with these concepts. For the schizophrenic patient, *constant* physical sanctuary in a neuropsychiatric hospital or sanitarium would seem to play a very important role, for here he is placed in a position where he cannot harm himself and where others will watch over him.

Two other tests were administered: the Hildreth Feeling and Attitude

Scale and the Minnesota Multiphasic Personality Inventory (MMPI). On the Feeling and Attitude Scale, he selected the lowest item of every one of the eight sets of scales, checking the following responses: "I wish I were dead; No hope; I hate everybody and everything; Completely worn out; Couldn't feel any worse; Don't know whether I'm coming or going; The longer I work at any job the more angry I feel; I hate the world." His MMPI profile was as follows:

53	80	40	93	94	78	82	61	105	101	120	80
L	F	K	Hs	D	Hy	Pd	Mf	Pa	Pt	Sc	Ma

In addition, it may interest the reader to know that he answered the following MMPI items, among others, as "true." The items below are not intended to imply a "suicidal scale," but rather to point up his feelings of psychotic disturbance and intense unworthiness.

13. I work under a great deal of tension.
16. I am sure I get a raw deal from life.
24. No one seems to understand me.
27. Evil spirits possess me at times.
33. I have had very peculiar and strange experiences.
35. If people had not had it in for me I would have been much more successful.
39. At times I feel like smashing things.
44. Much of the time my head seems to hurt all over.
50. My soul sometimes leaves my body.
61. I have not lived the right kind of life.
66. I see things or animals or people around me that others do not see.
67. I wish I could be as happy as others seem to be.
76. Most of the time I feel blue.
97. At times I have a strong urge to do something harmful or shocking.
106. Much of the time I feel as if I have done something wrong or evil.
110. Someone has it in for me.
115. I believe in a life hereafter.
121. I believe I am being plotted against.
138. Criticism or scolding hurts me terribly.
158. I cry easily.
168. There is something wrong with my mind.
182. I am afraid of losing my mind.
202. I believe I am a condemned person.
236. I brood a great deal.
252. No one cares much what happens to you.
265. It is safer to trust nobody.
301. Life is a strain for me much of the time.
315. I am sure I get a raw deal from life.

333. No one seems to understand me.
337. I feel anxiety about something or someone almost all the time.
339. Most of the time I wish I were dead.

Comment

The results on these two tests (the Feeling and Attitude Scale and the MMPI) complement and reinforce one another. They show that the subject could not feel worse, more useless, or more despondent; that he felt depressed, persecuted, hostile, evil, condemned, confused; and that he wished he were dead.

DOCTOR'S PROGRESS NOTES, CONTINUED, AND
NURSES' NOTES

1/25   To EEG laboratory.

1/27   EEG shows cortical abnormality in both parietal and right temporal areas. Spine X-ray negative.

1/29   Nurse's note. Seems more restful and in better contact. Has more confidence in self.

1/30   Nurse's note. Visited by parents.

2/1   Nurse's note. Quiet during night.

2/2   Being sent to shock board today for possible insulin consideration. Both patient and his parents have been pressing for treatment and practically demanding it. Father very abrupt, cold, and to the point in his demands. Patient has an abnormal EEG. Work-up sheet has been completed but in view of the abnormal EEG, patient was not accepted for EST. Is still on observation, but if can be given therapy other than EST, may be presented for removal from observation. Hears voices from the spiritual world which have told him to commit suicide. Illness apparently is deep seated, with periodic attacks 6 years ago and 4 years ago.

2/2   Nurse's note. Hyperactive and talkative. Walks about ward continually.

2/3   Nurse's note. Refused breakfast. Quiet this AM.

2/4   Nurse's note. Agitated, disturbed. Confused and restless.

2/5   Nurse's note. Visited by parents.

2/7   Nurse's note. Hyperactive, but not more so than usual. Complains of headache.

2/8   Patient placed on Phenurone to treat psychomotor equivalent. His restlessness, talkativeness, expressed hostility continue unchanged. [Nurse's note. Singing, shouting, and talking. Wants to send a secret message to the outside. Very noisy.]

2/9   Observation staff with consultant. Recommend removal from observation. [Nurse's note. Confused and restless.]

2/10   Nurse's note. Nervous and apprehensive. Anxious to be able to do some OT [occupational therapy] work today.

2/13   Nurse's note. Visited by parents.

2/14   Nurse's note. Patient likes being back on this ward. Hears and answers voices. Becomes noisy at times.

2/17   Nurse's note. Patient is friendly but states he wishes he were dead.

2/20   There is no change. He is seclusive, withdrawn, but if spoken to, is talkative, flighty. Wants to go home to play records and sing. He is being transferred to receive ENT [electronarcosis treatment].

2/21   Nurse's note. Visited by father. Patient seems to have suicidal ideas. He is quiet and cooperative.

2/27   Patient believes the ENT he has been receiving changed his mind as exemplified by the "nightmarish quality of my dreams" which try to tell him truths about himself and to advise him as to a course of action to take. He discusses his dreams at great length and is convinced that they are "messages." He also says he hears voices when he is conscious. However, he considers this to be unusual and knows "—that it's my mind playing tricks on me." He says he has been sick for 6 years with cowardice, mental confusion. This is due to one part of his brain, of which he is not aware, advising other parts of brain. He says he has studied psychiatry and psychoanalysis because he felt that sometime he might have to apply them to himself.

2/28   Nurse's note. Very active. Shows a flight of ideas. Fairly cooperative but seems rather apprehensive.

3/2   Nurse's note. Upon taking patient to recreation hall, the patient attempted to elope. Patient was caught before he could escape. Mother here to visit.

3/18   Nurse's note. Contact poor. Confused continually. Belligerent at times and again very calm and quiet. Tries to be quiet when asked, but can't remember for long at one time. Objects to treatments and ward routine. Visited by mother.

3/22   Doctor's order. Weekend passes with relatives.

3/23   Nurse's note. On weekend pass with mother.

4/14   Nurse's note. Visited by mother—went for automobile ride. Discusses sex at great length in minute detail. Pats head and says he is crazy, "more than halfway."

4/22   Patient has completed 20 EN treatments without much improvement. He still talks in a rambling and vague manner. He antagonizes the other patients on the ward.

4/27   Nurse's note. Has been rather upset about mother not taking him home for the weekend. Talks loudly and uses profanity.

5/2   Patient asked to see the ward doctor. He speaks under moderate pressure, in a slightly rambling but obviously goal-directed conversation.

The patient expressed a great deal of ambivalence toward his father who he feels has failed to give him the love, respect, and affection due the patient. Patient states he has frequent nightmares in which he is attacked physically or verbally by his father. At times the patient has aggressive, hostile feelings toward his father and feels he might kill the father. The patient brings out manifest oedipal rivalry with father for the mother, but the deeper content and effeminate mannerisms more likely indicate homosexual attachment to the father.

5/3   Nurse's note. On 72-hour pass with mother.

5/6   Nurse's note. On pass with parents.

5/7   No extension of pass to be granted 5/8.

5/7   Brought in by private ambulance accompanied by father at 10:30 PM. Was seen immediately while being wheeled inside building. He was ashy white, with cold perspiration, and not breathing. Artificial respiration was started immediately. Cardiac examination disclosed no heart tones. Intracardiac injection of Adrenalin was given, preceded by hypodermic Coramine. Father and ambulance driver stated he had been breathing while coming into reception building. Catholic priest called and administered last rites. Father states son was found at 6 PM in unconscious state. Believes he took overdose of sedative, as he had been talking of paying $50 for bottle of sedative pills. Was taken to emergency hospital where stomach was pumped about 9:30 PM. Patient was in home when found unconscious. Cause of death: cardiac failure from paralysis of respiratory center due to self-ingested unknown barbiturates with suicidal intent. Expired at 10:32 PM.

FINAL HOSPITAL SUMMARY

May 7. This patient was admitted on January 18, voluntarily. At that time he complained of nervousness, nightmares, fears of pain, and fear of people. He said he heard spirit voices telling him to commit suicide. He said he did not want to work, that "brushing my teeth is enough work." History from the family revealed that the patient had become shy, withdrawn, and seclusive. He had become very interested in religion, and was preoccupied with thoughts about hell. He had been talking about suicide rather frequently, but the family never took him seriously. At home he made several inadequate attempts at suicide, after which he gradually became more seclusive, depressed, and at times freely hallucinating. Soon after his admission here he was transferred to the observation ward. He was presented to the treatment staff and insulin convulsive therapy and electronarcosis were recommended. He was removed from observation status on February 8 and started on electronarcosis treatment on February 20. He received twenty electronarcosis treatments, without much improvement.

Treatments were discontinued on April 22, and a course of insulin convulsive therapy was being considered. The patient's parents insisted on taking him out on a weekend pass. Patient ingested an unknown number of barbiturates and was brought back to the hospital on May 7, by private ambulance. He was dead on arrival.

Diagnosis

(1) Schizophrenic reaction, mixed type, with paranoid features, manifested by seclusiveness, auditory hallucinations, ideas of reference and persecution.

(2) Poisoning, acute, barbiturate (type unknown), fatal.

Disposition

Patient died May 7 (listed as suicide by coroner's office).

NEWSPAPER CLIPPING

Autopsy Asked in Death of War Vet

A young war veteran undergoing treatment at the neuropsychiatric hospital died today at the hospital, and police asked for an autopsy to determine the cause of death.

Police said Henry White, 25, apparently died as the result of an overdose of sedatives at his home, 100 Main Street.

Police said the young man developed a fear complex after he was honorably discharged last year.

He arrived home on a pass, went to bed and said he didn't want to be disturbed. His father, William White, called police when he couldn't awaken his son last night. He died at the hospital.

IMPLICATIONS

Some possible implications of the above materials are as follows:

(1) Suicidal tendencies expressed by psychotic patients are of special importance and merit careful evaluation, largely because of the unpredictable element introduced by the psychosis itself.

(2) The neuropsychiatric hospital offers sanctuary and protection, the interruption of which—even for a weekend—must be evaluated carefully.

(3) The home environment from which a suicidal psychotic patient comes to the hospital may be the environment to which he should not be returned, even for a short period, while he is still psychotic and suicidal.

(4) The hospital may have to play important roles with relatives of

a suicidal patient. The hospital staff, particularly the psychiatric social worker, may need to help the family achieve a better understanding of the suicidal threats (and relieve their own feelings of guilt), and the physician may have to buffer the patient against the parents' denial of treatment through withholding of permission and against the demands of parents for premature release, inappropriate treatment, weekend pass, and so forth.

(5) The possibility of obtaining important clues about suicidal ideation and affect through the use of psychologic tests seems to be substantiated, even though the need for continued intensive research with such instruments is indicated.

(6) In the neuropsychiatric hospital setting, effective channels of communication to the physician (from the psychologist, nurse, social worker, psychiatric aide, and others) about the patient's suicidal verbalizations are the *sine qua non* for appropriate decisions concerning the overall treatment of the patient.

(7) When the psychotic patient expresses suicidal notions, he is a double-barrelled risk: not only may he respond to the injunctions of hallucinated voices to kill himself, but also he is in constant danger of taking his own life in order to expunge the specific aspects within himself that he finds intolerable. Further, the activating mechanism for this explosive mixture may depend on the hair trigger of a dereistic thought, a hallucinated command, or a fleeting affective state.

18

Suggestions for Suicide Prevention

The importance of suicide as a cause of death is gravely underestimated. Nor do the statistics on suicide represent the whole problem. Many suicides are not reported or pass as accidental death. The numbers do not include what Karl Menninger (5) calls chronic or partial suicide, such as the progressive self-destruction seen in chronic alcoholism. (For example, cirrhosis of the liver, mainly due to alcoholism, is the fifth ranking cause of death in San Francisco, where "suicide" is listed as the eighth most frequent cause of death.) Automobile accidents include a number of suicides or suicidal attempts. Families succeed in hiding a number of genuine suicides. It is estimated that self-destructive impulses or accident proneness are factors in about half of all nonfatal accidents. Many suicidal attempts are never recorded in vital statistics. In many of the cases in which death occurs, weeks or months after suicidal attempt, the death is not recorded as suicide.

At least five attempts at suicide are estimated to occur for every actual suicide, which means that there are a minimum of 100,000 attempted suicides in the United States each year. Daily we read in the newspapers of suicides that could have been prevented. These articles frequently describe despondent people who were under doctor's care or who had threatened suicide before—obvious danger signals often overlooked.

Complete figures would thus show perhaps as many as 50,000 suicides a year in the United States, instead of the 16,000 to 20,000 figure usually cited. In addition, there are all the suicidal attempts—a large area for preventive work.

Some practical aspects of suicide prevention, embodying suggestions made elsewhere (1, 2), can be listed:

(1) Persons who have attempted suicide offer a good chance for pre-

ventive work; but usually they get only emergency treatment and are discharged, although it is known that many will repeat the attempt. Many have been in hospitals several times yet never receive psychiatric treatment. They all need psychiatric evaluation and definitive treatment, or many will try again and succeed. For those who are potential suicides but have not attempted it, the problem is early recognition of mental depression—mainly a question of diagnosis.

(2) Often the doctor does not seem to feel the same deep concern for suicide as for medical and surgical fatalities. Even though suicide is preventable in most cases, there is a tendency to feel that suicide is the individual's own business and that he should be allowed to die if he wishes. Hence the failure to give the one who has attempted suicide a psychiatric consultation and follow-up treatment. Many physicians need better psychiatric orientation about psychiatric referrals. Often their influence is the most important factor in getting real protection for the patient.

(3) The basic problem is the diagnosis of depression. About half of all suicidal attempts are carried out by individuals with psychoneurotic depression. In this group, it is a question of evaluating a true depressive reaction, inasmuch as all such patients are potential suicides. In taking the patient's history, one must note the patient's description of changes within himself. Furthermore, he often complains only of physical symptoms, and the emotional reaction behind them must be unearthed by watching for changes in emotional reactions. To put it another way, in any patient's history, a functional complaint that is not backed up by true organic symptoms or findings should make a physician look for evidence of depression, including the depth and degree of handicap to the individual. In order to make the diagnosis (often missed), one must look for evidence of reduced energy output, changes in the way things appeal to the patient, his change of interest, and a pronounced change in feeling tone. It is important to keep in mind that psychogenesis is not always present. Many cases are spontaneous and of endogenous type, especially in the manic-depressive group. Indeed, about half of such patients have had previous attacks, with spontaneous recovery within a few months, even though a supposed chronic organic syndrome was treated. Symptoms may include:

(a) *Insomnia.* Especially characteristic is early morning awakening. Later on comes an inability to fall asleep. Insomnia is one of the most persistent complaints, about which patients are often very much concerned; and they may blame it for everything. Actually it is the depression that disturbs the sleep. Deeply depressed persons have bad thoughts at night. They may get up, pace the floor, smoke. These are highly significant signs of oncoming severe depression.

(b) *Anorexia.* With the oncoming depression, patients lose appetite and lack interest in food, with subsequent loss of weight. Frequently they seek medical aid for gastrointestinal upset which may be the first major complaint. Further inquiry brings out statements such as that all foods "taste the same" or "like sawdust." They have pronounced constipation and use laxatives or enemas for a condition owing only to the small residue in the bowel. The patient may claim that he eats enough, but careful investigation will show an inadequate, low calorie intake, with weight loss. It should be mentioned that hormone treatment is valueless as a cure for depression (3).

(c) *Loss of interest and drive.* The patient's formerly pleasurable interests no longer appeal to him. He will admit his loss of feeling in this regard. A deeper depression gradually engulfs everything, with loss of feeling for family, reading, hobbies, or recreation. The patient does not get his usual stimulation out of things; he may just sit and mope. At times, family informants can confirm this lack of interest if the patient covers it up. There is usually lack of libido or sex drive, to a degree of frigidity or impotence, depending upon the depth of the depression—and patients greatly concerned over this problem are especially prone to suicide. Patients also feel mental and physical sluggishness and retardation, so that they have to drive themselves to get to work in the morning or even to get up. As a rule, all these symptoms are exaggerated in the morning and lessen toward evening.

(d) *The mood reaction.* Many patients will not admit despondency and, when asked, will say they feel fine. Only further questions can bring out that they feel discouraged or disgusted and blame all their complaints upon some vague physical condition or upon insomnia. Occasionally, in a depressed mood, the patient may say that he feels "wretched," or "miserable," or "bad all over," or something like, "I just can't describe to you how bad I feel." It often requires various tactful questions to elicit the true undertone of depression and feelings of discouragement usually disguised by complaints about vague physical conditions.

(4) Use of barbiturates in these cases is dangerous, and it is a mistake to yield to the temptation to prescribe barbiturates indiscriminately for insomnia. Addiction may develop, and use of these drugs reduces inhibitions and thus increases the suicidal risks; or it may cause the confusion that results in an accidental overdose. Physicians may inadvertently increase the hazard by prescribing too large an amount. Patients may ac-

cumulate a supply of tablets by canvassing several physicians (one of our patients had obtained sedatives from fourteen physicians). About a fifth of all suicidal attempts are made with barbiturates, and these drugs account for at least one-twentieth of suicidal deaths a year. Suicide from overdoses of barbiturates is increasing. The same caution is indicated in the use of tranquilizing drugs in depressions.

Apropos of barbiturates, when a suicidal attempt has occurred, the emergency requires hospitalization of the patient and symptomatic treatment of the injury, to be followed by definitive psychiatric treatment. Since so many attempts are made with barbiturates, specific therapy for coma must be readily available. While treatment for barbiturate coma is not completely satisfactory, the following methods, described elsewhere in detail (4), have been found fairly adequate and at times lifesaving. A large dose may cause a condition that may not respond except to treatment with the artificial kidney, a device which is available only in a few places. Subconvulsive electrostimulation and intravenous administration of Metrazol both counteract the cerebral depressive action of the barbiturates and preserve the respiratory function. In our department we often combine the two methods. Recently we have had several patients respond favorably to Megimide.

(5) Once the physician establishes a diagnosis of depression, he must determine the degree of severity. Here psychologic tests like the Rorschach, the TAT, the MAPS test, or other projective tests are helpful. If the patient is not too hopeless and has made no definite threats or actual suicide attempt and the depression is reactive to emotional conflicts, outpatient or office treatment usually suffices. All threats and gestures of suicide, however insincere, should never be lightly dismissed. Shneidman and Farberow (6) report that although the patient may not carry out the threat, nearly everyone who does commit suicide has given some earlier warning of his intentions. In some cases the type of suicidal attempt gives an indication of the severity of risk. In more severe cases psychiatric consultation and hospitalization for a period is absolutely necessary to give the safest protection. The doctor should see that relatives make these arrangements, since patients are often too indecisive to do so themselves. Modern treatment of depression is almost uniformly successful.

The following cases are illustrative examples of recent suicidal problems we have treated.

A professional man, in his fifties, after a stroke, began to lose confidence in himself and interest in his work; he became extremely depressed, could not concentrate on anything, slept very poorly, and withdrew from all contacts. He felt he would never be able to work again, talked about suicide, and then attempted it with sleeping tablets. He lay in barbiturate coma for two days and almost died. After hospital treatment, including electroshock, and some follow-up interviews he was able to resume his professional work with considerable competence.

A young, single girl upon graduation was offered a position with considerable responsibility. She became greatly concerned and felt she was incapable. She slept poorly and felt increasingly inadequate, with suicidal thoughts. She sought medical help and told her physician of her suicidal ideation. She attempted suicide by slashing wrists and neck and was found almost exsanguinated in her bathroom. After emergency treatment in a hospital, she was transferred for psychiatric observation and after three weeks was dismissed to continue with office psychotherapy. She continued to be depressed and after five months of inactivity she was referred for evaluation. As is indicated in this type of case, we recommended electroshock therapy. Prompt clearing of the depression occurred and the patient resumed full occupation and normal social activities. This patient's true condition could have been recognized earlier and effective treatment given to spare a year of illness.

(6) The responsibility for suicide prevention does not lie wholly with physicians, although early detection of depression and prompt suitable treatment are especially important. Lay persons can also do a great deal of preventive work. Families must also be educated to the need for continued care of a depressive patient until he is fully recovered. Often suicide is attempted when the patient appears to be recovering (6). Near the end of hospital treatment of depression great caution must be exercised. Premature removal on the excuse of homesickness is common; the relatives give in to the patient's pleas and take him out too soon. Some patients conceal their real intent and use such pretexts as homesickness in order to get out and accomplish suicide. It is the physician's duty to warn families of this hazard.

(7) Lay associations, for instance, Save-a-Life League, organized some years ago on the East coast, should help with public education about motives for suicide and the recognition of signals of danger. Organizations can work out a program similar to that of Alcoholics Anonymous, for example. Individuals with suicidal impulses should be encouraged to come for help to psychiatric clinics.

(8) Peace officers and other police systems should have ample instruction on how to deal with suicidal attempts: not only how to give emergency first aid, but also how to procure psychiatric evaluation and help families

to procure it. In the Berkeley, California, Police Department, for example, all statements about suicide are treated as if the person were attempting to commit suicide, and he is talked to in private or his family is advised to take him to one of two hospitals or to his family physician for consultation. Police officers feel that all such persons should have the benefit of expert advice. A written report of the incident is prepared at once.

(9) Stricter controls and legal restraints over the promiscuous prescribing of lethal and addictive drugs, particularly barbiturates, are needed. In addition, the best laws regarding the use of barbiturates are not well enforced in this country. We have previously urged more careful controls (4).

(10) Hospital administrators should also accept their responsibility to include adequate, complete psychiatric consultation and follow-up treatment of all persons brought into hospital emergency departments because of attempted suicide.

(11) Registration of suicidal attempts, with the report of such attempts to public health officers, should be required in the same way as reportable diseases, with follow-up supervision by public health doctors and nurses in order to see that the patient is receiving psychiatric, as well as other adequate medical care.

(12) Both psychiatrists and other practitioners should keep ample case records in order to increase the understanding of various motives and thus to help with prevention. Complete studies of the presuicidal type of personality may also offer leads. The study by Shneidman and Farberow, previously mentioned, is a case in point.

(13) A logical source of help, especially in research, should be found in life insurance and accident insurance companies. Although these companies realize the extent of the problem of suicide and have kept accurate statistics, they have not, to date, made any studies in prevention. They must know that many cases of suicide are covered up and passed off as accidents, in order to collect insurance money. These companies contribute large sums for research to prolong life in such diseases as cardiovascular and kidney disease, chronic bronchitis, stomach and duodenal ulcers, and gallbladder disorders, and these data furnish valuable information on prognosis; but so far the companies have shown little interest in suicide prevention. A fund for psychiatric research and for lay education would be a constructive step in widening the preventive program.

(14) Another source of help would be the health insurance plans, most of which exclude benefits for costs of hospital and medical care in cases of

attempted suicide or self-inflicted injuries. Many health insurance policies have restrictions excluding shock therapy as a method of treatment, and yet at present this may be the only effective way of quickly terminating a depressive psychosis. This exclusion results from misunderstandings about convulsive therapy, a procedure that may be lifesaving for the patient. Ill-based criticisms and fear of hazards frequently tie the hands of the physician and prevent immediate treatment in emergency cases.

(15) Probably the greatest need for prevention of suicide is public education. In our efforts to give effective psychiatric treatment, we are still restrained by prejudice, the stigma that mental illness is disgraceful. People often feel that those who commit or try to commit suicide are weak, useless people. We need to educate people about the danger signals of suicide and to make psychiatric treatment readily available. Mental hygiene societies over the nation could greatly aid by tackling this practical problem and giving educational aid that would help us remove suicide from the list of major causes of death.

References

1. Bennett, A. E., Prevention of suicide. *California Medicine,* 81: 396–401, 1954.
2. ———, The physicians' responsibility in the prevention of suicides. *Diseases of the Nervous System,* 15: 207–210, 1954.
3. ——— and C. B. Wilbur, Convulsive shock therapy in involutional states after complete failure with previous estrogenic treatment. *American Journal of Mental Science,* 208: 170–176, 1944.
4. Hargrove, E. A., A. E. Bennett, and F. R. Ford, Acute and chronic barbiturate intoxication. *California Medicine,* 77: 383–386, 1952.
5. Menninger, K., *Man Against Himself.* New York: Harcourt, Brace and Company, Inc., 1938.
6. Shneidman, E. S., and N. L. Farberow, Clues to suicide. *United States Public Health Reports,* 71: 109–114, 1956.

Postscript

It is hoped that the reader has been as impressed as the editors by the seriousness of the entire suicide problem, the variety of thinking which has been expended on it, and the need for continued concentrated application of efforts in research, study, and understanding in this area. Of necessity, however, practice must often precede tested theory, and preventive measures must be thought of (and applied) even though the underlying theoretical issues are still not completely resolved. It is apparent that the attack on the problem of suicide prevention must be conducted simultaneously from both the theoretical and the practical points of view. Suggestions are offered to various groups for the thoughtful consideration of professional people and laymen as at least partial implementation of a multiple attack on this problem.

Universities and medical centers

Recognize that real advances in understanding of suicide can come only through systematic research, and that every effort should be made to encourage and foster both basic and practical research on the psychology, biology, and ecology of suicide.

Insurance companies

Recognize that they have a vast monetary as well as humanitarian stake in suicide prevention. Although insurance companies have granted large sums for research in cardiovascular diseases they have somehow not yet made tangible their interest in suicide prevention. The granting of funds for research and education would be an important step in any serious long-range program of suicide prevention.

Legislators

Become interested in laws designed to require the registration of suicide attempts with a report to and follow-up by public health officers, in order to ensure that the individual receives adequate professional care. Legislation is also needed to provide the framework for stricter control and legal restraint over the prescribing of all lethal drugs, including the barbiturates.

Mental hygiene societies

Establish organizations (like the Save-a-Life League) devoted to the prevention of suicide through continued education about danger signals and motives for suicide, and to encouraging those individuals with suicide impulses to seek professional help. Part of their responsibility might be the education of physicians in the recognition of the suicidal patient and in the safeguards to be used in the prescription of the various drugs.

Industry

Recognize that sometimes "self-punishing" behavior, such as continued accidents, alcohol addiction, multiple surgery, and so forth, can be related to *gradual* (unconscious) suicide, and that in these cases expert psychiatric or psychologic evaluations are also indicated.

Police and hospital personnel

Understand that individuals who attempt or threaten suicide are emotionally disturbed persons who need sympathetic professional care and are not criminals or bunglers to be treated in a perfunctory, uninterested, or hostile manner.

Journalists and newspapermen

Recognize that in reporting on attempted or completed suicides the reporter is dealing with emotional disturbances and not with sensational scandal. Recognize their responsibilities and their share in shaping the readers' attitudes and opinions about suicide and suicide prevention.

Everyman

Be aware, as indicated in the chapter, Clues to Suicide, of four important items of information about suicide prevention: (a) that individuals who threaten suicide are often more disturbed than people who attempt suicide; (b) that individuals who commit suicide almost always have previously threatened or attempted it, and therefore these attempts and threats must be taken seriously; (c) that most suicides seem to occur in the three-month period after the individual apparently has passed the suicidal crisis and appears to be recovering, and therefore physicians and relatives must be especially watchful (and willing to reenlist the services of a specialist) for at least ninety days after a person who has been suicidal appears to be improving; and (d) that calling, without delay, upon the services of professional psychiatric, psychologic, and social work specialists for the evaluation and treatment of a depressed or potentially suicidal relative or friend may mean the difference between life and death.

APPENDIX

Genuine and Simulated
Suicide Notes

Data about suicidal persons come from many different sources. For psychologic information, these data would include such sources as case histories, anamneses, psychologic tests, or psychotherapy notes, and would come from a variety of people, such as relatives, friends, family, or the suicidal subject himself. Of all these, the productions of the suicidal person himself are generally the most useful for an understanding of him, his personality structure, and his psychodynamics. In the case of the attempted or threatening suicidal person, such data are potentially available and are relatively easy to obtain. Where the person has already committed suicide, the problem of collecting significant data has always been a much more difficult one. Here the information has generally been obtained from other people, or from other data which may have inadvertently been gathered prior to his demise and which, therefore, may not be directly pertinent to his emotional state at the time of the suicidal crisis.

One possible source of information, however, that is a product of the suicidal person himself and is directly relevant to his emotional and ideational states at the time of his suicide, and that seems to express many facets of his personality structure and dynamics, is the suicide note he writes just before he takes his own life. Such notes, read in any quantity, strike the reader with the richness of the material for clues to the affect, conflicts, and motivations of the suicidal person. They strongly suggest the possibility of viewing them as projective devices (in much the same way as MAPS tests or TAT protocols are projective products) from which information may be inferred about the subject.

This Appendix contains some of the suicide notes which the editors of this book have collected and are a part of the data of a research project on the psychology of suicide which they are conducting. Specifically, it presents some selected genuine suicide notes which have been studied by a controlled experimental method, that is, by comparing them with stimulated suicide notes elicited from nonsuicidal people. This method also serves to illustrate a part of the experimental approach the investigators are attempting with this problem.

It is often instructive to compare that which one wishes to understand with something that is like it, yet not identical to it. Thus by focusing on the differences, the investigator may learn the essential characteristics of what he is examining. This, indeed, is the direct implication of John Stuart Mill's Method of Difference—which is really at the heart of scientifically controlled observation or experiment.

Believing that suicide notes might yield some clues for understanding the ideation, affect, logic, or psychodynamics of suicide, it was decided to analyze them by comparing them with a set of comparable, yet not identical, data. The first effort was to compare genuine suicide notes with suicide notes written by individuals who had attempted suicide, but this was not practical inasmuch as "attempt notes" are invariably destroyed upon recovery of the note writer and are thus impossible to obtain in sufficient number. Subsequently, a procedure was devised to elicit suicide-like notes from *nonsuicidal* subjects, and to use these for comparisons with the genuine notes. These elicited notes were called *simulated* or pseudosuicidal notes. The purpose of these comparisons is to point up the differences (or residues), albeit subtle, which characterize the genuine-note writer.

Each of the 33 pairs of notes reproduced below contains one genuine and one simulated suicide note. The genuine suicide notes were obtained from the files of the Office of the Coroner, Los Angeles County, where they are a matter of public record. This office keeps a file on every reported suicide committed in Los Angeles County. With the kind cooperation of the Coroner,[1] 721 suicide notes [2] have been collected from the folders of all the recorded suicide cases in Los Angeles County for the ten-year period, 1945 to 1954. In each year of this ten-year period, between 12 and 15 per cent of those who committed suicide left suicide notes.[3] These notes are

[1] This opportunity is taken to thank the personnel of the Los Angeles County Coroner's Office, particularly Messrs. Ben Brown, Victor Wallage, Forrest A. Huntley, and the late William G. McFarlane.

[2] The only known previously published source devoted primarily to suicide notes in any number is the following: W. Morgenthaler, Letzte aufzeichnungen von selbstmoerdern. *Beiheft zur Schweizerischen Zeitschrift fuer Psychology und Ihre Anwendungen,* no. 1: 1–150, Bern: Hans Huber, 1945. Morgenthaler's monograph contains 47 suicide notes obtained in Berne, Switzerland, during the period 1928 to 1935.

[3] This fact introduces sampling problems which must be pointed out, but which can hardly be overcome. However, the socioeconomic statistics of the note-writing

from both sexes—almost three males to every one female—and from individuals who ranged in age from thirteen to ninety-six.

The simulated suicide notes were obtained from *nonsuicidal* individuals contacted in labor unions, fraternal groups, and the general community. Recognizing the moral, ethical, and taboo overtones associated with suicide, several precautions were exercised in eliciting these pseudosuicidal notes. Each individual was given a personality questionnaire and was interviewed briefly. If he indicated any signs of personality disturbance or tendencies toward morbid content of thought he was diverted by being asked to write about "the happiest experience of his life," and he was not given the suicide-note task; however, if he indicated that he was reasonably well adjusted, not depressed, not concerned with suicide, and would not be upset by thinking about suicide, he was instructed as follows:

A study is being done on the prevention of suicide. For this, it is necessary to obtain many suicide notes written by normal people! For this reason, you are asked to write below, in your own words, the suicide note that you would write if you were going to take your own life. Make your note sound as real as you possibly can. Write what you think *you* would write if you were planning to commit suicide. Before you write the note, answer these two questions first: (a) What method would you use to take your own life? (b) To whom would you address the note you are writing?

In order to keep the two groups homogeneous (and to emphasize whatever differences might exist in the notes), all 66 genuine and simulated notes were selected from those written only by individuals who were male, Caucasian, Protestant, native-born, and between the ages of twenty-five and fifty-nine. In addition, each of the 33 simulated-note writers was matched, *man-for-man*, with a genuine-note writer who was not only of a similar chronologic age (within five years) but also of the same occupational level.

The reader can, if he wishes, indicate which of each pair, A or B, he thinks is the *genuine* suicide note. The "key" indicating which note is genuine is given on the last page of this section. Further, the reader can even perform a little experiment on the value that this volume has had for him by checking the paired notes (and not looking up the "key") before he reads the book thoroughly and then duplicating the task (and looking up the "key") after he has gone through the book carefully. It is hoped that the difference will be in the direction of his greater perspicacity.

---

group have been compared with the similar data from the non-note-writing group and the two groups have been found to be essentially the same.

PAIRED NOTES

1-A To the Police. No note—one was written before this. Los Angeles Police already have a record of one attempt. Notify—Anne M. Jones, 100 Main St., Los Angeles, tel. BA 00000. I live at 100 Spring St., Los Angeles. I work at Ford, 100 Broadway. That is all.

I can't find my place in life.

J. William Smith

1-B Dear Mom, In the last week a number of occurrances have forced me into a position where I feel my life is not worth continuing.

Friday I lost the job I have held for the past seven years. When I told my wife she packed her bags and left me. For six years she has been living with me, not for me but for my money.

Mom please take care of Mary for me. I'm leaving and I don't want Betty to have her.

I have nothing left to live for so I'm just checking out.

I love you Mom, *Bill*

2-A I hope this is what you wanted.

2-B Dear, please forgive me for leaving you with all the responsibilities that this is certain to bring on you. If there is anything of me that can be used in any medical or scientific way please dont refuse to let them as my last request. I am very proud of our son, and his high potential in his chosen field for which he has real talent. Bye for the last time, and never forget that you were the best thing that ever happened to me. Have my brother help you, I know he will want to very much.

3-A Dearest Mary. This is to say goodbye. I have not told you because I did not want you to worry, but I have been feeling bad for 2 years, with my heart. I knew that if I went to a doctor I would lose my job. I think this is best for all concerned. I am in the car in the garage. Call the police but please don't come out there. I love you very much darling. Goodbye,

Bill

3-B   I am tired of living so I decided to end it all, hope this will not distress anybody.

4-A   Dear Mary. I regret that things have reached such a state that this is the only way out for me and my family. I apologize for the trouble I've caused.

4-B   This is the last note I shall ever wright. No one should feel bad about my going as I am not worth it. I don't want to go but there is nothing else to do.

My Love kept after me until I lost control and struck at the only one I ever loved. The only thing that meant anything to me. Then I got tight. When I struck at her something snapped inside my head. I could feel it. I didn't want to hurt her ever. She is Mary Jones of 100 Main St. Los Angeles. Her aunt's phone is BA 00000. She lives close by. Please get in tutch with them at once. She keped after me until this is all I can do. I must.

My last request is not to be put 6 ft. under but burned and my ashes scattered over the mountains.

Please don't let my brother know how or why I died. To her it must be an acident. Mary is the most wonderful person on earth. I just wasn't the right one for her. It is not her fault I fell so madly in Love with her.

I have never been much good. I have only hurt everyone.

Well at least I have loved. I loved her and her two girls more than words could ever tell. They were like my own girls to me.

Well, that's it.

                                                          John W. Smith

Get in touch with Mary Jones at once. Call BA 00000. Tell Mrs. Brown. She will see Mary. Thank you.

                                                          John William Smith

5-A   Dearest: Not being of sound mind I have decided to leave this world by electrocuting myself.

                                                          Bill

5-B   Honey I got you into this thing and it was no fault of yours—so I am taking the only way out and I leave everything which has all been acquired since we were married to you my darling wife—Mary Smith—and God Bless You Darling. Forgive me—goodbye dear. You trusted me and I thought I was doing everything for the best but I used poor judgment and poor management on my part and bit off more than I could chew but didn't know it at the time I did it. Sell everything before winter sets in— I leave everything of value of any kind or nature including real estate— home—and all to my darling wife. Tell my mother—sister I said God bless them all and forgive me— Goodbye darling and God bless you all.

Your loving husband always, William J. Smith

6-A Dear Mary, The reason for my despondency is that you'd prefer the company of almost anyone to mine. 2. You told me you had nothing to look forward to on week ends. You told me you preferred living alone. This led to more sedatives. I have lost the love of my two children. You blamed me for your vaginal bleeding. Your first husband was denied normal sexual intercourse because you said it hurt. I received the same accuse. You said it hurt even out of wedlock. This you cant help. But affection would have been harmless. I had little of that. But gaiety you saved for strangers, but even so I loved you. My salary wasn't enough for a large family, with the car upkeep. I was happy regardless. So were you between moods also. You are free now to frequent the places where they drink and indulge in loose talk. Please refrain from giving Betty sips of beer, after all she is only 12. Make her love you some other way. Soon she'll dominate you and one thing leads to another. You don't want another child where your boy is. Your love for me would have endured if it had been the real thing.

Dr. Jones did all he could for my internal trouble. When we quarrel over other and younger men it was silly but you would have been hurt too. It's O.K. to be friendly but not hilarious. Nembutal has a tendency to make you tolerant rather than jealous. It headed off many a quarrel because its quieting to the nerves. As you know I took them for sleep and spastic colon at nite; also migraine headache.

Well, I've loved you through 3 years of quarreling, adjusting the sex angle the way you said it pleased you. Your word for it was "ecstacy." Farewell and good fortune. I hope you find someone who doesn't "hurt" you as you said 3 of us did. All the love I have,

Bill

Notify my kin by mail. Call Georgia St. Hosp. Ambulance.

6-B Dear Mary: I am sorry to cause you a lot of trouble and grife but I think this is best for all of us.

Dad

7-A Dear Mary. I don't know why I am doing this unless my reasoning has gone all to pot. Something must have slipped.

Bill

7-B My Dearest Wife: I cannot endure this situation any longer. I cannot believe I have been so bad a husband as to merit this. Something is certainly wrong. I honestly don't know what it is.

Whatever you may be searching for I hope with all my heart you find. Please be good to little Betty, our daughter, I love her so.

I am talking over this Cyanide deal to myself. God knows what I'll do. I have it here. Possibly 20 grains—5 more than is necessary. I still love you. Be good to Betty Please.

8-A Dear Mary. You have been the best wife a man could want and I still love you after fifteen years.

Don't think to badly of me for taking this way out but I can't take much more pain and sickness also I may get to much pain or so weak that I can't go this easy way. With all my love forever—

Bill

8-B Goodbye dear wife. I cannot stand the suffering any longer. I am doing this by my own free will. You will be well taken care of.

Love and goodbye

9-A My Darling: I'm sorry to leave you this way, but it looks like the only way out for me. Things have become so uncertain and unbearable, that I believe it will be better this way. Have the kids remember me, and don't be grevious because I took this way out. Never forget that I love you with all my heart and soul.

Bill

9-B   Dear Mother. I just cannot take it any more this is no way out but this has me down. I Joseph William Smith give ever thing to Henry Jones my car and what ever I have.

Joseph Smith

10-A   This is the end. Ive had enough. Cant take anymore.

10-B   Dear Mother and Mary, I am sorry to tell you this but Jo told you that I was drinking again. I won't lie about it. Because I quit for 5 week and never taken a drink. But Jo had come up home two nite a week after she got off from work and she would stay with me. But ever nite she came up she was drunk, and I would put her to bed. And on the nite of 12 of March she came drunk and when I went to work I left her in my bed and when she got up that was Wed. She went home she told me. But she didn't go home she went and got drunk, and I had been give her money to pay her room, and I give her money before I went that morning. But she go to the tavern and she got drunk and she got in a fight. I don't no who with, but it was on the street and she eather fell or got nook down and she got a black and blue place on her hip big as a teacup. I asked her how she got that but she said she done it on the ice box and she said it was like that and I no difference. The one that told me didn't no Jo was my wife. He seen it and told her she could do better then that. He said she was to drunk. I saw this and this made me mad and I did start drinking because she told me that she love me and I was so nice to give her money. I do love her and she love me. But I can't stand for her to drink like she does and do the way she do. Jo was up at my house Sun March 31, and she went home about 4 o'clock to go to work and I tryed to get to strating up. But she won't. If you can do anything with her I wish you would. Because I love her so much and she is killing herself. I wouldn't wrote you this if she hadn't told you I had started to drink again. I told her Sun. I would help her and I will if she will be half way write with me.

11-A   Dearest darling i want you to know that you are the only one in my life i love you so much i could not do without you please forgive me i drove myself sick honey please beleave me i love you again an the baby honey don't be mean with me please I have lived fifty years since i met you, **I love you**—I love you. Dearest darling i love you i love you. Please don't discraminat me darling i know that i will die dont be mean with me please i love you more than you will ever know darling please an honey Tom i know don't tell Tom why his dady said good by honey. Can't stand it any more. Darling i love you. Darling i love you.

11-B I am Sorry Mary But i just Can't Stand Life Any Longer.

William Smith

12-A To Mary Jones. Please take care of my bills. Tell Tom I made enough money for him. He can take care of these small bills. Mary, I love Betty and I can't stand being without her. She's something I spoiled myself.

Love, *Bill*

Mary take this pen as Helen gave it to me when I went to the army.

12-B Dear Mary. Although in the past you may have thought the idea of suicide had never entered my mind, I will tell you now that it has. I have given every other way my utmost but this seems to be the only solution—No doubt you remember times in the past when I have said, "I am worth a lot more dead than alive." Well, I wasn't just kidding—My insurance will leave you well provided for and you now can have all those things I could never give you—you see, I know now that I can never hope to really make a success of life and I see no use to continue and drag you down with me, although the years we have been together have been the happiest of my life, I want it to stop here. I want you to marry again as soon as possible and the next time choose someone who can make it. I love you deeply.

Bill

13-A Dear Mary. Im sorry for all the trouble Ive caused you. I guess I can't say any more. I love you forever and give Tom my love. I guess I've disgraced myself and John I hope it doesn't reflect on you.

13-B Darling: It's been great but I just can't go on for reasons you may know but I can't explain. There's enough insurance for all of you. Be happy and all my love always to you and our three.

Remember me as your adoring

Bill

14-A Mary Darling. It's all my fault. I've thought this over a million times and this seems to be the only way I can settle all the trouble I have caused you and others. This is only a sample of how sorry I am. This should cancel all.

Bill

14-B Dear Mary. I can go on no longer so will take the easy way out. I've taken care of everything. Sorry

Bill

15-A I'm tired. There must be something fine for you. Love.

Bill

15-B Darling: All of my life I have looked upon suicide as a weak and cowardly way out but after thinking it out carefully I honestly believe that this is the best way. I realize that this will be quite a shock to you but as you know, time heals all wounds, and as time goes on I hope you will realize that this was the best solution of our problems. Please try to explain to Tom and teach him to grow into a fine man, far better I hope than his Dad has been.

My insurance will take care of both of you at least until Tom is through school. God bless and keep you both. All of my love is for you and Tom Forever and ever.

Bill

16-A To Tom, Betty, John—The stigma I bring upon you cannot be much more than has already been done. Be good to your mother and do all you can to help as she is a wonderful person. Tom—a rather gruesome thought— Remember when we worked in the yard and you asked to see a cadaver at the College? Little did we know that I would be the first deceased for you to encounter. I love you and know you will make a wonderful man. Betty—We have been very close to each other. Please don't think too harshly of my actions. Stabilization takes place in time, and I know you will grow up to be one of the best women in the world. My love, dear. Johnny— You came last in our offspring so couldn't know me as well as your brother and sister. Just follow your brother's example, love your sister and help Mother. Remember, I love you, Johnny. Mary— There is no more or less to say than I have already told you— Truth will triumph eventually.

Bill

16-B Dear Mary: As we both might reasonable recognize this is not the right way to solve any situation. Lord how I wish it could be done in any other way. No use of thinking about that now, its like a dead end road in the middle of the night. Confusion, bewilderment, questions with no answers. What can a person say? How do you lift yourself up again and try to keep going? The will is gone, reason is gone, there is only one answer. You'll probably ask why—over and over again—I've been doing that and only creating more confusion. Continue with your will to live, fill any emptiness with your love for our children, find a new live for yourself and forgive me for whatever results to you from this. Love,

Bill

17-A Dear Wife; I am sorry to cause you this embarrassment but I can't seem to stand life this way. This is the easy way for me. You will get over it in time too.

17-B Dearest Mary—I just can't go on without Tom, John and you. I hope some day you can forgive me. I know you will find someone better for you and the boys. God bless you all.

Love, *Bill*

18-A My dear wife: I never thought that I'd write a suicide note but life can throw some unexpected curves. This note has two purposes, first, to make certain that this is a suicide and not murder so that in no way can some unforeseen circumstantial evidence point suspicion at some innocent person. Secondly, to give you my reasons for this drastic action and to assure you that you are in no way responsible for my action.

As you will recall, I've always said that I'd rather be dead than be a hopeless and helpless burden upon you. Fate has decreed that I be just that. I have considered this action carefully and prayerfully. I know that you, in your great unselfish love, would have voted against me in this.

My continued living, though you would be quick to deny this, would be a continuing depressant, because of my condition, upon you and the kids. Facts are facts and a "head in the sand" attitude is only kidding ourselves. After the first shock of my death has worn away, I'm sure that you will see the logic of my decision—even though you may not admit it—and life will be much easier and happier for you.

My undying love to you and the kids. Please tell them I'm doing this because I think it is best for all of us. With my love,

Bill

18-B Dearest Mary: Well, dear—it's the end of the trail for me. It has been a fairly long and reasonably pleasant life, all in all—especially fine that part in which you played a part. You have been wonderful. No man could have asked for a better wife than you have been.

Please understand that if I didn't feel that this course would be the best for you and the girls I certainly would have waited for nature to take her course. It would not have been long, anyhow, for the clot I coughed up was from the lungs and I know there's activity there—of an ominous nature.

Be good to your mother girls. You have the finest mother in the world; even as I have had the most wonderful wife and two wonderful daughters. Bye-by Mary, Betty, and Helen. How I do love you all. And may God help and guide you from here on in.

"Daddy"

19-A Dearest Wife. I am writing this to explain why I am going to end it all. I know that this is a cowardly way and I am sorry but I just haven't the will to do otherwise. Please forgive me if you can and believe that I loved you to the end.

Bill

19-B Dear Mary. Since you are convinced that you are an invalid and no one can help you, I hope my $3000 insurance will help you to see the truth about yourself and get rid of your mental sickness. You are now free to marry Joe. Remember you will never have any happiness with anyone until you learn to help yourself. I have no regrets and hold no malice or unkind thoughts toward you. We would have had a happy life together if you had wanted to help yourself. I hope you eventually will find happiness. Love, *Bill*.

Tell my folks I'm sorry I couldn't see them before I went.

20-A I'm tired of being sick and in pain and can see no use in prolonging it as they say there is no hope of recovery.

20-B I specifically request that my body be disposed of by cremation. To my good friends, Joe Smith and Mary Jones I give my deep and undying affection. My dear parents, Henry W. and Betty C. Brown have done their best for me and it is my failure, rather than anything they have failed to offer that has brought this about. My sister, Helen White of 100 Main Street, New York, is closest and dearest to me and, with her consent, I ask that she take and raise my son. My phongraph records, now in storage with my parents, I give to my former wife, Wilma Brown, 200 Broadway, Los Angeles, Calif.

Explanations would be useless, suffice to say I have tried and failed. Given unto my hand this ninth day of June in the year of 1943, A.D., in the city of Los Angeles, California.

Jack Brown

21-A Some where in this pile is your answers. I couldn't find it. Mom, you should have known what was about to happen after I told you my troubles now I will get my rest.

Dad, I am in this jam because I trusted people (namely you) and some people trusted me, because I am, in my present state a menace to me and my customers I think this is the best way out, and out of my insurance if you ever take a drink I hope you drown yourself with it.

21-B Dear Mary. Things are piling up too high for me. I love you but I know our basic difficulties are not soluable. Please don't think too harshly of me if I take this way out. You have insurance and your health to help get started again. Tell the kids I had an accident so they wont be ashamed of their daddy.

Love, *Bill*

22-A Dearest Wife: I'm sorry I had to do this but I know you will be happier as a result. I hope you will be married as soon as it is proper to be, and I feel sure that you and Fred will have a full and happy life together. Love always,

Bill

22-B My dearest family: I am terribley sick and it is all my fault. I blame no one but myself. I know it is going to go hard with Tommy and Sister. Please see that Tommy gets a Mickey Mouse Watch for his birthday. Helen I am counting on you to take care of Mother. Please do not follow in my fottsteps.

Mary my darling I know you did everything possible to avoid this, but please forgive me, as I think it was the only way out. God forgive me and help take care of my family.

23-A Dear Mary. Honey I hope you will forgive me for being the way I was this AM. I honestly love you with all my heart and I thought we would understand things together. I didn't know you felt the way you did about everything. I really thought we were the "happily married couple." Too bad you just keep everything inside you.

For the first time in my life I was really in love, and I thought you were too. I had hopes that you would forget your feelings and we would try to be happy together.

My bonus should take care of things so you contact Joe. Sorry to end things this way now to you—I wish you the best of everything.

I did and do think you the nicest person ever. Good by and thanks for everything.

Bill

23-B Dearest One, This world is too cruel for me. I am in search of peace—eternal peace where I will not be a burden to you and all the world.

This world was not meant for me. I was never wanted or able to place myself in any good position. I am only a handicap to you and your life will be better without me. I love you, but my love has brought you nothing but saddness and despair.

Forgive, Dearest, but since I was very young, everyone considered me a failure and over the years it has proven to be so. I have done nothing to make life seem worthwhile. Mother meant good, but she drove me to my grave. Forgive me for not being what you exspected. I do love you. Do not think badly of me. I am better off dead, no one will miss me. Until later, when we can be happy.

Your Desperate Husband, *Bill Smith*

24-A My Dearest Mary. For many months now the pain of my illness has been unberable and since none of the specialists could give me any hope whatsoever I have decided to end my suffering forever. I Love You,

Bill

24-B To my wife Mary: As you know, like we've talked over before our situation, I'll always love you with all my heart and soul. It could have been so simple if you had have given me the help that you alone knew I needed.

This is not an easy thing I'm about to do, but when a person makes a few mistakes and later tried to say in his own small way with a small vocabulary that he is sorry for what has happened and promises to remember what has happened and will try to make the old Bill come home again, and do his best to start all over again, and make things at home much better for all concerned, you still refuse to have me when you as well as I know that I can't do it by myself, then there's only one thing to do.

I'm sorry honey, but please believe me this is the only way out for me as long as you feel as you do— This will put you in good shape. Please always take care of Betty and tell her that her Daddy wasn't too bad a guy after all. With all the love that's in me. *Bill*

Yes, Mommie, now you have your car and a lot more too, even more than you had hoped for. At least you are better off financially than you were 6 years ago. The only pitiful thing about the whole situation is the baby and the nice car that I bought with blood money. I only hope I do a good job of it. Then your troubles will be over with. I know this is what you have been hoping for for a long time. I'm not crazy, I just love you too much!!!

I love you—*Daddy*—Goodbye forever.

25-A To the Police. I can see no reason to battle the elements of life any longer with no progress being made.

25-B Mary: The only thing you never called me was crazy. Now you can do that. I loved you so.

Bill

26-A Dear Mary. Everything is kind of mixed up with me and what I am doing is the only way out I guess I can think of no other I am very sorry I got you in the shape we are in but I did I love you very much. It is going to hurt my mother and Dad to and also you I think. I hope you all the luck in the world.

With all my love, *Bill*. Goodbye

26-B Dear Mary. I have decided to end my life. Things are not going right and don't look as though they ever will. I'm doing this to help you, so that you may continue unhampered.

Love, *Bill*

27-A To my kids— This is a lousy way to leave you, but I can no longer help you in any way. It's better for us all that the burden of caring for me be lifted—you will have sufficient problems of your own. You must face these problems intelligently, squarely, couragously, rather than running away from them, as I am from this one insolvable problem of my disability. Remember me as I was—as we enjoyed life together—as we worked out your small problems—which seemed so large—and above all remember I would never under any circumstances run out on you if there remained any chance that I could be of help to you.

Daddy

27-B Mary dear. Im sorry that I have been making you unhappy—I'm all twisted up inside. You and Joe will be better off this way—start over.

Love, *Bill*

28-A Darling wife, Mary Helen Smith I'm sorry for everything I did please don't be angry at me my sweet wife. You left me and did not say anything So darling this is your divorce my darling wife Mary. I wish you get the rings back my dear wife. Goodby my dear wife Mary. I love you more than anything in the hold world my sweet wife.

William Smith

28-B Dear wife. It seems that fate has destined me to be a failure. All at once it appears that I can no longer face the problems and responsibility of trying to get ahead only to see us struggle along in poverty. So as usual I have taken the easy way out and left you to finish the job I have so poorly started. With money from our Life Insurance program you will be able to give the children and yourself the things you have always wanted for us all. Possibly we will all meet again sometime where we will be able to live in the peaceful way we all deserved so much here on earth.

Your ever loving husband

29-A Mary—I know this is a terrible thing to do but believe me, dear, it is for the best. The events of the last few months have left me at my wit's end and I see no other way out. I am sorry I was such a trial to you and the children, please forgive me.

Bill

29-B Dear Mary; I'm just to tired and to sick of trying to continue. Sorry it had to be this way. I'm sure everything will work out for the best. Keep everything quiet as possible. Say I had a heart attack.

As Ever, *Bill*

God forgive me. God bless you and John.

30-A Dear Wife. My health has broken and I no longer feel that I can be of help in the Support of the family therefore becoming a burden— So Im ending it all. Sorry to leave in this manner but feel that it is best for all concerned—Love.

30-B Honey. I am sorry this is the only way I know. I am all wrong. I love you very much.

Bill

31-A Dear Mary. I am writeing you, as our Divorce is not final, and will not be till next month, so the way things stand now you are still my wife, which makes you entitled to the things which belong to me, and I want you to have them. Don't let anyone take them from you as they are yours. Please see a lawyer and get them as soon as you can. I am listing some of the things, they are: A Blue Davenport and chair, a Magic Chef Stove, a large mattress, an Electrolux cleaner, a 9 x 12 Rug redish flower design and pad. All the things listed above are all most new. Then there is my 30-30 rifle, books, typewriter, tools and a hand contract for a house in Chicago, a Savings account in Boston, Mass.

Your husband, *William H. Smith*

31-B Dearest Mary. As I sit here with this gun in my Hand, which in a few minutes I will take my life I am thinking of all the wonderful minutes, Days, years, I have spent with you. I know if I talked all this over again with you, you would talk me out of what I am about to do.

I know the mistakes I have made are not in the least bit your fault. But as you know in my small way I will always try to place part of the Blame on you. So I hope you will forgive me all or partly for what I am about to do.

Goodby dear I hope we will meet again in some other place, where we can be as happy as I have been since I have been married to you. Goodby sweetheart. Yours as always,

Bill

32-A I'm tired of it all. I Love you and God Bless you.

32-B Good bye my Dear. I am very sorry but it is just too hard to breathe.

Love, *Bill*

Dearest have someone at the Legion call the V.A. I think they will take care of me.

33-A To the police. please tell family that I love them why say more.

33-B Good by Kid. You couldn't help it. Tell that brother of yours,

When he gets where I'm going. I hope I'm a foreman down there. I might be able to do something for him.

Bill

NOTE: The following is the "key" for the 33 pairs of genuine and simulated suicide notes. The letter *A* or *B* refers in each case to the genuine note:

1-A	6-A	11-A	16-A	21-A	26-A	31-A
2-A	7-B	12-A	17-B	22-B	27-B	32-B
3-A	8-A	13-A	18-B	23-A	28-A	33-B
4-B	9-B	14-A	19-B	24-B	29-B	
5-B	10-B	15-A	20-B	25-B	30-B	

Name Index

Subject Index

Abandonment, 19, 24, 129, 165–167
Abortion, 92
Accidents and accident proneness, 15, 91, 138, 187, 195
Accomplice in suicide, 84, 88, 89
Acute phase in suicide, 103–104
Adolescence, 101, 132, 136, 138
Affective tension, 132, 186
Age and suicide, 41, 43, 47, 49, 62, 63, 143
(*See also* Middle age; Old age; Young age)
Aggression, 13, 14, 15, 16, 58, 65, 67, 91, 133, 136
Agitation, 105, 106, 108, 125, 145
Alcoholics Anonymous, 191
Alcoholism and suicide, 108, 113, 114, 147, 148, 152, 155, 156, 160–163, 187, 195
Altruistic suicide, 12, 60
Ambivalence, 114, 121, 137, 148, 184
Anger (*see* Hostility)
Anniversaries and suicide, 18, 26
Anomic suicide, 12, 59
Anorexia, 111, 189
Anticipation, role of, 34
Antisocial behavior, 132, 138
Anxiety, 23, 28, 100, 103, 115, 120, 121, 124, 126, 127, 136, 137, 140, 144, 147, 158, 160, 161, 169
Arteriosclerosis, 145, 155, 156, 157, 158, 159
Athens, 79
Atmosphere effect, 33
Attempted suicide (*see* Suicide attempts)
Austen Riggs Center, 115
Austria, 83, 84

Barbiturates (*see* Drugs)
Bedford, Massachusetts, 153
Berkeley, California, 191

Bible, 80
Birth and suicide, 18
(*See also* Rebirth)
Brahman sects, 79
Brittany, 82
Buddhism, 79, 92
Burial of suicide, 30, 73, 81–83, 92, 93
Business cycles (*see* Economic factors and suicide)

California, 89
Canon Law, 72, 81, 82, 88
"Catalogic" thinking, 32, 36, 180
Catharsis, 76, 77
Catholicism and suicide, 70–73, 75–77, 80, 82, 92, 108, 123
Character neurosis, 138
Chicago, 61, 67
Childhood patterns in suicide, 126, 144, 165
Children, suicide in, 15–17, 100, 101, 131–141
Christian doctrine, 81, 82, 85
Chronic brain syndrome, 157, 160, 162
Chronic suicide, 187
Church (*see* Catholicism and suicide)
Cities, 61, 63
Climate in suicide, 12, 151
Clinic, therapy in, 119, 120
Clinical records (*see* Psychiatric histories)
Clues to suicide (*see* Danger signals of suicide)
"Code of Social Defense," 87
Coma, barbiturate, 115, 190
Common law, 81, 82, 85
Communication, in hospital, 186
in psychotherapy, 19, 117, 118
Compulsive neurosis, 136